George Lovett Bennett

First Latin Writer

With Accidence, Syntax Rules & Vocabularies

George Lovett Bennett

First Latin Writer

With Accidence, Syntax Rules & Vocabularies

ISBN/EAN: 9783337157999

Printed in Europe, USA, Canada, Australia, Japan

Cover: Foto ©ninafisch / pixelio.de

More available books at **www.hansebooks.com**

Mr. BENNETT'S LATIN BOOKS.

16mo. Cloth. 75 cents.

EASY LATIN STORIES FOR BEGINNERS,
With Vocabulary and Notes.

16mo. Cloth. $1.00.

FIRST LATIN WRITER,
Comprising Accidence, the Easier Rules of Syntax illustrated by copious Examples, and Progressive Exercises in Elementary Latin Prose, with Vocabularies.

16mo. Cloth. 75 cents.

FIRST LATIN EXERCISES,
Containing all the Rules, Exercises, and Vocabularies of the FIRST LATIN WRITER, but omitting the Accidence.

16mo. $1.00.

SECOND LATIN WRITER,
Containing Hints on Writing Latin Prose, with Graduated Continuous Exercises.

JOHN ALLYN, PUBLISHER,
30, *FRANKLIN STREET, BOSTON.*

WITH ACCIDENCE, SYNTAX RULES AND VOCABULARIES

BY

GEORGE L. BENNETT, M.A.

HEAD MASTER OF SUTTON VALENCE SCHOOL

NEW EDITION

Boston
JOHN ALLYN, PUBLISHER
MDCCCLXXXVIII

CONTENTS.

	PAGE
PREFACE, . . .	vii
ACCIDENCE, ...	1
EXERCISES ON THE SYNTAX:—	
THE SIMPLE SENTENCE, *Ex.* 1-150, .	53
THE COMPOUND SENTENCE, . .	117
Adjectival Clauses, *Ex.* 151-175, . . .	117
Adverbial Clauses, *Ex.* 176-200, . .	126
Substantival Clauses, *Ex.* 201-270, . . .	136
LATIN-ENGLISH VOCABULARY, . . .	161
ENGLISH-LATIN VOCABULARY, . .	174

PREFACE.

I HAVE prepared this First Latin Writer in the hope that it may prove helpful to those who agree with me that it is quite useless to attempt the difficulties of the Compound Sentence before the Simple Sentence has been thoroughly mastered. The Accidence and Syntax rules are on the lines of the Public School Latin Primer; I have attempted to make them easier for beginners, but little explanation has been given, as the rules are put shortly in plain English. I have not been able to make the disconnected sentences illustrating the Syntax Rules interesting, but I hope the large collection of pieces for translation into Latin will prove so. Difficulties of rare occurrence have been avoided as much as possible. I have to acknowledge some valuable assistance from my friend Mr. E. D. Mansfield of Clifton College.

GEORGE L. BENNETT.

HIGH SCHOOL, PLYMOUTH,

ACCIDENCE.

THE LETTERS.

1. The Latin Alphabet is the same as the English without *w*. The letters are divided into

(*a*) VOWELS, sounding by themselves, *a, e, i, o, u, y*. *I* (*j*), and *u* (*v*), are called semi-consonants.

(*b*) CONSONANTS, sounding with vowels:—

	MUTES.		SEMIVOWELS.			DOUBLE.
	HARD.	SOFT.	NASALS.	SPIRANTS.	LIQUIDS.	
Guttural, or Throat Sounds,	c k q	g	n	h		x = cs
					r l	
Dental, or Teeth Sounds,	t	d	n	s		z = ds
Labial, or Lip Sounds,	p	b	m	f v		

A dental mute drops out before *s:* so, *pes* is written instead of *peds*.

QUANTITY.

2. The QUANTITY of syllables is short (˘), long (-), or doubtful (⁔).

(*a*) A vowel coming before another vowel is *short*.

(*b*) A vowel coming before two consonants or a double letter is *long*.

(*c*) All diphthongs are *long*.

(*d*) A short vowel is *doubtful* if followed by a mute with a liquid after it.

PRONUNCIATION.

3. Pronounce *a*, *i* as in French.
      ē as English *a*.
      ĕ as in English.
      ae like *ai* in French *Mai*.
      au like *ow* in *cow*.
      oe like *ae*.
      c like *k*.
      g as in *get*.

PARTS OF SPEECH.

4. There are eight Parts of Speech:

1. SUBSTANTIVE.	5. ADVERB.
2. ADJECTIVE.	6. PREPOSITION.
3. PRONOUN.	7. CONJUNCTION.
4. VERB.	8. INTERJECTION.
These change according to their meaning.	These always remain the same.

A Substantive names a thing.

An Adjective describes a substantive.

A Pronoun is used to prevent the repetition of a substantive.

A Verb states what a thing is, does, or suffers.

An Adverb qualifies a verb or adjective, showing Where, When, How.

A Preposition governs different cases of substantives.
A Conjunction joins words or clauses together.
An Interjection is an exclamation.

DECLENSION OF SUBSTANTIVES.

5. There are three Genders, *Masculine*, *Feminine*, and *Neuter*.

Some substantives may be either masculine or feminine. These are called *Common*.

Substantives are declined by Number and Case.
There are two Numbers, Singular and Plural.
There are six Cases:

1. NOMINATIVE, answering the question, Who? or What?
2. VOCATIVE, used in addressing a person, or thing.
3. ACCUSATIVE, answering the question, Whom? or What?
4. GENITIVE, ,, ,, Whose?
5. DATIVE, ,, ,, To, or for, whom? or what?
6. ABLATIVE, ,, ,, By, with, or from, whom? or what?

STEM-CHARACTER.

6. The Stem is that part of a word from which the different cases are formed.

The stem of a substantive can be found by cutting off the syllable *-rum* or *-um* from the genitive plural.

The last letter of the stem is called the Character.

So, from the stem *ped* (foot), we have

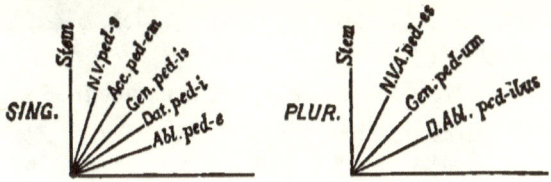

(*a*) In the Nominative Singular *pes* is written for *peds*, because it sounds better. See 1, (*b*.)

(*b*) Case means a falling away from the stem.

THE FIVE DECLENSIONS.

7. There are five Declensions of Substantives, distinguished by their Character.

First Declension—character, **A.**
Second   „   „   **O.**
Third   „   „   Consonant or **I.**
Fourth   „   „   **U.**
Fifth   „   „   **E.**

The Vocative is the same as the Nominative, except in words of the Second Declension ending in *-us*.

In Neuter Substantives the Nominative, Vocative, and Accusative are the same, and in the plural end in *a*.

The Dative and Ablative Plural of all genders are the same.

FIRST DECLENSION (Character, A).

8. The Nominative ends in *a* (usually feminine), except a few Greek words, in *ăs, ēs* (masculine), and *ē* (feminine).

Singular.	Plural.
Nom. Mensă, *a table*	Mensae, *tables*
Voc. Mensă, *O table*	Mensae, *O tables*
Acc. Mensam, *a table*	Mensas, *tables*
Gen. Mensae, *of a table*	Mensārum, *of tables*
Dat. Mensae, *to or for a table*	Mensīs, *to or for tables*
Abl. Mensā, *by, with,* or *from a table*	Mensīs, *by, with,* or *from tables*

(*a*) Some few words that have a corresponding masculine form in the Second Declension take *-ăbŭs* instead of *-is* in the Dative and Ablative Plural. So deă, *a goddess*, deābŭs; fīliă, *a daughter*, fīliābŭs.

(*b*) Greek words in *as, es, e*, are thus declined :—

Nom.	*Voc.*	*Acc.*	*Gen.*	*Dat.*	*Abl.*
Aenēas	-ā	-ān	-ae	-ae	-ā
Anchīsēs	-ē *or* -ă	-ēn	-ae	-ae	-ā
Cўbĕlē	-ē	-ēn	-ēs	-ae	-ē

(*c*) Derived from the Greek we have a few masculine forms ending in *a ;* so poētă, *poet ;* naută, *sailor*.

SECOND DECLENSION (Character, O).

9. The Nominative ends in *us, er* (masculine), *um* (neuter).

a. *MASCULINE.*

Singular.		Plural.	
Nom.	Dŏmĭnŭs, *a lord*	Nom.	Dŏmĭnī, *lords*
Voc.	Dŏmĭnĕ	Voc.	Dŏmĭnī
Acc.	Dŏmĭnum	Acc.	Dŏmĭnōs
Gen.	Dŏmĭnī	Gen.	Dŏmĭnōrum
Dat.	Dŏmĭnō	Dat.	Dŏmĭnīs
Abl.	Dŏmĭnō	Abl.	Dŏmĭnīs
Nom.	Măgistĕr, *a master*	Nom.	Măgistrī, *masters*
Voc.	Măgistĕr	Voc.	Măgistrī
Acc.	Măgistrum	Acc.	Măgistrōs
Gen.	Măgistrī	Gen.	Măgistrōrum
Dat.	Măgistrō	Dat.	Măgistrīs
Abl.	Măgistrō	Abl.	Măgistrīs
Nom.	Pŭĕr, *a boy*	Nom.	Pŭĕrī, *boys*
Voc.	Pŭĕr	Voc.	Pŭĕrī
Acc.	Pŭĕrum	Acc.	Pŭĕrōs
Gen.	Pŭĕrī	Gen.	Pŭĕrōrum
Dat.	Pŭĕrō	Dat.	Pŭĕrīs
Abl.	Pŭĕrō	Abl.	Pŭĕrīs

b. *NEUTER.*

Singular.		Plural.	
Nom. Voc. Acc.	Bellum, *war*	Nom. Voc. Acc.	Bellă, *wars*
Gen.	Bellī	Gen.	Bellōrum
Dat. Abl.	Bellō	Dat. Abl.	Bellīs

Fīlĭŭs, *son*, gĕnĭŭs, *familiar spirit*, and Roman proper names ending in *iŭs*, make vocative in *ī*.

Dĕŭs, *God*, makes vocative Dĕŭs.

Words ending in *iŭs* or *ium* have genitive either *iī* or *ī*.

Greek words with nominative ending in *os* have *on* sometimes in accusative instead of *um*.

THIRD DECLENSION
(Character, Consonant or I).

10. Nouns with Consonant Character usually have more syllables in other cases than the nominative and vocative.

Consonant-Nouns.

a. *MASCULINE AND FEMININE.*

	Singular.		Plural.
Nom. Voc.	Iŭdex, *judge*	Nom. Voc.	Iŭdĭcēs, *judges*
Acc.	Iŭdĭcem	Acc.	Iŭdĭcēs
Gen.	Iŭdĭcĭs	Gen.	Iŭdĭcum
Dat.	Iŭdĭcī	Dat.	Iŭdĭcĭbŭs
Abl.	Iŭdĭcĕ	Abl.	Iŭdĭcĭbŭs

	Singular.		Plural.
Nom. Voc.	Aetās, *age*	Nom. Voc.	Aetātēs, *ages*
Acc.	Aetātem	Acc.	Aetātēs
Gen.	Aetātĭs	Gen.	Aetātum
Dat.	Aetātī	Dat.	Aetātĭbŭs
Abl.	Aetātĕ	Abl.	Aetātĭbus

	Singular.		Plural.
Nom. Voc.	Lĕō, *lion*	Nom. Voc.	Lĕōnĕs, *lions*
Acc.	Lĕōnem	Acc.	Lĕōnēs
Gen.	Lĕōnĭs	Gen.	Lĕōnum
Dat.	Lĕōnī	Dat.	Lĕōnĭbŭs
Abl.	Lĕōnĕ	Abl.	Lĕōnĭbŭs

b. *NEUTER.*

	Singular.		Plural.
Nom. Voc. Acc.	Nōmĕn, *name*	Nom. Voc. Acc.	Nōmĭnă, *names*
Gen.	Nōmĭnĭs	Gen.	Nōmĭnum
Dat.	Nōmĭnī	Dat.	Nōmĭnĭbŭs
Abl.	Nōmĭnĕ	Abl.	Nōmĭnĭbŭs

Nom. Voc. Acc.	Ŏpŭs, *work*	Nom. Voc. Acc.	Ŏpĕră, *works*
Gen.	Ŏpĕrĭs	Gen.	Ŏpĕrum
Dat.	Ŏpĕrī	Dat.	Ŏpĕrĭbŭs
Abl.	Ŏpĕrĕ	Abl.	Ŏpĕrĭbŭs

c. *IRREGULAR.*

	Old man	Pig	Ox or cow	Jupiter	
Singular.	M.	C.	C.	M.	
Nom. Voc.	Sĕnex	Sus	Bōs	Iuppĭtĕr	—
Acc.	Sĕn-	Su-	Bŏv-	Iŏv-	ēm
Gen.	Sĕn-	Su-	Bŏv-	Iŏv-	ĭs
Dat.	Sĕn-	Su-	Bŏv-	Iŏv-	ī
Abl.	Sĕn-	Su-	Bŏv-	Iŏv-	ĕ
Plural.					
Nom. Voc. Acc.	Sĕn-	Su-	Bŏv-	—	ēs
Gen.	Sĕn-	Su-	—	—	ūm
Dat. Abl.	Sĕn-	Su-	—	—	ĭbŭs

I-Nouns.

Sus has also Dative and Ablative Plural *sūbŭs*.
Bos has Genitive Plural *boum*, Dative and Ablative *bōbŭs* or *būbŭs*.
The following are declined like Consonant Nouns:—

pătĕr, *father*	accĭpĭtĕr, *hawk*	vātēs, *seer*
mātĕr, *mother*	cănĭs, *dog*	vŏlŭcrĭs, *bird*
frātĕr, *brother*	iŭvĕnĭs, *youth*	

Greek consonant-nouns form Accusative Singular in *ă* or *em*; Accusative Plural usually in *ăs*: as, gĭgas, *giant*; Accusative Singular, gĭgantă or gĭgantem; Accusative Plural, gĭgantăs.

Some Greek words in *eus* form Accusative Singular *eum* or *ea*; Genitive Singular *eī* or *eŏs*: as, Orpheus; Accusative, Orpheum *or* Orpheă; Genitive, Orpheī *or* Orpheŏs.

I-Nouns.

11. Nouns with character I usually have the same number of syllables throughout, except in the Gen. Dat. Abl. Plural.

a. *MASCULINE AND FEMININE.*

Singular.		Plural.	
Nom. Voc.	Ŏvĭs, *sheep*	*Nom. Voc.*	Ŏvēs, *sheep*
Acc.	Ŏvem	*Acc.*	Ŏvēs, or ŏvīs
Gen.	Ŏvĭs	*Gen.*	Ŏvĭum
Dat.	Ŏvī	*Dat.*	Ŏvĭbŭs
Abl.	Ŏvĕ	*Abl.*	Ŏvĭbŭs

Nom. Voc.	Nūbĕs, *cloud*	*Nom. Voc.*	Nūbes, *clouds*
Acc.	Nūbem	*Acc.*	Nūbēs, *or* nūbīs
Gen.	Nūbĭs	*Gen.*	Nūbĭum
Dat.	Nūbī	*Dat.*	Nūbĭbŭs
Abl.	Nūbĕ	*Abl.*	Nūbĭbŭs

b. *NEUTER.*

Singular.		Plural.	
Nom. Voc. Acc.	Os, *bone*	*Nom. Voc. Acc.*	Ossă, *bones*
Gen.	Ossĭs	*Gen.*	Ossĭum
Dat.	Ossī	*Dat.*	Ossĭbŭs
Abl.	Ossĕ	*Abl.*	Ossĭbŭs

Nom. Voc. Acc.	Mărĕ, *sea*	*Nom. Voc. Acc.*	Mărĭă
Gen.	Mărĭs	*Gen.*	Mărĭŭm
Dat. Abl.	Mărī	*Dat. Abl.*	Mărĭbŭs

c. *IRREGULAR.*

Accusative *em* or *im;* Ablative *ĭ* or *ĕ*—
Classis, *fleet;* febrĭs, *fever;* messis, *harvest;* clāvĭs, *key;* nāvĭs, *ship;* puppĭs, *stern.*

Accusative *im ;* Ablative *ī*—
Tussĭs, *cough ;* sĭtĭs, *thirst ;* ămussĭs, *carpenter's rule.*

Accusative *em;* Ablative *ī*—
Canālĭs, *canal;* aedīlĭs, *aedile.*

Accusative *em;* Ablative *ī* or *ĕ*—
Imbĕr, *shower;* ūtĕr, *wine-skin;* ventĕr, *belly;* lintcr, *boat.*

Like I-nouns are declined :—

 1. Words with stem ending in two consonants.
 2. The following words :—

Glis, *dormouse,* stem glir-	Nix, *snow,* stem niv-
Lis, *strife,* ,, lit-	Strix, *owl,* ,, strig-
Mas, *male,* ,, mar-	Faux, *jaw,* ,, fauc-
Mus, *mouse,* ,, mur-	Vis, *force,* ,, vir- (*in plural*)

FOURTH DECLENSION (Character, U).

12. Masculine and Feminine have Nominative in *us*, Neuter in *u*.

Singular.		Plural.	
Nom. Voc.	Grădŭs, *step*	*Nom. Voc.*	Grădūs, *steps*
Acc.	Grădum	*Acc.*	Grădūs
Gen.	Grădūs	*Gen.*	Grădŭum
Dat.	Grăduī	*Dat.*	Grădĭbŭs (ŭbŭs)
Abl.	Grădū	*Abl.*	Grădĭbŭs (ŭbŭs)
N.V.A.	Gĕnū, *knee*	*N.V.A.*	Gĕnŭă, *knees*
Gen.	Gĕnūs	*Gen.*	Gĕnŭum
Dat. Abl.	Gĕnū	*Dat. Abl.*	Gĕnĭbŭs (ŭbŭs)

Dŏmŭs, *a house:* Dative Singular, *uī* or *ō*, Ablative *ō ;* Accusative Plural, *ūs* or *ōs ;* Genitive Plural, *uum* or *ōrum.*

Adjectives.

FIFTH DECLENSION (Character, E).
13. Only Feminine nouns. Nominative ends in *-ēs*.

Singular.		Plural.	
Nom. Voc.	Dĭēs, *day*	*Nom. Voc.*	Dĭēs, *days*
Acc.	Dĭem	*Acc.*	Dĭēs
Gen.	Dĭēī	*Gen.*	Dĭērum
Dat.	Dĭēī	*Dat.*	Dĭēbŭs
Abl.	Dĭē	*Abl.*	Dĭēbŭs

Res, *thing*, is the only other that has the increasing cases in the plural.

ADJECTIVES.

14. Adjectives of three endings in *us, a, um*, or *er, a, um*, follow the Second Declension in Masculine and Neuter; the First Declension in Feminine: as, bonus, *good;* niger, *black;* tener, *tender.*

	Singular.			Plural.		
	MAS.	FEM.	NEUT.	MAS.	FEM.	NEUT.
Nom.	Bŏnŭs	bŏnă	bŏnum	Bŏnī	bŏnae	bŏnă
Voc.	Bŏnĕ	bŏnă	bŏnum	Bŏnī	bŏnae	bŏnă
Acc.	Bŏnum	bŏnam	bŏnum	Bŏnōs	bŏnās	bŏnă
Gen.	Bŏnī	bŏnae	bŏnī	Bŏnōrum	bŏnārum	bŏnōrum
Dat.	Bŏnō	bŏnae	bŏnō	Bŏnīs	bŏnīs	bŏnīs
Abl.	Bŏnō	bŏnā	bŏnō	Bŏnīs	bŏnīs	bŏnīs
Nom.	Nĭgĕr	nigră	nigrum	Nigrī	nigrae	nigră
Voc.	Nĭgĕr	nigră	nigrum	Nigrī	nigrae	nigră
Acc.	Nigrum	nigram	nigrum	Nigrōs	nigrās	nigră
Gen.	Nigrī	nigrae	nigrī	Nigrōrum	nigrārum	nigrōrum
Dat.	Nigrō	nigrae	nigrō	Nigrīs	nigrīs	nigrīs
Abl.	Nigrō	nigrā	nigrō	Nigrīs	nigrīs	nigrīs
Nom.	Tĕnĕr	tĕnĕră	tĕnĕrum	Tĕnĕrī	tĕnĕrae	tĕnĕră
Voc.	Tĕnĕr	tĕnĕră	tĕnĕrum	Tĕnĕrī	tĕnĕrae	tĕnĕră
Acc.	Tĕnĕrum	tĕnĕram	tĕnĕrum	Tĕnĕrōs	tĕnĕrās	tĕnĕră
Gen.	Tĕnĕrī	tĕnĕrae	tĕnĕrī	Tĕnĕrōrum	tĕnĕrārum	tĕnĕrōrum
Dat.	Tĕnĕrō	tĕnĕrae	tĕnĕrō	Tĕnĕrīs	tĕnĕrīs	tĕnĕrīs
Abl.	Tĕnĕrō	tĕnĕrī	tĕnĕrō	Tĕnĕrīs	tĕnĕrīs	tĕnĕrīs

15. All other Adjectives follow the Third Declension.

Singular.

	MAS. FEM.	NEUT.		MAS. FEM.	NEUT.
Nom. Voc.	Mĕlĭŏr	mĕlĭŭs, *better*	*Nom. Voc.*	Tristĭs	tristĕ, *sad*
Acc.	Mĕlĭōrem mĕlĭŭs		*Acc.*	Tristem	tristĕ
Gen.	Mĕlĭōrĭs		*Gen.*	Tristĭs	
Dat.	Mĕlĭōrī		*Dat.*	Tristī	
Abl.	Mĕlĭōrĕ *or* i		*Abl.*	Tristī	

10 Numeral and Pronominal Adjectives.

Plural.

	MAS. FEM. NEUT.		MAS. FEM.	NEUT.
Nom. Voc. Acc.	Mĕliōrēs mĕliōră	Nom. Voc. Acc.	Tristēs	tristiă
Gen.	Mĕliōrum	Gen.	Tristium	
Dat. Abl.	Mĕliōrĭbŭs	Dat. Abl.	Tristĭbŭs	

Singular.

	MAS. FEM. NEUT.		MAS. FEM. NEUT.
Nom. Voc.	Fēlix, *happy*.	Nom. Voc.	Ingens, *huge*.
Acc.	Fēlīcem fēlix	Acc.	Ingentem ingens
Gen.	Fēlīcĭs	Gen.	Ingentĭs
Dat.	Fēlīcī	Dat.	Ingentī
Abl.	Fēlīcī	Abl.	Ingentī or ĕ

Plural.

Nom. V. A.	Fēlīcēs	fēlīciă	Nom. V. A.	Ingentēs	ingentĭa
Gen.	Fēlīcium		Gen.	Ingentium	
Dat. Abl.	Fēlīcĭbŭs		Dat. Abl.	Ingentĭbŭs	

Adjectives in *er* of Third Declension have three endings in Nominative Singular.

Singular.

Nom. Voc. Cĕlĕr, cĕlĕrĭs, cĕlĕrĕ, *swift* | *Nom. Voc.* Ācĕr, acrĭs, acrĕ, *keen*

	MAS. FEM.	NEUT.		MAS. FEM.	NEUT.
Acc.	Cĕlĕrem	cĕlĕrĕ	Acc.	Acrem	acrĕ
Gen.	Cĕlĕrĭs		Gen.	Acrĭs	
Dat. Abl.	Cĕlĕrī		Dat. Abl.	Acrī	

Plural.

N. V. A.	Cĕlĕrēs, cĕlĕriă		N. V. A.	Acrēs acriă
Gen.	Cĕlĕrium		Gen.	Acrium
Dat. Abl.	Cĕlĕrĭbŭs		Dat. Abl.	Acrĭbŭs

16. NUMERAL AND PRONOMINAL ADJECTIVES.

	Singular.				Plural.		
	MAS.	FEM.	NEUT.		MAS.	FEM.	NEUT.
Nom.	Ūnŭs	ūnă	ūnum, *one*	Nom.	Ūnī	ūnae	ūnă
Acc.	Ūnum	ūnam	ūnum	Acc.	Ūnōs	ūnās	ūnă
Gen.	Ūnĭŭs (all genders)			Gen.	Ūnōrum	ūnārum	ūnōrum
Dat.	Ūnī (all genders)			Dat.	Ūnīs (all genders)		
Abl.	Ūnō	ūnā	ūnō	Abl.	Ūnīs (all genders)		

Numeral and Pronominal Adjectives. 11

Unus is used in Plural with Substantives that have Plural only, or have a different meaning in Plural. Like unus, decline ullus, *any;* nullus, *none, no;* totus, *whole;* solus, *alone.*

	Singular.			Plural.		
	MAS.	FEM.	NEUT.	MAS.	FEM.	NEUT.
Nom.	Ălĭŭs	ălĭă	ălĭud, *other, another*	Ălĭī	ălĭae	ălĭă
Acc.	Ălĭŭm	ălĭam	ălĭud	Ălĭōs	ălĭās	ălĭă
Gen.	Ălĭŭs (all genders)			Ălĭōrum ălĭārum ălĭōrum		
Dat.	Ălĭī (all genders)			Ălĭīs (all genders)		
Abl.	Ălĭō	ălĭā	ălĭō	Ălĭīs (all genders)		

	Singular.					
	MAS.	FEM.	NEUT.	MAS.	FEM.	NEUT.
Nom.	Altĕr	altĕră	altĕrum, *other, the other*	Ŭtĕr	utră	utrum, *which (of two)*
Acc.	Altĕrum altĕram altĕrum			Utrum utram utrum		
Gen.	Altĕrĭŭs (all genders)			Utrĭŭs (all genders)		
Dat.	Altĕrī (all genders)			Utrī (all genders)		
Abl.	Altĕrō	altĕrā	altĕrō	Utrō	utrā	utrō

	Plural.					
	MAS.	FEM.	NEUT.	MAS.	FEM.	NEUT.
Nom.	Altĕrī	altĕrae	altĕră	Utrī	utrae	utră
Acc.	Altĕrōs	altĕrās	altĕră	Utrōs	utrās	utră
Gen.	Altĕrōrum altĕrārum altĕrōrum			Utrōrum utrārum utrōrum		
Dat. Abl.	Altĕrīs (all genders)			Utrīs (all genders)		

	Plural.					
	MAS.	FEM.	NEUT.	MAS.	FEM.	NEUT.
Nom.	Dŭŏ	duae	dŭŏ, *two*	Trēs	trēs	trĭă, *three*
Acc.	Duōs *or* duŏ	duās	dŭŏ	Trēs	trēs	trĭă
Gen.	Duōrum	duārum	duōrum	Trium (all genders)		
Dat. Abl.	Duōbŭs	duābŭs	duōbŭs	Trĭbus (all genders)		

Ambō, *both,* is declined like duŏ.
Other cardinal numbers, from 4 to 200, are undeclined.
From 200 to 900, cardinal numbers, are declined like the plural of *bonus.*
Millĕ, 1000, is an undeclined Adjective.
Millĭă, millium, millĭbŭs, *thousands,* is a Substantive.
Ordinal numbers are declined like *bonus.*
Distributive numbers are declined like the plural of *bŏnŭs.*

17. NUMERALS.

	CARDINAL, answering the question, how many?	ORDINAL, answering the question, which in numeric order?	DISTRIBUTIVE, answering the question, how many each?	ADVERBS, answering the question, how often?
1	ūnŭs	prīmŭs	singŭlī	sĕmĕl
2	duŏ	sĕcundŭs or altĕr	bīnī	bĭs
3	trēs	tertiŭs	ternī or trīnī	tĕr
4	quātuŏr	quartŭs	quăternī	quătĕr
5	quinquĕ	quintŭs	quīnī	quinquiēs
6	sex	sextŭs	sēnī	sexiēs
7	septem	septĭmŭs	septēnī	septiēs
8	octō	octāvŭs	octōnī	octiēs
9	nŏvem	nōnŭs	nŏvēnī	nŏviēs
10	dĕcem	dĕcĭmŭs	dēnī	dĕciēs
11	undĕcim	undĕcĭmŭs	undēnī	undĕciēs
12	duŏdĕcim	duŏdĕcĭmŭs	duŏdēnī	duŏdĕciēs
13	trĕdĕcim	tertiŭs dĕcĭmŭs	ternī dēnī	trĕdĕciēs
14	quătuordĕcim	quartŭs dĕcĭmŭs	quăternī dēnī	quătuordĕciēs
15	quindĕcim	quintŭs dĕcĭmŭs	quīnī dēnī	quindĕciēs
16	sēdĕcim	sextŭs dĕcĭmŭs	sēnī dēnī	sēdĕciēs
17	septemdĕcim	septĭmŭs dĕcĭmŭs	septēnī dēnī	septies dĕciēs
18	duodēvīgintī	duŏdēvīcesĭmŭs	duŏdēvīcēnī	duŏdēvīciēs
19	undēvīgintī	undēvīcēsĭmŭs	undēvīcēnī	undēviciēs
20	vīgintī	vīcēsĭmŭs	vīcēnī	vīciēs
21	ūnŭs et vīgintī	prīmŭs et vīcēsĭmŭs	vīcēnī singŭlī	sĕmĕl et vīciēs
30	trīgintā	trīcēsĭmŭs	trīcēnī	trīciēs
40	quadrāgintā	quadrāgēsĭmŭs	quadrāgēnī	quadrāgiēs
50	quinquāgintā	quinquāgēsĭmŭs	quinquāgēnī	quinquāgiēs
60	sexāgintā	sexāgēsĭmŭs	sexāgēnī	sexāgiēs
70	septuāgintā	septuāgēsĭmŭs	septuāgēnī	septuāgiēs
80	octōgintā	octōgēsĭmŭs	octōgēnī	octōgiēs
90	nōnāgintā	nōnāgesĭmŭs	nōnāgēnī	nōnāgiēs
100	centum	centēsĭmŭs	centēnī	centiēs
101	centum et ūnŭs	centēsĭmŭs prīmŭs	centēnī singŭlī	centiēs sĕmĕl
200	dūcentī	dūcentēsĭmŭs	dūcēnī	dūcentiēs
300	trĕcentī	trĕcentēsĭmŭs	trĕcēnī	trĕcentiēs
400	quadringentī	quadringentēsĭmŭs	quadringēnī	quadringentiēs
500	quingentī	quingentēsĭmŭs	quingēnī	quingentiēs
600	sexcentī	sexcentēsĭmŭs	sēcēnī	sexcentiēs
700	septingentī	septingentēsĭmŭs	septingēnī	septingentiēs
800	octingentī	octingentēsĭmŭs	octingēnī	octingentiēs
900	nongentī	nongentēsĭmŭs	nongēnī	nongentiēs
1000	millĕ	millēsĭmŭs	singŭlā milliă	milliēs
2000	duŏ milliă	bis millēsĭmŭs	bīnă milliă	bis milliēs

COMPARISON OF ADJECTIVES.

18. The Adjective has three degrees of comparison, the Positive, the Comparative, and the Superlative. So :—

Positive.	Comparative.	Superlative.
dūrŭs	dūrĭŏr	dūrissĭmŭs
hard	harder	hardest

GENERAL RULE.

Change *i* or *is* of the Genitive into *iŏr* for comparative, and into *issĭmŭs* for superlative.

Exceptions.

1. Adjectives with Nominative in *ĕr* form superlative by adding *rĭmŭs*.
So crēbĕr, *frequent*, crebrĭŏr, crēberrĭmŭs. Vĕtŭs, *ancient*, forms vĕterrĭmŭs, from stem *vĕter*.

2. Six adjectives form the superlative by changing *ĭs* into *lĭmus* :—

Făcĭlĭs, *easy*	Sĭmĭlĭs, *like*	Grăcĭlĭs, *slender*
Diffĭcĭlĭs, *difficult*	Dissĭmĭlĭs, *unlike*	Hŭmĭlĭs, *lowly*

Superlative *facil-lĭmŭs*, etc.

3. Adjectives ending in *dĭcŭs, fĭcŭs, vŏlŭs*, are compared in *entĭŏr, entissĭmŭs*.
So mălĕdĭcus, *abusive*, mălĕdĭcentĭŏr, mălĕdĭcentissĭmŭs.

4. Adjectives ending in *us* pure (preceded by a vowel), generally use in comparison *măgĭs, maxĭmĕ*.
So dŭbĭŭs, *doubtful*, măgis dŭbĭŭs, maxĭmĕ dŭbĭŭs.

19. IRREGULAR COMPARISON.

Positive.		Comparative.	Superlative.
bŏnŭs,	*good*	mĕlĭŏr	optĭmŭs
mălŭs,	*bad*	pejor	pessĭmŭs
magnŭs,	*great*	major	maxĭmŭs
parvŭs,	*small*	mĭnŏr	mĭnĭmŭs
multŭs,	*much.*	plūs	plŭrĭmŭs
nēquam,	*worthless.*	nēquĭŏr	nēquissĭmŭs

(*a*) *Plus* is only Neuter in Singular; but has full Plural.

(b) Dīvĕs, *rich*, dīvĭtiŏr *or* dītiŏr, dīvĭtissĭmŭs *or* dītissĭmŭs.

(c) Sĕnex, *old*, sĕniŏr, nātū maiŏr, *or* maiŏr, *superlative* nātū maxĭmŭs *or* maxĭmŭs.

Iŭvĕnĭs, *young*, iūniŏr, nātū mĭnŏr, *or* mĭnŏr, *superlative* nātū mĭnĭmŭs *or* mĭnĭmŭs. *Natu* means 'by birth.'

20. Adjectives of position derived from prepositions.

Preposition.	Positive.	Comparative.	Superlative.
ē, ex, *out of*	extĕrŭs, *outside*	extĕriŏr	extrēmŭs *or* extĭmŭs
sŭpĕr, *above*	sŭpĕrŭs, *high*	sŭpĕriŏr	suprēmŭs *or* summŭs
infrā, *below*	infĕrŭs, *deep*	infĕriŏr	infĭmŭs *or* ĭmŭs
post, *after*	postĕrus, *next after*	postĕriŏr	postrēmus *or* postŭmus.
intrā, *within*	—	intĕriŏr	intĭmŭs
prae, *before*	—	priŏr	prīmŭs
citrā, *on near side of*	—	cĭtĕriŏr	cĭtĭmŭs
ultrā, *beyond*	—	ultĕriŏr	ultĭmŭs, *last*
prŏpĕ, *near*	—	prŏpiŏr	proxĭmŭs
dē, *down from*	—	dētĕriŏr, *worse*	dēterrĭmŭs, *worst*

COMPARISON OF ADVERBS.

21. Adverbs derived from adjectives are compared in the same way, as is stated in the GENERAL RULE on p. 13, and have their endings *ŭs* for Comparative and *ē* for Superlative.
So :—

Positive.	Comparative.	Superlative.
dignŭs (*adj.*), *worthy*	digniŏr	dignissĭmŭs
dignē, *worthily*	digniŭs	dignissĭmē
audax (*adj.*), *bold*	audāciŏr	audācissĭmŭs
audacter, *boldly*	audāciŭs	audācissĭmē
grăvĭs (*adj.*), *heavy*	grăviŏr	gravissĭmŭs
grăvĭtĕr, *heavily*	grăviŭs	gravissĭmē

So :—

saepĕ, *often*	saepiŭs	saepissĭmē
diū, *long*	diūtiŭs	diūtissĭmē

IRREGULAR COMPARISON.

multum, *much*	plūs	plūrĭmum
magnŏpĕrĕ, *greatly*	măgĭs	maxĭmē

PRONOUNS.

22. Personal or Reflexive Pronouns are Substantival; that is to say, they take the place of a Substantive: the rest are generally Adjectival; that is to say, they take the place of an Adjective.

PERSONAL.
1. *FIRST PERSON.*

Singular.
Nom. Ĕgŏ, *I*
Acc. Mē
Gen. Meī
Dat. Mĭhī
Abl. Mē

Plural.
Nom. Nōs, *we*
Acc. Nōs
Gen. Nostrī, *or* nostrum
Dat. Nōbīs
Abl. Nōbīs

2. *SECOND PERSON.*

Nom. Voc. Tū, *thou*
Acc. Tē
Gen. Tuī
Dat. Tĭbī
Abl. Tē

Nom. Voc. Vōs, *you*
Acc. Vōs
Gen. Vestrī, *or* vestrum
Dat. Vōbīs
Abl. Vōbīs

REFLEXIVE.
SINGULAR AND PLURAL.

Nom. (Wanting)
Acc. Sē, *or* sēsē, *himself, herself, itself, themselves*
Gen. Suī
Dat. Sĭbī
Abl. Sē, *or* sēsē

POSSESSIVE.

23. Like *bŏnŭs.*
    Mĕus, meă, meum, *my, mine*
    Tuŭs, tuă, tuum, *thy, thine*
    Suŭs, suă, suum, *his, her, its, their own*

Like *nĭgĕr.*
    Nostĕr, nostră, nostrum, *our*
    Vestĕr, vestră, vestrum, *your*

Mĕŭs has vocative singular, *mī, meă, meum*; *tuŭs, suŭs* have none.

Demonstrative.

24.   Is, *that*, or *he, she, it*.

	Singular.				Plural.		
Nom.	Ĭs	eă	ĭd	*Nom.*	Iī	eae	eă
Acc.	Eum	eam	ĭd	*Acc.*	Eōs	eās	eă
Gen.	Eĭŭs ⎫	all genders		*Gen.*	Eōrum	eārum	eōrum
Dat.	Eī ⎬			*Dat.*	Iīs *or* ēīs ⎫	all genders	
Abl.	Eō	eā	eō	*Abl.*	Iīs *or* eīs ⎭		

Hic, *this* (near me).

	Singular.				Plural.		
Nom.	Hīc	haec	hōc	*Nom.*	Hī	hae	haec
Acc.	Hunc	hanc	hōc	*Acc.*	Hōs	hās	haec
Gen.	Hŭĭŭs ⎫	all genders		*Gen.*	Hōrum	hārum	hōrum
Dat.	Huīc ⎬			*Dat.*	Hīs ⎫	all genders	
Abl.	Hōc	hāc	hōc	*Abl.*	Hīs ⎭		

Ille, *that* (yonder).

	Singular.				Plural.		
Nom.	Illĕ	illă	illŭd	*Nom.*	Illī	illae	illă
Acc.	Illum	illam	illŭd	*Acc.*	Illōs	illās	illă
Gen.	Illĭŭs ⎫	all genders		*Gen.*	Illōrum	illārum	illōrum
Dat.	Illī ⎬			*Dat.*	Illīs ⎫	all genders	
Abl.	Illō	illā	illō	*Abl.*	Illis ⎭		

Istĕ, *that* (near you), is declined like *illĕ*.

Definitive.

25.   Idem, *same*.

	Singular.				Plural.		
Nom.	Īdem	eădem	ĭdem	Iīdem	eaedem	eădem	
Acc.	Eundem	eandem	ĭdem	Eōsdem	eāsdem	eădem	
Gen.	Ēiusdem ⎫	all genders		Eōrundem	eārundem	eōrundem	
Dat.	Eīdem ⎬			Iisdem *or* ĕisdem ⎫	all genders		
Abl.	Eōdem	eădem	ĕōdem	Iisdem *or* ĕisdem ⎭			

Ipsĕ, *self*, is declined like *illĕ*, but with neuter singular Nominative, Accusative, *ipsum*.

Relative.

26.   Qui, *who*, or *which*.

	Singular.				Plural.		
Nom.	Quī	quae	quŏd	*Nom.*	Quī	quae	quae
Acc.	Quem	quam	quŏd	*Acc.*	Quōs	quās	quae
Gen.	Cūĭŭs ⎫	all genders		*Gen.*	Quōrum	quārum	quōrum
Dat.	Cuī ⎬			*Dat.*	Quĭbŭs *or* quīs ⎫	all genders	
Abl.	Quō	quā	quō	*Abl.*	Quĭbŭs *or* quīs ⎭		

Compounded Pronouns.

INTERROGATIVE.			INDEFINITE.		
27.	Quis, *who?*			Quis, *any one.*	
Nom. Quis	(quis)	quid	*Nom.* Quis	quă	quid
Acc. Quem	quam	quid	*Acc.* Quem	quam	quid

In other forms, as Relative.
Indefinite Nominative Plural Neuter, *quă* or *quae.*

The form *qui, quae, quŏd*, declined as the Relative, is used in agreement with a Substantive, either as Interrogative or Indefinite.

COMPOUNDED PRONOUNS.

28. Some pronouns are strengthened by a syllable added to them, which remains invariable. So quīdam, *a certain one,* Genitive, cūiusdam; ecquĭs, *any one?* Genitive, eccūiŭs?

29.   TABLE OF PRONOUNS.

PERSONAL.
1st Pers.	ĕgŏ			*I*
	nōs			*we*
2d Pers.	tū			*thou*
	vōs			*you*
3d Pers. (supplied by Demonstratives)				*he, she, it*

REFLEXIVE.
1st Pers.	(me)	ipsum	ipsam	*myself*
2d Pers.	(te)	ipsum	ipsam	*yourself*
3d Pers.	se			*him, her, its, self, themselves*

POSSESSIVE.
1st Pers.	meŭs	meă	meum	*my, mine*
	nostĕr	nostră	nostrum	*our*
2d Pers.	tuŭs	tuă	tuum	*thy, thine*
	vestĕr	vestră	vestrum	*your*
3d Pers.	suŭs	suă	suum	*his, her, its, their, own*

DEMONSTRATIVE.
All Pers.	ĭs	eă	ĭd	*that, or he, she, it*
	hīc	haec	hōc	*this (near me)*
	illĕ	illă	illŭd	*that (yonder)*
	istĕ	istă	istŭd	*that (near you)*

DEFINITIVE.
| All Pers. | ĭdem | eădem | ĭdem | *the same* |
| | ipsĕ | ipsă | ipsum | *self* |

RELATIVE.
Relative	quī	quae	quŏd	*who, which*
Interrogative	quĭs	(quĭs)	quid	*who?*
Indefinite	quĭs	quă	quĭd	*any*

B. L. W.   B

THE VERB.

30. In the Latin Verb there are—
1. Three Persons—First, Second, and Third.
2. Two Numbers—Singular and Plural.
3. Seven Tenses—four Primary and three Historic.

  PRIMARY.—*Present;* as, ămō, *I love.*
    Future Simple; as, ămābō, *I shall love.*
    Future Perfect; as, ămāvĕrō, *I shall have loved.*
    Perfect; as, ămāvī, *I have loved.*
  HISTORIC.—*Imperfect;* as, ămābam, *I was loving.*
    Aorist; as, ămāvī, *I loved.*
    Pluperfect; as, ămāvĕram, *I had loved.*

NOTE.—There is only one form for the Perfect and Aorist; so *amavi* either = *I have loved,* or *I loved.*

4. Three Moods of the Verb Finite.
  Indicative; as, ămō, *I love.*
  Imperative; as, ămā, *love thou.*
  Conjunctive; as, ămem, *I may love.*

5. Verb-Nouns of the Verb Infinite.
  Infinitive, with the Gerunds and Supines which act as its cases.
  Participles, declined like Adjectives.

6. Two Voices—Active and Passive; as
  Ămo, *I love;* ămŏr, *I am loved.*

CONJUGATIONS.

31. There are four Conjugations of Regular Verbs.

  First Conjugation—character, A
  Second ,,   ,, E.
  Third   ,,   ,, Consonant or U.
  Fourth ,,   ,, I.

To conjugate a verb, the Present, Perfect, and Supine Stems must be known.

1. The Present Stem in the First, Second, and Fourth Conjugations is found by taking the syllable *rĕ* from the Present Infinitive Active; in the Third Conjugation by taking away the syllable *ĕrĕ.*

2. The Perfect Stem is found by taking the syllable *ī* from the Perfect Indicative Active.

3. The Supine Stem is found by taking the syllable *um* from the Supine.

DEPONENT VERBS.

32. Deponent Verbs (with a few exceptions) are passive in form, active in meaning; as, ūtŏr, *I use*.

1. The Present Stem in the First, Second, and Fourth Conjugations is found by taking the syllable *ri* from the Present Infinitive; in the Third Conjugation by taking away the syllable *i*.

2. The Supine Stem is found by taking the syllable *um* from the Supine.

Deponent Verbs are conjugated like Passive Verbs, but have also Gerunds, Supines, Participles, and Future Infinitives of active form.

Intransitive Deponents have no Supine in *ū*, nor Gerundive.

POWERS.

33. Active and Deponent Verbs are either—

Transitive, acting on an object; as, amo te, *I love thee*, or Intransitive, not acting on an object; as, sto, *I stand*.

Intransitive Verbs are not used in the Passive except impersonally, that is to say, without a subject—as, pugnātum est, *he*, or *they fought* (lit. *there was fighting*).

34. FORMATION OF TENSES.

Present Stem.	Perfect Stem.	Supine Stem.
All Presents.	All Perfects Active.	Supines.
All Futures Simple.	All Pluperfects Active.	Fut. Participle Active.
All Imperfects.	Future Perfect Active.	Perf. Participle Passive.
Gerund and Gerundive.		

35. ENGLISH MEANINGS OF THE

	Name of Tense.	Active Voice.
PRESENT STEM TENSES.	*Present Indic.*	I love, am loving, do love. Thou lovest, art loving, dost love, etc.
	Present Conj.	I may love. Thou mayst love. He may love, etc.
	Present Imper.	Love (thou). Love (ye).
	Present Infinitive	To love.
	Present Partic.	Loving (*adjective*).
	Imperf. Indic.	I was loving. Thou wast loving, etc.
	Imperf. Conj.	I might, should love. Thou mightst, shouldst love, etc.
	Fut. Simp. Indic.	I shall love. Thou wilt love. He will love, etc.
	Fut. Simp. Imper.	Thou must love. He must love, etc.
	Gerund	Loving (*substantive*).
	Gerundive	
PERFECT STEM TENSES.	*Perfect Indic.*	I have loved. Thou hast loved. He has loved.
	Aorist	I loved. Thou lovedst. He loved, etc.
	Perfect Conj.	I may have loved. Thou mayst have loved, etc.
	Perfect Infin.	To have loved.
	Imperf. Indic.	I had loved. Thou hadst loved, etc.
	Pluperf. Conj.	I should have loved. Thou wouldst have loved, etc.
	Future Perfect	I shall have loved. Thou wilt have loved, etc.
SUPINE STEM TENSES.	*Supine in* um	To love (*substantive*).
	Supine in u	In loving (*substantive*).
	Future Participle	About to love.
	Future Infinitive	To be about to love.
	Perfect Participle	*None.*

LATIN TENSES. VERB 'To Love.'

PASSIVE VOICE.

I am being loved.   Thou art being loved.   He is being loved, etc.

I may be loved.   Thou mayest be loved.   He may be loved, etc.

             Be (thou) loved.   Be (ye) loved.
To be loved.
  None.
I was being loved.
I might, should be loved.   Thou mightst, shouldst be loved, etc.

I shall be loved.   Thou wilt be loved.   He will be loved.

             Thou must be loved.   He must be loved, etc.

Meet to be loved (*adjective*).

I have been loved.   Thou hast been loved.   He has been loved, etc.

I was loved.   Thou wast loved.   He was loved, etc.
I may have been loved.   Thou mayst have been loved, etc.

To have been loved.
I had been loved.   Thou hadst been loved.   He had been loved, etc.
I should have been loved.   Thou wouldst have been loved, etc.

I shall have been loved.   Thou wilt have been loved, etc.

  None.
  None.
  None.
To be about to be loved.
Loved, *or* Having been loved.

36. TENSE-ENDINGS OF THE

	Tense.	Conjugation.	ACTIVE ENDINGS.					
PRESENT STEM TENSES.	*Pres. Indic.*	1, 2, 4 3	-o -o	-s -is	-t -it	-mus -ĭmus	-tis -ĭtis	-nt[2] -unt
	Pres. Conj.	1 2, 3, 4	-em[1] -am	-es -as	-et -at	-ēmus -āmus	-ētis -ātis	-ent -ant
	Pres. Imper.	1, 2, 4 3	 e				-te -ite	
	Pres. Infin.	1, 2, 4 3	-re -ĕre					
	Pres. Partic.	1, 2 3, 4	-ns -ens					
	Impf. Indic.	1, 2 3, 4	-bam -ēbam	-bas -ēbas	-bat -ēbat	-bāmus -ēbāmus	-bātis -ēbātis	-bant -ēbant
	Impf. Conj.	1, 2, 4 3	-rem -ĕrem	-res -ĕres	-ret -ĕret	-rēmus -ĕrēmus	-retis -ĕrētis	-rent -ĕrent
	Future Indic.	1, 2 3, 4	-bo -am	-bis -es	-bit -et	-bĭmus -ēmus	-bĭtis -ētis	-bunt -ent
	Future Imp.	1, 2, 4 3	-to -ito	-to -ito			-tote -itote	-nto[2] -unto
	Gerund	1, 2 3, 4	-ndum -endum					
PERFECT STEM TENSES.	*Perf. Ind. Aor.*	all	-i	-isti	-it	-ĭmus	-istis	-ērunt or ēre
	Perfect Conj.	all	-ĕrim	-ĕris	-ĕrit	-ĕrĭmus	-ĕrĭtis	-ĕrint
	Perfect Infin.	all	-isse					
	Pluperf. Indic.	all	-ĕram	-ĕras	-ĕrat	-ĕrāmus	-ĕrātis	-ĕrant
	Pluperf. Conj.	all	-issem	-isses	-isset	-issēmus	-issētis	-issent
	Fut. Perf. Indic.	all	-ĕro	-ĕris	-ĕrit	-ĕrĭmus	-ĕrĭtis	-ĕrint
SUPINE STEM TENSES.	*Supine*	all	*Acc.* -um ; *Abl.* -u.					
	Future Partic.	all	-urus -ura -urum					
	Future Infin.	all	-urus -ura -urum esse					
	Perfect Partic.	all						

[1] In *A*-Verbs the *a* is lost in these endings, as *amo* (for *ama-o*). *amem*, etc.
[2] *I*-Verbs insert *u*, as *audi-unt, audi-unto.*

FOUR REGULAR CONJUGATIONS.

PASSIVE ENDINGS.

-or[1]	-ris[2]	-tur	-mur	-mĭni	-ntur[3]
-or	-ĕris[2]	-itur	-imur	-ĭmĭni	-untur
-er[1]	-ĕris[2]	-ĕtur	-ĕmur	-ĕmĭni	-entur
-ar	-āris[2]	-ātur	-āmur	-āmĭni	-antur
	-re			-mĭni	
	-ĕre			-ĭmĭni	
-ri					
-i					
None					
None					
-bar	-bāris[2]	-batur	-bāmur	-bāmĭni	-bantur
-ēbar	-ēbāris[2]	-ēbātur	-ēbāmur	-ēbāmĭni	-ēbantur
-rer	-rēris[2]	-rctur	-rēmur	-rēmĭni	-rentur
-ĕrer	-ĕrēris[2]	-ĕrētur	-ĕrēmur	-ĕrēmĭni	-ĕrentur
-bor	-bĕris[2]	-bĭtur	-bĭmur	-bĭmĭni	-buntur
-ar	-ēris[2]	-ētur	-ēmur	-ēmĭni	-entur
	-tor	-tor			-ntor[3]
	-itor	-itor			-untor
Gerundive -ndus					
-endus					

[In the PASSIVE VOICE these are COMPOUND TENSES, being formed by the Past Participle with the tenses of the Verb SUM.]

-us -a -um

---

[1] In *A*-Verbs the *a* is lost in these endings, as *amor* (for *ama-or*), *amer*.
[2] There is an alternative form, *re* for *ris*.
[3] *I*-Verbs insert *u*, as *audi-untur*, *audi-untor*.

37. THE VERB SUM, 'I Am.'

		PRESENT.	IMPERFECT.	FUTURE SIMPLE.

VERB FINITE	*INDICATIVE.*	*I am.*
		S. 1. Sum
		  2. ĕs
		  3. es -t
		Pl. 1. sŭmus
		  2. es -tis
		  3. sunt
			I was.
			ĕram
			ĕras
			ĕrat
			ĕrāmus
			ĕrātis
			ĕrant
				I shall be.
				ĕro
				ĕris
				ĕrit
				ĕrĭmus
				ĕrĭtis
				ĕrunt

	CONJUNCTIVE.	*I may be.*
		S. 1. sim
		  2. sis
		  3. sit
		Pl. 1. sīmus
		  2. sītis
		  3. sint
			I might, should, would be.
			es -sem *or* fŏrem
			es -ses ,, fŏres
			es -set ,, fŏret
			es -sēmus ,, fŏrēmus
			es -sētis ,, fŏretis
			es -sent ,, fŏrent	

	IMPERATIVE.	*Be thou.*
		S. 2. es
		  3. —
		Pl. 2. es -te
		  3. —
				Thou must be.
				es -to
				es -to
				es -tōte
				sunto

VERB INFINITE	*INFIN.*		*To be.* es -se	
	PARTIC.			

PRESENT STEM Es-

Prosum takes *d* before *e*; so, prosum, pro-d-es,
Absum, praesum, have Present

THE VERB SUM, 'I Am.'

PERFECT STEM Fu-

Perfect and Aorist.	Pluperfect.	Future Perfect.
I have been. I was.	*I had been.*	*I shall have been.*
S. 1. fu -i	fu -ĕram	fu -ĕro
2. fu -isti	fu -ĕras	fu -ĕris
3. fu -it	fu -ĕrat	fu -ĕrit
Pl. 1. fu -ĭmus	fu -ĕrāmus	fu -ĕrĭmus
2. fu -istis	fu -ĕrātis	fu -ĕrĭtis
3. fu -ērunt or -ēre	fu -ĕrant	fu -ĕrint
I may have been.	*I might, would, should have been.*	
S. 1. fu -ĕrim	fu -issem	
2. fu -ĕris	fu -isses	
3. fu -ĕrit	fu -isset	
Pl. 1. fu -ĕrĭmus	fu -issēmus	
2. fu -ĕrĭtis	fu -issētis	
3. fu -ĕrint	fu -issent	
To have been. fu -isse		

Future Participle—futūrus, *about to be.*
Future Infinitive—fŏre *or* futūrus esse, *to be about to be.*

pro-d-est, prósumus, pro-d-estis, prosunt.
Participles—absens, praesens.

38. A-VERBS—ACTIVE VOICE.

		PRESENT STEM Ama-		
		PRESENT.	IMPERFECT.	FUTURE SIMPLE.
VERB FINITE	INDICATIVE	*I love, am loving, do love.* S. 1. Amo 2. ama -s 3. ama -t Pl. 1. ama -mus 2. ama -tis 3. ama -nt	*I was loving.* ama -bam ama -bas ama -bat ama -bāmus ama -bātis ama -bant	*I shall love.* ama -bo ama -bis ama -bit ama -bĭmus ama -bĭtis ama -bunt
	CONJUNCTIVE	*I may love.* S. 1. amem 2. ames 3. amet Pl. 1. amēmus 2. amētis 3. ament	*I might, would, should love.* ama -rem ama -res ama -ret ama -rēmus ama -rētis ama -rent	
	IMPERATIVE	*Love thou.* S. 2. ama 3. — Pl. 2. ama -tŏ 3. —		*Thou must love.* ama -to ama -to ama -tōte ama -nto
VERB INFINITE	INFIN.	*To love.* ama -re		
	PARTIC.	*Loving.* ama -ns		
	GERUND	*Acc.* ama -ndum, *loving.* *Gen.* ama -ndi *Dat.* ama -ndo *Abl.* ama -ndo		

A-VERBS—ACTIVE VOICE.

PERFECT STEM **Amav-**		
PERFECT AND AORIST.	PLUPERFECT.	FUTURE PERFECT.
I have loved. I loved. S. 1. amav -i 2. amav -isti 3. amav -it Pl. 1. amav -ĭmus 2. amav -istis 3. amav -ērunt *or* -ēre	*I had loved.* amav -ĕram amav -ĕras amav -ĕrat amav -ĕrāmus amav -ĕrātis amav -ĕrant	*I shall have loved.* amav -ĕro amav -ĕris amav -ĕrit amav -ĕrĭmus amav -ĕrĭtis amav -ĕrint
I may have loved. S. 1. amav -ĕrim 2. amav -ĕris 3. amav -ĕrit Pl. 1. amav -ĕrĭmus 2. amav -ĕrĭtis 3. amav -ĕrint	*I might, would, should have loved.* amav -issem amav -isses amav -isset amav -issēmus amav -issētis amav -issent	
To have loved. amav -isse		

SUPINE STEM **Amat-**
Supine { *Accusative,* amat -um, *to love.* { *Ablative,* amat -u, *in loving.* Future Participle, amat -urus, *about to love.* Future Infinitive, amat -urus esse, *to be about to love.*

39. E-VERBS—ACTIVE VOICE.

PRÈSENT STEM Mone-

Present.	Imperfect.	Future Simple.
I advise, am advising, dò advise.	*I was advising.*	*I shall advise.*
S. 1. Mone -o	mone -bām	mone -bo
2. mone -s	mone -bas	mone -bis
3. mone -t	mone -bat	mone -bit
Pl. 1. monē -mus	mone -bāmus	mone -bĭmus
2. monē -tis	mone -bātis	mone -bĭtis
3. mone -nt	mone -bant	mone -bunt
I may advise.	*I might, would, should advise.*	
S. 1. mone -am	mone -rem	
2. mone -as	mone -res	
3. mone -at	mone -ret	
Pl. 1. mone -amus	mone -rēmus	
2. mone -atis	mone -rētis	
3. mone -ant	mone -rent	
Advise thou.		*Thou must advise.*
S. 2. mone		mone -to
3. —		mone -to
Pl. 2. monē -te		mone -tōte
3. —		mone -nto

To advise.
mone -re

Advising.
mone -ns

Acc. mone -ndum, *advising.*
Gen. mone -ndi
· *Dat.* mone -ndo
Abl. mone -ndo

E-VERBS—ACTIVE VOICE.

PERFECT STEM Monu-

Perfect and Aorist.	Pluperfect.	Future Perfect.
I have advised. I advised.	*I had advised.*	*I shall have advised.*
S. 1. monu -i	monu -ĕram	monu -ĕro
2. monu -isti	monu -ĕras	monu -ĕris
3. monu -it	monu -ĕrat	monu -ĕrit
Pl. 1. monu -ĭmus	monu -ĕrāmus	monu -ĕrĭmus
2. monu -istis	monu -ĕrātis	monu -ĕrĭtis
3. monu -ērunt *or* -ēre	monu -ĕrant	monu -ĕrint
I may have advised.	*I might, would, should have advised*	
S. 1. monu -ĕrim	monu -issem	
2. monu -ĕris	monu -isses	
3. monu -ĕrit	monu -isset	
Pl. 1. monu -ĕrĭmus	monu -issēmus	
2. monu -ĕrĭtis	monu -issētis	
3. monu -ĕrint	monu -issent	

To have advised.
monu -isse

SUPINE STEM Monit-

Supine { *Accusative*, monit -um, *to advise.*
{ *Ablative*, monit -u, *in advising.*

Future Participle, monit -ūrus, *about to advise.*
Future Infinitive, monit -ūrus esse, *to be about to advise.*

40. CONSONANT-VERBS—ACTIVE VOICE.

		PRESENT STEM Reg-		
		Present.	Imperfect.	Future Simple.
VERB FINITE	*INDICATIVE*	*I rule, am ruling, do rule.* S. 1. Reg -o 2. reg -is 3. reg -it Pl. 1. reg -ĭmus 2. reg -itis 3. reg -unt	*I was ruling.* reg -ēbam reg -ēbas reg -ēbat reg -ēbāmus reg -ēbātis reg -ēbant	*I shall rule.* reg -am reg -es reg -et reg -ēmus reg -ētis reg -ent
	CONJUNCTIVE	*I may rule.* S. 1. reg -am 2. reg -as 3. reg -at Pl. 1. reg -āmus 2. reg -ātis 3. reg -ant	*I might, would, should rule.* reg -ĕrem reg -ĕres reg -ĕret reg -ĕrēmus reg -ĕrētis reg -ĕrent	
	IMPERATIVE	*Rule thou.* S. 2. reg -ĕ 3. — Pl. 2. reg -ĭte 3. —	—	*Thou must rule.* reg -ĭto reg -ĭto reg -ĭtōte reg -unto
VERB INFINITE	*INFIN.*	*To rule.* reg -ĕre		
	PARTIC.	*Ruling.* reg -ens		
	GERUND	*Acc.* reg -endum, *ruling.* *Gen.* reg -endi *Dat.* reg -endo *Abl.* reg -endo		

CONSONANT-VERBS—ACTIVE VOICE.

PERFECT STEM Rex-

Perfect and Aorist.	Pluperfect.	Future Perfect.
I have ruled. I ruled.	*I had ruled.*	*I shall have ruled.*
S. 1. rex -i	rex -ĕram	rex -ĕro
2. rex -isti	rex -ĕras	rex -ĕris
3. rex -it	rex -ĕrat	rex -ĕrit
Pl. 1. rex -ĭmus	rex -ĕrāmus	rex -ĕrĭmus
2. rex -istis	rex -ĕrātis	rex -ĕrĭtis
3. rex -ĕrunt *or* -ēre	rex -ĕrant	rex -ĕrint
I may have ruled.	*I might, would, should have ruled.*	
S. 1. rex -ĕrim	rex -issem	
2. rex -ĕris	rex -isses	
3. rex -ĕrit	rex -isset	
Pl. 1. rex -ĕrĭmus	rex -issēmus	
2. rex -ĕrĭtis	rex -issētis	
3. rex -ĕrint	rex -issent	
To have ruled: rex -isse		

SUPINE STEM Rect-

Supine { *Accusative,* rect -um, *to rule.*
{ *Ablative,* rect -u, *in ruling.*

Future Participle, rect -ūrus, *about to rule.*
Future Infinitive, rect -ūrus esse, *to be about to rule.*

41. I-VERBS—ACTIVE VOICE.

		PRESENT STEM Audi-		
		PRESENT.	IMPERFECT.	FUTURE SIMPLE.
VERB FINITE.	INDICATIVE.	*I hear, am hearing, do hear.* S. 1. Audi -o 2. audī -s 3. audi -t Pl. 1. audi -mus 2. audi -tis 3. audi -unt	*I was hearing.* audi -ēbam audi -ēbas audi -ēbat audi -ēbāmus audi -ēbātis audi -ēbant	*I shall hear.* audi -am audi -es audi -et audi -ēmus audi -ētis audi -ent
	CONJUNCTIVE.	*I may hear.* S. 1. audi -am 2. audi -as 3. audi -at Pl. 1. audi -āmus 2. audi -ātis 3. audi -ant	*I might, would, should hear.* audi -rem audi -res audi -ret audi -rēmus audi -rētis audi -rent	
	IMPERATIVE.	*Hear thou.* S. 2. audi 3. — Pl. 2. audi -te 3. —		*Thou must hear.* audi -to audi -to audi -tōte audi -unto
VERB INFINITE.	INFIN.	*To hear.* audi -re		
	PARTIC.	*Hearing.* audi -ens		
	GERUND.	*Acc.* audi -endum, *hearing.* *Gen.* audi -endi *Dat.* audi -endo *Abl.* audi -endo		

I-VERBS—ACTIVE VOICE.

PERFECT STEM Audiv-

Perfect and Aorist.	Pluperfect.	Future Perfect.
I have heard. I heard.	*I had heard.*	*I shall have heard.*
S. 1. audiv -i	audiv -ĕram	audiv -ĕro
2. audiv -isti	audiv -ĕras	audiv -ĕris
3. audiv -it	audiv -ĕrat	audiv -ĕrit
Pl. 1. audiv -ĭmus	audiv -ĕrāmus	audiv -ĕrĭmus
2. audiv -istis	audiv -ĕrātis	audiv -ĕrītis
3. audiv -ērunt or -ēre	audiv -ĕrant	audiv -ĕrint
I may have heard.	*I might, would, should have heard.*	
S. 1. audiv -ĕrim	audiv -issem	
2. audiv -ĕris	audiv -isses	
3. audiv -ĕrit	audiv -isset	
Pl. 1. audiv -ĕrĭmus	audiv -issēmus	
2. audiv -ĕrītis	audiv -issētis	
3. audiv -ĕrint	audiv -issent	
	To have heard. audiv -isse	

SUPINE STEM Audit-

Supine { *Accusative,* audit -um, *to hear.*
{ *Ablative,* audit -u, *in hearing.*
Future Participle, audit -ūrus, *about to hear.*
Future Infinitive, audit -urus esse, *to be about to hear.*

42. A-VERBS—PASSIVE VOICE.

PRESENT STEM Ama-

		PRESENT.	IMPERFECT.	FUTURE S[...]
VERB FINITE.	*INDICATIVE.*	*I am being loved.* S. 1. Amor 2. ama -ris *or* -re 3. ama -tur *Pl.* 1. ama -mur 2. ama -mĭni 3. ama -ntur	*I was being loved.* ama -bar ama -bāris *or* -bāre ama -bătur ama -bāmur ama -bāmĭni ama -bantur	*I shall be* ama -bor ama -bĕris ama -bĭtur ama -bĭmu[r] ama -bĭmĭn[i] ama -buntu[r]
	CONJUNCTIVE.	*I may be loved.* S. 1. amer 2. amēris *or* -re 3. amētur *Pl.* 1. amēmur 2. amēmĭni 3. amentur	*I might, would, should be loved.* ama -rer ama -rēris *or* -rēre ama -rētur ama -rēmur ama -rēmĭni ama -rentur	
	IMPERATIVE.	*Be thou loved.* S. 2. ama -re 3. — *Pl.* 2. ama -mĭni 3. —		*Thou must b[e]* áma -t[o] ama -t[o] — ama -n[t]
VERB INFINITE.	*INFIN.*	*To be loved.* ama -ri		
	PARTIC.			
	GERUNDIVE.	ama -ndus, -nda, -ndum, *meet to be loved.*		

A-VERBS—PASSIVE VOICE.

SUPINE STEM Amat-

Perfect and Aorist.	Pluperfect.	Future Perfect.
I have been, I was, loved.	*I had been loved.*	*I shall have been loved.*
S. 1. amat -us sum	amat -us ĕram	amat -us ĕro
2. amat -us es	amat -us ĕras	amat -us ĕris
3. amat -us est	amat -us ĕrat	amat -us ĕrit
Pl. 1. amat -i sumus	amat -i ĕrāmus	amat -i ĕrĭmus
2. amat -i estis	amat -i ĕrātis	amat -i ĕrĭtis
3. amat -i sunt	amat -i ĕrant	amat -i ĕrunt
I may have been loved.	*I might, would, should have been loved.*	
S. 1. amat -us sim	amat -us essem	
2. amat -us sis	amat -us esses	
3. amat -us sit	amat -us esset	
Pl. 1. amat -i simus	amat -i essēmus	
2. amat -i sitis	amat -i essētis	
3. amat -i sint	amat -i essent	
To have been loved. amat -us esse		
Loved or *having been loved.* amat -us		

A Future Infinitive can be formed by *iri* with the Supine: amat -um iri, *to be about to be loved.*

43. E-VERBS—PASSIVE VOICE.

PRESENT STEM Mone-

	Present.	Imperfect.	Future Simple.
	I am being advised.	*I was being advised.*	*I shall be advised.*
S. 1.	Mone -or	mone -bar	mone -bor
2.	mone -ris *or* re	mone -bāris *or* bāre	mone -bĕris *or* bĕre
3.	mone -tur	mone -bātur	mone -bĭtur
Pl. 1.	mone -mur	mone -bāmur	mone -bĭmur
2.	mone -mĭni	mone -bāmĭni	mone -bĭmini
3.	mone -ntur	mone -bantur	mone -buntur
	I may be advised.	*I might, would, should be advised.*	
S. 1.	mone -ar	mone -rer	
2.	mone -āris *or* āre	mone -rēris *or* rēre	
3.	mone -ātur	mone -rētur	
Pl. 1.	mone -āmur	mone -rēmur	
2.	mone -āmĭni	mone -rēmĭni	
3.	mone -antur	mone -rentur	
	Be thou advised.		*Thou must be advised.*
S. 2.	mone -re		mone -tor
3.	—		mone -tor
Pl. 2.	mone -mĭni		—
3.	—		mone -ntor
	To be advised. mone -ri.		

mone -ndus, -nda, -ndum, *meet to be advised.*

E-VERBS—PASSIVE VOICE.

SUPINE STEM Monit-

Perfect and Aorist.	Pluperfect.	Future Perfect.
I have been, I was, advised.	*I had been advised.*	*I shall have been advised.*
S. 1. monit -us sum	monit -us ĕram	monit -us ĕro
2. monit -us es	monit -us ĕras	monit -us ĕris
3. monit -us est	monit -us ĕrat	monit -us ĕrit
Pl. 1. monit -i sumus	monit -i ĕrāmus	monit -i ĕrĭmus
2. monit -i estis	monit -i ĕrātis	monit -i ĕrĭtus
3. monit -i sunt	monit -i ĕrant	monit -i ĕrunt
I may have been advised.	*I might, would, should have been advised.*	
S. 1. monit -us sim	monit -us essem	
2. monit -us sis	monit -us esses	
3. monit -us sit	monit -us esset	
Pl. 1. monit -i simus	monit -i essēmus	
2. monit -i sitis	monit -i essētis	
3. monit -i sint	monit -i essent	

To have been advised.
monit -us esse

Advised or *having been advised.*
monit -us

A Future Infinitive can be formed by *iri* with the Supine: monit -um iri *to be about to be advised.*

44. CONSONANT-VERBS—PASSIVE VOICE.

PRESENT STEM Reg-

		Present.	Imperfect.	Future Simple.
VERB FINITE.	*INDICATIVE.*	*I am being ruled.* S. 1. Reg -or 2. reg -ĕris *or* ĕre 3. reg -ĭtur *Pl.* 1. reg -ĭmur 2. reg -ĭmĭni 3. reg -untur	*I was being ruled.* reg -ēbar reg -ēbāris *or* ebāre reg -ēbātur reg -ēbāmur reg -ēbāmĭni reg -ēbantur	*I shall be ruled* reg -ar reg -ēris *or* ēr reg -ētur reg -ēmur reg -ēmĭni reg -entur
	CONJUNCTIVE.	*I may be ruled.* S. 1. reg -ar 2. reg -āris *or* āre 3. reg -atur *Pl.* 1. reg -āmur 2. reg -āmĭni 3. reg -antur	*I might, would, should be ruled.* reg -ĕrer reg -ĕrēris *or* erēre reg -ĕrētur reg -ĕrēmur reg -ĕrēmĭnĭ reg -ĕrentur	
	IMPERATIVE.	*Be thou ruled* S. 2. reg -ĕre 3. — *Pl.* 2. reg -ĭmĭni 3. —		*Thou must be rul* reg -ĭtor reg -ĭtor — reg -untor
VERB INFINITE.	*INFIN.*		*To be ruled.* reg -i	
	PARTIC.			
	GERUNDIVE.	reg -endus, -enda, -endum, *meet to be ruled.*		

CONSONANT-VERBS—PASSIVE VOICE.

SUPINE STEM **Rect-**		
PERFECT AND AORIST.	PLUPERFECT.	FUTURE PERFECT.
I have been, I was, ruled.	*I had been ruled.*	*I shall have been ruled.*
S. 1. rect -us sum	rect -us ĕram	rect -us ĕro
2. rect -us es	rect -us ĕras	rect -us ĕris
3. rect -us est	rect -us ĕrat	rect -us ĕrit
Pl. 1. rect -i sumus	rect -i ĕrāmus	rect -i ĕrĭmus
2. rect -i estis	rect -i ĕrātis	rect -i ĕrĭtis
3. rect -i sunt	rect -i ĕrant	rect -i ĕrunt
I may have been ruled.	*I might, would, should have been ruled.*	
S. 1. rect -us sim	rect -us essem	
2. rect -us sis	rect -us esses	
3. rect -us sit	rect -us esset	
Pl. 1. rect -i simus	rect -i essēmus	
2. rect -i sitis	rect -i essētis	
3. rect -i sint	rect -i essent	
To have been ruled. rect -us esse		
Ruled or *having been ruled.* rect -us		
A Future Infinitive can be formed by *iri* with the Supine: rect -um iri, *to be about to be ruled.*		

45. I-VERBS—PASSIVE VOICE.

		PRESENT STEM **Audi-**		
		PRESENT.	IMPERFECT.	FUTURE SIMPLE.
VERB FINITE.	INDICATIVE.	*I am being heard.* S. 1. Audi -or 2. audi -ris *or* re 3. audi -tur Pl. 1. audi -mur 2. audi -mĭni 3. audi -untur	*I was being heard.* audi -ēbar audi -ēbāris *or* ebāre audi -ēbātur audi -ēbāmur audi -ēbāmĭni audi -ēbantur	*I shall be heard.* audi -ar audi -ēris *or* ēre audi -ētur audi -ēmur audi -ēmĭni audi -entur
	CONJUNCTIVE.	*I may be heard.* S. 1. audi -ar 2. audi -āris *or* āre 3. audi -ātur Pl. 1. audi -āmur 2. audi -āmĭni 3. audi -antur	*I might, would, should be heard.* audi -rer audi -rēris *or* ĕrēre audi -rētur audi -rēmur audi -rēmĭni audi -rentur	
	IMPERATIVE.	*Be thou heard.* S. 2. audi -re 3. — Pl. 2. audi -mĭnı 3. —		*Thou must be heard.* audi -tor audi -tor — audi -untor
VERB INFINITE.	INFIN.	*To be heard.* audi -ri		
	PARTIC.			
	GERUNDIVE.	audi -endus, -enda, -endum, *meet to be heard.*		

I-VERBS—PASSIVE VOICE.

SUPINE STEM **Audit-**		
PERFECT AND AORIST.	PLUPERFECT.	FUTURE PERFECT.
I have been, I was, heard. S. 1. audit -us sum 2. audit -us es 3. audit -us est Pl. 1. audit -i sumus 2. audit -i estis 3. audit -i sunt	*I had been heard.* audit -us ĕram audit -us ĕras audit -us ĕrat audit -i ĕrāmus audit -i ĕrātis audit -i ĕrant	*I shall have been heard.* audit -us ĕro audit -us ĕris audit -us ĕrit audit -i ĕrĭmus audit -i ĕrĭtis audit -i ĕrunt
I may have been heard. S. 1. audit -us sim 2. audit -us sis 3. audit -us sit Pl. 1. audit -i simus 2. audit -i sitis 3. audit -i sint	*I might, would, should have been heard.* audit -us essem audit -us esses audit -us esset audit -i essēmus audit -i essētis audit -i essent	
To have been heard. audit -us esse		
Heard or *having been heard.* audit -us		
A Future Infinitive can be formed by *iri* with the Supine : audit -um iri, *to be about to be heard.*		

46. EXAMPLE OF DEPONENT VERB.

			PRESENT.	IMPERFECT.	FUTURE SIMPLE.
VERB FINITE.	INDICATIVE		*I am using.* S. 1. Ut-or 2. ut -ĕris *or* ĕre 3. ut -ĭtur Pl. 1. ut -ĭmur 2. ut -ĭmĭni 3. ut -untur	*I was using.* ut -ēbar ut -ēbāris *or* ebāre ut -ēbātur ut -ēbāmur ut -ēbāmĭni ut -ēbantur	*I shall use.* ut -ar ut -ēris *or* ēre ut -ētur ut -ēmur ut -ēmĭni ut -entur
	CONJUNCTIVE		*I may use.* S. 1. ut -ar 2. ut -āris *or* āre 3. ut -ātur Pl. 1. ut -āmur 2. ut -āmĭni 3. ut -antur	*I might, would or should use.* ut -ĕrer ut -ĕrēris *or* erēre ut -ĕrētur ut -ĕrēmur ut -ĕrēmĭni ut -ĕrentur	
	IMPERATIVE		*Use thou.* S. 2. ut -ĕre 3. — Pl. 2. ut -ĭmĭni 3. —		*Thou must use.* ut -ĭtor ut -ĭtor — ut -untor
VERB INFINITE.	INFIN.		*To use.* ut -i		
	PARTIC.		*Using.* ut -ens.		
	GERUND		*Acc.* ut -endum, *using.* *Gen.* ut -endi *Dat.* ut -endo *Abl.* ut -endo *Gerundive.*—ut -endus, -enda, -endum, *meet to be used.*		

CONSONANT CONJUGATION.

SUPINE STEM Us-

Perfect and Aorist.	Pluperfect.	Future Perfect.
I have used. I used.	*I had used.*	*I shall have used.*
S. 1. us -us sum	us -us ĕram	us -us ĕro
2. us -us es	us -us ĕras	us -us ĕris
3. us -us est	us -us ĕrat	us -us ĕrit
Pl. 1. us -i sumus	us -i ĕrāmus	us -i ĕrĭmus
2. us -i estis	us -i ĕrātis	us -i ĕrĭtis
3. us -i sunt	us -i ĕrant	us -i ĕrunt
I may have used.	*I might, would, should have used.*	
S. 1. us -us sim	us -us essem	
2. us -us sis	us -us esses	
3. us -us sit	us -us esset	
Pl. 1. us -i simus	us -i essēmus	
2. us -i sitis	us -i essētis	
3. us -i sint	us -i essent	

To have used.
us -us esse

Having used.
us -us

Supine { us -um, *to use.*
{ us -u, *in using.*

Future Participle, us -ūrus, *about to use.*
Future Infinitive, us -ūrus esse, *to be about to use.*

VERBS IN *IO* OF THE THIRD CONJUGATION.

47. Verbs in *io* of the Third Conjugation in their tenses derived from the Present stem throw away *i* before another *i*, *ĕr*, and *e* at the end of the word. So:—

ACTIVE—
INDIC. *Pres.* căpĭō, căpĭs, căpĭt, căpĭmŭs, căpĭtĭs, căpiunt.
     Fut. căpiam, căpiēs, căpiĕt, căpiēmŭs, căpiētĭs, căpient.
     Imp. căpiēbam, căpiēbas, etc.
CONJ. *Pres.* căpiam, căpiās, căpiăt, căpiāmŭs, căpiātĭs, căpiant.
     Imp. căpĕrem, căpĕrēs, etc.
IMPER. *Pres.* căpĕ, căpĭtĕ.
     Fut. căpĭtō, căpĭtōtĕ, căpĭuntō.
INF. *Pres.* căpĕrĕ. *Gerund.* căpĭendum, -endī, -endō.

PASSIVE—
INDIC. *Pres.* căpĭŏr, căpĕrĭs, căpĭtŭr, căpĭmŭr, căpĭmĭnī, căpiuntŭr.
     Fut. căpiăr, căpiērĭs, etc.
     Imp. căpiēbăr, căpiēbārĭs, etc.
CONJ. *Pres.* căpiăr, căpiārĭs, etc.
     Imp. căpĕrĕr, căpĕrēris, etc.
IMPER. *Pres.* căpĕrĕ, căpĭmĭnī.
     Fut. căpĭtŏr, căpiuntŏr.
INF. *Pres.* căpi. *Gerundive*, căpiendŭs.

MOODS.

48. The Indicative Mood affirms and questions.
The Imperative Mood commands.
The Conjunctive Mood has two general uses:—

    1. Pure, or not depending on another verb.
    2. Subjunctive, or depending on another verb.

The Pure Conjunctive has the signs *would, should; can, could; may, might.*

The Subjunctive is generally translated like the Indicative; but sometimes (after Conjunctions) it takes the signs of the Conjunctive, as

    Ĕdĕ ŭt vīvās, *eat that you may live.*

Gerund, Supines, Participles. 45

In prohibitions (*commands* with a negative), use
Perfect (Aorist) Conjunctive with Second Person.
Present Conjunctive with First and Third Persons.

The Infinitives ending in *rĕ*, *ī* are Present or Imperfect; Infinitives in *issĕ*, *ŭs esse*, Perfect or Pluperfect.

GERUND, SUPINES, PARTICIPLES.

49. The Gerund is the Neuter Gerundive Participle declined as a Verb-Noun.

The Supines are cases (Accusative and Ablative) of a Verb-Noun of the Fourth Declension.

The Gerundive is used to express fitness or necessity, either

Personally; as, vītă tŭendă est, *life should be protected;* or Impersonally; as, eundum est, *one must go.*

The other Participles are

Act. Pres. ămans, *loving*
Fut. ămātūrŭs, *about to love*
Perf. wanting

Pass. Pres. wanting
Fut. wanting
Perf. ămatŭs, *loved.*

DERIVED VERBS.

50. *Frequentative Verbs* (First Conj.)—

Express repeated or more vigorous action; they end in *tŏ, sŏ, ĭtŏ, ĭtŏr;* as,

Cantō, *I sing out,* from cănō, *I sing.*
Rŏgĭtō, *I ask often,* from rŏgō, *I ask.*

Inceptive Verbs (Third Conj.)—

Express beginning of action. They end in *scō;* as,

Pallescō, *I turn pale,* from palleō, *I am pale.*

Desiderative Verbs (Fourth Conj.)—

Express desire of action. They end in *ūriō;* as,

Esūriō, *I am hungry,* from ĕdō, *I eat.*

QUASI-PASSIVE AND SEMI-DEPONENT VERBS.

51. *Quasi-Passive Verbs*—
have an Active form with Passive meaning; as,
Vāpŭlō, *I am beaten.*

Semi-Deponent Verbs—
have 1. Active Present with a Perfect of Passive form; as,
Audeō, *I dare,* ausŭs sum, *I dared.*

2. Active Perfect with Deponent Perfect Participle; as,
Prandeō, *I dine,* prandī, pransŭs, *having dined.*

DEFECTIVE VERBS.

52. Defective Verbs are incomplete, having only some tenses or parts of tenses.

The Verbs coepī, *I have begun,* ōdī, *I hate,* měmĭnī, *I remember,* have no Present-Stem tenses.

Aiō, *I say 'ay,' affirm.*

INDIC. *Pres.* aiŏ	aīs	aīt	—	—	aiunt
Imp. aiēbam *complete*					
CONJ. *Pres.* —	aiās	aiăt	—	—	aiant

Inquam, *I say.*

INDIC. *Pres.* inquam	inquĭs	inquĭt	inquĭmŭs	—	inquiunt
Imp. —	—	inquiēbăt	—	—	inquiēbant
S. Fut. —	inquiēs	inquiĕt	—	—	—
Perf. —	inquistī	inquĭt	—	—	—
IMPER. *Pres.* —	inqŭe	—	—	inquĭte	—

In Latin as in Greek there was an older conjugation of Verbs ending in *mi,* of which *sum* and *inquam* are traces.

IMPERSONAL VERBS.

53. Impersonal Verbs are conjugated only in the Third Person Singular of the Finite Verb, and in the Infinitive.

Impersonal Verbs.

Active Impersonals have no Passive voice.
They are principally of the Second Conjugation.

With Acc.	Ŏportĕt	*it behoves*	dĕcĕt	*becomes*	dēdĕcĕt	*misbecomes*
	Pĭgĕt	*it irks*	pŭdĕt	*shames*	poenĭtĕt	*repents*
	Taedĕt	*it disgusts*	mĭsĕrĕt	*moves pity*	—	—
With Dat.	Lĭbĕt	*it pleases*	lĭcĕt	*is lawful*	lĭquĕt	*is clear*
With ad and Acc.	Attĭnĕt	*it relates*	pertĭnĕt	*belongs*	—	—

The Persons are expressed by the cases following the Verb, as:—

Ŏportĕt {
 mē, *It behoves me*
 tē, ,, *thee*
 eum, ,, *him*
 nōs, ,, *us*
 vōs, ,, *you*
 eōs, ,, *them*
} or {
 I ought
 thou oughtest
 he
 we
 you
 they
} *ought*

Lĭcĕt {
 mĭhĭ, *It is lawful for me*
 tĭbĭ, ,, *thee*
 eī, ,, *him*
 nōbīs, ,, *us*
 vōbīs, ,, *you*
 iīs, ,, *them*
} or {
 I may
 thou mayest
 he
 we
 you
 they
} *may*

Intransitive Verbs may be used impersonally in the Passive, as, lūdĭtŭr, *it is played*. The persons are expressed by an Ablative with the Preposition *ā, ăb*, following the verb, as:—

Lūdĭtŭr {
 ā mē, *It is played by me*, or, *I play*
 ā tē, ,, *thee*, or, *thou playest*
 ăb eō, ,, *him*, or, *he plays*
 ā nōbīs, ,, *us*, or, *we play*
 ā vōbīs, ,, *you*, or, *you play*
 ăb iīs, ,, *them*, or, *they play*
}

The Neuter of the Gerundive Participle is used impersonally in the same way with a Dative, as:—

Lūdendum est {
 mĭhĭ, *It must be played by me*, or, *I*
 tĭbĭ, ,, *thee*, or, *thou*
 eī, ,, *him*, or, *he*
 nōbīs, ,, *us*, or, *we*
 vōbīs, ,, *you*, or, *you*
 iīs, ,, *them*, or, *they*
} *must play*

54. VERBS IN COMMON USE.

Present.	Infinitive.	Perfect.	Supine.	
Do	-ărĕ	dĕdi	dătum	*give*
Sto	-ărĕ	stĕtī	stătum	*stand*
Măneo	-ērĕ	mansi	mansum	*remain*
Iŭbeo	-ērĕ	iussi	iussum	*order*
Pendeo	-ērĕ	pĕpendi	pensum	*hang*
Sĕdeo	-ērĕ	sēdi	sessum	*sit*
Vĭdeo	-ērĕ	vīdi	vīsum	*see*
Dīco	-ĕrĕ	dixi	dictum	*say*
Dūco	-ĕrĕ	duxi	ductum	*lead*
Fīgo	-ĕrĕ	fixi	fixum	*fix*
Fingo	-ĕrĕ	finxi	fictum	*fashion*
Vīvo	-ĕrĕ	vixi	victum	*live*
Mergo	-ĕrĕ	mersi	mersum	*drown*
Mitto	-ĕrĕ	mīsi	missum	*send*
Scrībo	-ĕrĕ	scripsi	scriptum	*write*
Prĕmo	-ĕrĕ	pressi	pressum	*press*
Gĕro	-ĕrĕ	gessi	gestum	*carry on*
Răpio	-ĕrĕ	răpui	raptum	*seize*
Cŏlo	-ĕrĕ	cŏlui	cultum	*till*
Sperno	-ĕrĕ	sprēvi	sprētum	*despise*
Quaero	-ĕrĕ	quaesīvi	quaesītum	*seek*
Pendo	-ĕrĕ	pĕpendi	pensum	*weigh*
Disco	-ĕrĕ	dĭdĭci	—	*learn*
Curro	-ĕrĕ	cŭcurri	cursum	*run*
Parco	-ĕrĕ	pĕperci	parsum	*spare*
Cădo	-ĕrĕ	cĕcĭdi	căsum	*fall*
Caedo	-ĕrĕ	cĕcĭdi	caesum	*beat, kill*
Căno	-ĕrĕ	cĕcĭni	cantum	*sing*
Făcio	-ĕrĕ	fēci	factum	*make, do*
Vinco	-ĕrĕ	vīci	victum	*conquer*
Ago	-ĕrĕ	ēgi	actum	*do, drive*
Căpio	-ĕrĕ	cēpi	captum	*catch*
Solvo	-ĕrĕ	solvi	sŏlūtum	*loose, pay*
Apĕrio	-īrĕ	ăpĕrui	ăpertum	*open*
Vincio	-īrĕ	vinxi	vinctum	*bind*
Vĕnio	-īrĕ	vēni	ventum	*come*

DEPONENTS.

	Perf. Part.		
Reor		rătus	*think*
Lŏquor	,,	,,	lŏcūtus *speak*
Sĕquor	,,	,,	sĕcūtus *follow*
Quĕror	,,	,,	questus *complain*
Mŏrior	,,	,,	mortuus *die*
Nascor	,,	,,	nātus *be born*
Nanciscor	,,	,,	nactus *find*

ANOMALOUS VERBS.

55. Anomalous Verbs do not form all their parts according to rule.

Conjugation-Form.

	Be able.	Wish.	Not-wish.	Wish-rather.
1 Pers. Pres.	Possum	Vŏlŏ	Nōlŏ	Mālŏ
2 Pers. „	pŏtĕs	vīs	nonvīs	māvīs
Infin. „	possĕ	vellĕ	nollĕ	mallĕ
Perfect	pŏtŭ-ī	vŏlŭ-ī	nōlŭ-ī	mālŭ-ī
Ger. in dī	—	vŏlend-ī	nōlend-ī	mālend-ī
„ · dō	—	vŏlend-ō	nōlend-ō	mālend-ō
Part. Pres.	—	vŏlens	nōlens	mālens

Pŏtens, *able, powerful*, is used as an Adjective.

	Bear.	Be made.	Go.	Can.
1 Pers. Pres.	Fĕrŏ	Fīŏ	Ĕŏ	Quĕŏ
2 Pers. „	fers	fīs	īs	quīs
Infin. „	ferrĕ	fĭĕrī	īrĕ	quīrĕ
Perfect	tŭlī	factŭs sum	īvī	quīvī
Ger. in dum	fĕrend-um	—	ĕund-um	
„ dī	fĕrend-ī	—	ĕund-ī	
„ dō	fĕrend-ō	—	ĕund-ō	
Supine in um	lāt-um	—	ĭt-um	
„ ū	lāt-ū	—	ĭt-ū	
Part. Pres.	fĕr-ens	—	īens (ĕunt-ĭs)	
„ Fut.	lāt-ūrŭs	—	ĭt-ūrŭs	

Fĕrŏr (Passive) has *Pres. Ind. 2d Pers.* ferrĭs; *3d Pers.* fertŭr; *Imperf. Conj.* fĕr-r-ĕr, ferrērĭs, etc., and *Inf.* ferrī. Supino-stem forms, lātŭs sum, etc.

Fīŏ in the Present-stem forms is the Passive of făcĭŏ, which is regular in the Active, and in the Supine-stem forms of the Passive.

Quĕo and its compound nĕquĕŏ (*cannot*) form their tenses like ĕŏ.

Edō, *I eat*, often changes some of its forms as follows :—

Pres. 2d Pers. Sing. ĕdĭs or ēs; *3d Pers. Sing.* ĕdĭt or est; *Infin.* ĕdĕrĕ or essĕ; *Imperf. Conj.* ĕdĕrem or essem.

Pres. Conj. ĕdim, ĕdīs, ĕdīt, is used. Other forms are regular.

56. Anomalous Verbs.

TENSE-FORMATION.
Indicative Mood.
Present.

S.	1. Possum	Vŏlŏ	Nōlŏ	Mălŏ	Fĕrō	Fĭō		Ĕō
	2. Pŏtĕs	Vīs	Nonvīs	Māvis	Fers	Fīs		Īs
	3. Pŏtest	Vult	Nonvult	Māvult	Fert	Fĭt		Ĭt
Pl.	1. Possŭmŭs	Vŏlŭmŭs	Nōlŭmŭs	Mālŭmŭs	Fĕrĭmŭs	—		Īmŭs
	2. Pŏtestĭs	Vultĭs	Nonvultĭs	Māvultĭs	Fertĭs	—		Ītĭs
	3. Pŏssunt	Vŏlunt	Nōlunt	Mālunt	Fĕrunt	Fīunt		Ĕunt

Imperfect.

S.	1. Pŏt-ĕram	Vŏlē-bam	Nōlē-bam	Mālē-bam	Fĕrē-bam	Fīē-bam	Ī-bam	
	2.	-ĕrās	-bās	-bās	-bās	-bās	-bās	-bās
	3.	-ĕrăt	-băt	-băt	-băt	-băt	-băt	-băt
Pl.	1.	-ĕrāmŭs	-bāmŭs	-bāmŭs	-bāmŭs	-bāmŭs	-bāmŭs	-bāmŭs
	2.	-ĕrātĭs	-bātĭs	-bātĭs	-bātĭs	-bātĭs	-bātĭs	-bātĭs
	3.	-ĕrant	-bant	-bant	-bant	-bant	-bant	-bant

Future Simple.

S.	1. Pŏt-ĕrō	Vŏl-am	Nōl-am	Māl-am	Fĕr-am	Fī-am		Ī-bō
	2.	-ĕrĭs	-ēs	-ēs	-ēs	-ēs	-ēs	-bĭs
	3.	-ĕrĭt	-ĕt	-ĕt	-ĕt	-ĕt	-ĕt	-bĭt
Pl.	1.	-ĕrĭmŭs	-ēmŭs	-ēmŭs	-ēmŭs	-ēmŭs	-ēmŭs	-bĭmŭs
	2.	-ĕrĭtĭs	-ētĭs	-ētĭs	-ētĭs	-ētĭs	-ētĭs	-bĭtĭs
	3.	-ĕrunt	-ent	-ent	-ent	-ent	-ent	-bunt

Perfect and Aorist.

S.	1. Pŏtŭ-ī	Vŏlŭ-ī	Nōlŭ-ī	Mālŭ-ī	Tŭl-ī		Īv-ī	
	2.	-istī	-istī	-istī	-istī	-istī	—	-istī
	3.	-ĭt	-ĭt	-ĭt	-ĭt	-ĭt	—	-ĭt
Pl.	1.	-ĭmŭs	-ĭmŭs	-ĭmŭs	-ĭmŭs	-ĭmŭs	—	-ĭmŭs
	2.	-istĭs	-istĭs	-istĭs	-istĭs	-istĭs	—	-istĭs
	3.	-ērunt	-ērunt	-ērunt	-ērunt	-ērunt	—	-ērunt
		or ērĕ	*or* ērĕ	*or* ērĕ	*or* ērĕ	*or* ērĕ		*or* ērĕ

Pluperfect.

S.	1. Pŏtŭ-ĕram	Vŏlŭ-ĕram	Nōlŭ-ĕram	Mālŭ-ĕram	Tŭl-ĕram		Īv-ĕram	
	2.	-ĕrās	-ĕrās	-ĕrās	-ĕrās	-ĕrās	—	-ĕrās
	3.	-ĕrăt	-ĕrăt	-ĕrăt	-ĕrăt	-ĕrăt	—	-ĕrăt
Pl.	1.	-ĕrāmŭs	-ĕrāmŭs	-ĕrāmŭs	-ĕrāmŭs	-ĕrāmŭs	—	-ĕrāmŭs
	2.	-ĕrātĭs	-ĕrātĭs	-ĕrātĭs	-ĕrātĭs	-ĕrātĭs	—	-ĕrātĭs
	3.	-ĕrant	-ĕrant	-ĕrant	-ĕrant	-ĕrant	—	-ĕrant

Future Perfect.

S.	1. Pŏtŭ-ĕrō	Vŏlŭ-ĕrō	Nōlŭ-ĕrō	Mālŭ-ĕrō	Tŭl-ĕrō		Īv-ĕrō	
	2.	-ĕrĭs	-ĕrĭs	-ĕrĭs	-ĕrĭs	-ĕrĭs	—	-ĕrĭs
	3.	-ĕrĭt	-ĕrĭt	-ĕrĭt	-ĕrĭt	-ĕrĭt	—	-ĕrĭt
Pl.	1.	-ĕrĭmŭs	-ĕrĭmŭs	-ĕrĭmŭs	-ĕrĭmŭs	-ĕrĭmus	—	-ĕrĭmŭs
	2.	-ĕrĭtĭs	-ĕrĭtĭs	-ĕrĭtĭs	-ĕrĭtĭs	-ĕrĭtĭs	—	-ĕrĭtĭs
	3.	-ĕrint	-ĕrint	-ĕrint	-ērint	-ĕrint	—	-ĕrint

Anomalous Verbs.

TENSE-FORMATION.
Conjunctive Mood.
Present.

1.Poss -im	Vĕl -im	Nōl -im	Māl -im	Fĕr -am	Fī -am	É -am
2. -īs	-īs	-īs	-īs	-ās	-ās	-ās
3. -It	-It	-It	-It	-ăt	-ăt	-ăt
1. -īmŭs	-īmŭs	-īmŭs	-īmŭs	-āmŭs	-āmŭs	-āmŭs
2. -ītĭs	-ītĭs	-ītĭs	-ītĭs	-ātĭs	-ātĭs	-ātĭs
3. -int	-int	-int	-int	-ant	-ant	-ant

Imperfect.

1.Poss -em	Vell -em	Noll -em	Mall -em	Ferr -em	Fĭĕr -em	Īr -em
2. -ēs	-ēs	-ēs	-ēs	-ēs	-ēs	-ēs
3. -ĕt	-ĕt	-ĕt	-ĕt	-ĕt	-ĕt	-ĕt
1. -ēmŭs	-ēmŭs	-ēmŭs	-ēmŭs	-ēmŭs	-ēmŭs	-ēmŭs
2. -ētĭs	-ētĭs	-ētĭs	-ētĭs	-ētĭs	-ētĭs	-ētĭs
3. -ent	-ent	-ent	-ent	-ent	-ent	-ent

Perfect and Aorist.

1.Pŏtŭ -ĕrim	Vŏlŭ -ĕrim	Nōlŭ -ĕrim	Mālŭ -ĕrim	Tŭl -ĕrim	—	Īv -ĕrim
2. -ĕrĭs	-ĕrĭs	-ĕrĭs	-ĕrĭs	-ĕrĭs	—	-ĕrĭs
3. -ĕrĭt	-ĕrĭt	-ĕrĭt	-ĕrĭt	-ĕrĭt	—	-ĕrĭt
1. -ĕrĭmŭs	-ĕrĭmŭs	-ĕrĭmŭs	-ĕrĭmŭs	-ĕrĭmŭs	—	-ĕrĭmŭs
2. -ĕrĭtĭs	-ĕrĭtĭs	-ĕrĭtĭs	-ĕrĭtĭs	-ĕrĭtĭs	—	-ĕrĭtĭs
3. -ĕrint	-ĕrint	-ĕrint	-ĕrint	-ĕrint	—	-ĕrint

Pluperfect.

1.Pŏtŭ -issem	Vŏlŭ -issem	Nōlŭ -issem	Mālŭ -issem	Tŭl -issem	—	Īv -issem
2. -issēs	-issēs	-issēs	-issēs	-issēs	—	-issēs
3. -issĕt	-issĕt	-issĕt	-issĕt	-issĕt	—	-issĕt
1. -issēmŭs	-issēmŭs	-issēmŭs	-issēmŭs	-issēmŭs	—	-issēmŭs
2. -issētĭs	-issētĭs	-issētĭs	-issētĭs	-issētĭs	—	-issētĭs
3. -issent	-issent	-issent	-issent	-issent	—	-issent

Imperative Mood.
Present.

Sing. 2d Pers. Nōlī   Fĕr   Fī   Ī
Pl.   ,,   Nōlītŏ   Fertŏ   Fītŏ   Ītŏ

Future.

Sing. 2d Pers. Nōlītō   Fertō   Ītō
       3d Pers. Nōlītō   Fertō   Ītō
Pl.   2d Pers. Nōlītōtĕ   Fertōtĕ   Ītōtĕ
       3d Pers. Nōluntō   Fĕruntō   Euntō

(For the Parts of Verb Infinite, see **55**.)

PREPOSITIONS.

57. The following Prepositions take the Accusative:—

Ăd, *to, at, near, off*
Adversŭs, } *toward, against*
Adversum, }
Antĕ, *before*
Apŭd, *at, in, among, with*
Circum, *around*
Circā, } *about*
Circĭter, }
Cĭs, } *on the near side of*
Cītrā, }
Contrā, *against, over against*
Ergā, *towards*
Extrā, *outside of, without, out of*
Infrā, *below*
Inter, *between, among, amidst*
Intrā, *within*

Iuxtā, *adjoining to, beside*
Ob, *over against, by reason of*
Pĕnĕs, *in the power of*
Pĕr, *through*
Pōnĕ, *behind*
Post, *after, behind*
Praetĕr, *beside*
Prŏpĕ, *near*
Proptĕr, *nigh, on account of*
Sĕcundum, *next, along, according to*
Suprā, *above*
Trans, *across*
Ultrā, *beyond*
Versŭs, } *towards*
Versum, }

The following take the Ablative:—

A, ăb, abs, *by, from*
Absquĕ, *without*
Clam, *without the knowledge of*
Cōram, *in the presence of*
Cum, *with*
Dē, *down from, down, concerning*
Ē, ex, *out of, from*

Pălam, *in sight of*
Prae, *before, owing to, compared with*
Prō, *before, for, instead of*
Sĭnĕ, *without*
Tĕnŭs, *as far as*

Cum is attached to the Personal, Reflexive, and Relative Pronouns; as, *mēcum, tēcum, sēcum, nōbiscum, vōbiscum, quōcum, quācum, quĭbuscum.*

The following take Accusative or Ablative:—

In, *into, against* (Acc.), *in, upon, among* (Abl.)
Sŭb, *up to, under* (Acc.), *under* (Abl.)
Sŭpĕr, *over, upon*
Subtĕr, *under*

In, sŭb, with Accusative imply motion; with Ablative, rest.

CONJUNCTIONS.

58. Conjunctions either (*a*) join words and sentences without influencing mood: as, ĕt, quĕ, ac, atquĕ (*and*); aut, vĕl, vĕ (*either, or*); sĕd, autem (*but*); nam, ĕnim (*for*); or (*b*) join sentences, influencing mood: as, ut (*that*); nē (*lest*); quum (*when, since*), etc.

SYNTAX

WITH EXERCISES.

THE SIMPLE SENTENCE.

a. A Simple Sentence is the expression of a simple thought.

b. That of which something is said is called the Subject. The Subject must be a Substantive, or something which can take its place.

The following can take the place of a Substantive :—

    1. An Adjective.   3. An Infinitive.
    2. A Pronoun.   4. A Clause.

c. A Clause is a sentence which cannot stand by itself.

d. The Finite Verb which declares what is said of the Subject is called the Predicate.

Instead of the Finite Verb we often find the Copula or link (some part of the verb *sum*), and a word (called the Complement) linked by it to the Subject, both together forming the Predicate.

Some other verbs link the Complement to the Subject; such as, fīō, *I become*, nascŏr, *I am born*, vĭdeŏr, *I seem*, and verbs of calling, making, thinking, in the Passive Voice.

e. Some Verbs (called Transitive), require an object to complete the sense.

f. Every sentence in English or Latin must contain a Subject and Predicate, and can be analysed in the following form :—

Subject.	Predicate.	
Socrates	docet	
Socrates	teaches	
	Copula.	Complement.
Socrates	erat	sapiens
Socrates	*was*	*a wise man*

With an object—

Subject.	Predicate.	
	Verb.	Object.
Socrates	docebat	iuvenes
Socrates	*used to teach*	*young men*

With Adverbial Expressions (Extension of Predicate) qualifying the Verb—

Subject.	Predicate.		
	Verb.	Object.	Extension.
Socrates	docebat	iuvenes	Athenis
Socrates	*used to teach*	*young men*	*at Athens*

Exercise 1.

AGREEMENT OF ADJECTIVE.

An Adjective or Participle agrees in Gender, Number, and Case with the Substantive which it describes.

'Very' is often a sign of the Superlative.

1. Bona regina. 2. Fortes milites. 3. Longae hastae. 4. Parvorum puerorum. 5. Vir bonus. 6. Bonam uxorem. 7. Cari parentes. 8. Cara patria. 9. Magnis deabus. 10. Docti pueri. 11. Dulcius carmen. 12. Rex amatus. 13. Levi opere. 14. Maximorum regum. 15. Atrocis proelii.

1. A-short letter. 2. Of-a-wise father. 3. To-a-fortified city. 4. Great gifts. 5. Of-a-good queen. 6. A-brave soldier. 7. Great cities. 8. Of the-black slave. 9. To-the-beautiful sister. 10. Of-the-green grass. 11. Of-useful works. 12. By-the-sharp sword. 13. Sweet songs. 14. A-very-wise man. 15. A-shorter song.

Exercise 2.

AGREEMENT OF VERB.

A Verb Finite agrees with the Nominative of its Subject in Number and Person.

The word which answers to the question 'Who?' or 'What?' is the Nominative Case to the Verb.

On Agreement.

If a Pronoun is the subject, it is usually understood.

1. Mater amat. 2. Puer audit. 3. Rex vocabat. 4. Dux regit. 5. Pater monebat. 6. Matres amantur. 7. Cives reguntur. 8. Vox audita est. 9. Milites pugnaverant. 10. Hostes vincuntur. 11. Magister docebat. 12. Puer discit. 13. Laudavimus. 14. Regina laudabit. 15. Urbs munita erat.

1. Trees grow. 2. They-have-been-called. 3. The-spears wound. 4. The-kings are-praising. 5. The-soldier will-have-fought. 6. The-city is-being-fortified. 7. The-enemies have-been-conquered. 8. The-enemy will-be-conquered. 9. The-boys were-calling. 10. The-soldier is-fighting. 11. The-soldier was-fighting. 12. The-girls had-danced. 13. The-master walks. 14. The-boys are-being-taught. 15. The-girl is-praised.

Exercise 3.

APPOSITION.

a. If two or more Substantives refer to or describe the same thing they are put in the same case. This is called Apposition.

b. When two Substantives not referring to the same thing come together, the latter is put in the Genitive, and generally has the sign 'of' in English.

The Verb, etc., sometimes agrees with the word in apposition.

1. Urbs Roma. 2. Pyrenaei montes. 3. Romulus rex. 4. Flumen Tamesis. 5. Philosophi morum magistri sunt. 6. Philosophia morum magistra est. 7. Romulus Remi frater erat. 8. Roma urbs est antiquissima. 9. Libri nostra gaudia sunt. 10. Oppidum Gabii captum est. 11. Thebae, urbs validissima, Boeotiae caput est. 12. Aurum res pretiosa est. 13. Vos iudices estis. 14. Dolor est magnum malum. 15. Avus eius praetor erat.

1. Of-the-city (of) Rome. 2. For-King Romulus. 3. Of-the-river Tiber. 4. Hope is the-expectation of-good. 5. Caius is our father. 6. The-Nile is a-very-great river. 7. Britain is an-island. 8. Athens is the-capital of-Attica. 9. Gold, the-cause of-crime, has been found. 10. Pompeius will-be-made general. 11. The-sun, a-great-light, is shining. 12. He-was-made praetor and consul. 13. Horses are useful animals. 14. Experience is the-best mistress. 15. The-town of-Gabii will be taken.

Exercise 4.
RECAPITULATORY.

If the subject consists of more than one person, words applying to them are put in the Plural.

1. Servus timebat. 2. Puellae canebant. 3. Britannia est patria nostra. 4. Bona lex lata est. 5. Arbores crescent. 6. Epistola scribebatur. 7. Opus confectum est. 8. Grave onus relictum erat. 9. Boni pueri, discipuli nostri, laudabantur. 10. Urbs Roma incensa est. 11. Sidera micabant. 12. Velox cervus currebat. 13. Aurum et argentum, optima dona, missa sunt. 14. Fortissimi milites pugnabant. 15. Patres matresque amantur.

1. To-learn is useful. 2. Brutus, the-consul, was-sent. 3. The-Tiber is a-great river. 4. The-city of-Carthage was-destroyed. 5. Good gifts are very-useful. 6. To-read well is difficult. 7. A-great battle was-being-fought. 8. Catiline, a-wicked man, was-condemned. 9. Brave men are-always praised. 10. Iron is useful. 11. The-master was-reading. 12. The time was very-short. 13. These books are easier. 14. Augustus, the-emperor of-Rome, is dead. 15. Caesar and Brutus are dead.

Exercise 5.
RECAPITULATORY.

Verbs agree with the First Person rather than with the Second, and with the Second rather than with the Third.

1. Ego et Cicero valemus. 2. Tu et Tullia valetis. 3. Urbs Roma bene munita est. 4. Multae epistolae scriptae sunt. 5. Fortes milites laudabuntur. 6. Nos pueri felicissimi sumus. 7. Numa, rex Romanorum, vir erat sapientissimus. 8. Maxima dona missa erunt. 9. Carmina pulcherrima cantantur. 10. Tuus canis amissus est. 11. Magister irascitur. 12. Hostium exercitus fusus est. 13. Athenae urbs pulcherrima erat. 14. Ignavi milites non laudabuntur. 15. Socrates, philosophus doctissimus, mortuus est.

1. Happy boys are playing. 2. The walls of this town are very high. 3. We consuls are wanting. 4. The cowardly soldiers would have fled. 5. Manlius, a Roman soldier, was wounded. 6. Archimedes, a very wise man, was killed. 7. You and your son are happy. 8. A most loving wife was weeping. 9. You and I will come hither, my friend Brutus. 10. This river is called the Thames. 11. Sparta is the capital of Laconia. 12. Brutus, the consul, had fled. 13. This girl, my sister, will come very quickly. 14. A disgraceful crime was being committed. 15. The cavalry and infantry of the enemy were defeated.

Exercise 6.
RECAPITULATORY.

Adjectives agree with the Masculine rather than with the Feminine.

1. Numantia urbs quotidie diripitur. 2. Signa inferuntur. 3. Galli manserant. 4. Requiescat Italia. 5. Brutus Caiusque, consules Romani, veniebant. 6. Gramen est viride. 7. Amavissemus. 8. Tu vicisti, ego vincam. 9. Exercitus noster devictus erat. 10. Tu vales, ego quoque valeo. 11. Iuba, rex fortissimus, captus est. 12. Consul fio. 13. Certior facta est. 14. Regeremus. 15. Frater et soror pulcherrimi sunt.

1. My father and mother are dead. 2. I am the cause of this war. 3. He is the master of these learned boys. 4. Camillus was called the father of his country. 5. The Belgae are the bravest of the Gauls. 6. The battle had begun. 7. Many beautiful girls were standing around. 8. The camp was being attacked. 9. Sparta, the capital of Laconia, is being besieged. 10. Caesar, the leader of the Romans, is coming. 11. This beautiful city will be laid waste. 12. Saguntum, a wealthy city, is being plundered. 13. Lions are very fierce animals. 14. Very many fishes were being caught. 15. A loud voice might have been heard.

Exercise 7.
RECAPITULATORY.

If the things are lifeless, the Adjectives are often neuter.

1. Caius et Balbus eo profecti erant. 2. Aurum et argentum pretiosissima sunt. 3. Ego et tu redibimus. 4. Tarquinius rex vocatus est Superbus. 5. Diu erat anceps fortuna belli. 6. Cives Romani vocabuntur Quirites. 7. Urbs Roma Italiae caput est. 8. Murus et porta fracta sunt. 9. Urbs nostra et nomen deleta sunt. 10. Huc venistis, amici carissimi. 11. Acre telum volat. 12. Maximum flumen traiectum erat. 13. Galli, gens fortissima, devicti sunt. 14. Orationes facundissimae audiantur. 15. Vos omnes et liberi vestri condemnantur.

1. Gates and walls will have been broken. 2. You and your wife are very wicked. 3. His opinion will soon be changed. 4. A great quantity of gold has been found. 5. Riches, honour, glory, are very pleasant things. 6. The enemy is running away. 7. These towns will have been fortified. 8. This city will be plundered and burnt. 9. The island of Cyprus is very rich. 10. A disgraceful crime had been punished. 11. Both we and our children are poor. 12. Better gifts will have been sent. 13. The kings will be wise. 14. Romulus and Remus were brothers. 15. All the burdens are very heavy.

Exercise 8.

QUESTIONS.

In questions the Verb is usually in the Indicative.

In addition to the note of interrogation, there must be an interrogative word.

If the answer 'yes' is expected, use *nonnĕ*.

If the answer 'no' is expected, use *num*.

If merely information is required, use *nĕ*.

Nĕ cannot stand by itself; it is always joined to the end of the first word of the sentence.

Whether—or, to be translated by *utrum—an*.

'Whether' is often omitted in English; for example, we say, 'Is he poor or not?' The Latins say, 'Whether is he poor or not?'

1. Quis es? 2. Num huc venies? 3. Num hoc utile est? 4. Egone sum fortis? 5. Quota hora est? 6. Quot sunt milites? 7. Utrum Galli sunt an Romani? 8. Quid vis, mi fili? 9. Uter horum victor erit? 10. Nonne fortes erant? 11. Num totum opus confectum est? 12. Nonne aurum et argentum pretiosa sunt? 13. Nonne fortiter pugnabamus? 14. Utrum dives est annon? 15. Quale fuit negotium?

1. Who are you? 2. Are not fathers and mothers loved? 3. Who is the leader of this army? 4. Was the town of Gabii taken? 5. Was not the money paid? 6. Is she not beautiful? 7. Are you rich or poor? 8. Is he poor or not? 9. Did he come to-day? 10. What o'clock was it? 11. Who was Caesar? 12. How many sailors were there? 13. Are crocodiles fishes? 14. When will the Romans come? 15. Were not the Gauls conquered?

Exercise 9.

COMMANDS.

In Commands use the Imperative Mood.

If there is a Negative, the Perfect Conjunctive of the Second

Person must be used; the Present Conjunctive of other persons.

Translate 'not' in Negative Commands by *nē*.

1. Amamini. 2. Monemini. 3. Ne recti sitis. 4. Ne fugiant hostes. 5. Ne cucurreris. 6. Huc veni celeriter. 7. Pecunia ne solvatur. 8. Monentor. 9. Regitote. 10. Italia et Aegyptus, provinciae ditissimae, vastentur. 11. Oppidum Gabii diripiatur. 12. Veni, mi fili. 13. Ne mentiti sitis. 14. Captivi interficiantur. 15. Ne timueritis.

1. Love thou. 2. Don't love. 3. Rule ye. 4. Do not rule. 5. Let me go. 6. Let me not go. 7. Let them not be warned. 8. Hear ye. 9. Let them escape. 10. Let Caesar and Brutus be slain. 11. Be ye not conquered. 12. Let Italy at length rest. 13. Let these rich cities be plundered. 14. Soldiers, fight bravely. 15. Do not set out to-day.

Exercise 10.

The Accusative.

Transitive Verbs govern an Accusative of the object.

The object of a Verb can be discovered by asking the question 'whom?' or 'what?'

1. Latrones magnam praedam abstulerunt. 2. Caesar equites praemisit. 3. Hostium exercitum devicimus. 4. Latronis manus vinximus. 5. Audi meam vocem, mi fili. 6. Deum veneramur. 7. Ne hoc feceris. 8. Servi agros colebant. 9. Nonne hostes aciem instruxerunt? 10. Quid habes, mi care frater? 11. Omnes libros amisistis. 12. Sextus, Tarquinii Superbi filius, urbem ceperat. 13. Audistine vocem meam? 14. Romam non videmus. 15. Altissima moenia urbem muniunt. 16. Patrem suum imitabitur.

1. The master teaches the boys. 2. The boys hear the master. 3. She had written a long letter. 4. Are you writing a letter? 5. Do not kill me. 6. She was singing sweet songs. 7. We shall conquer our enemies. 8. Follow your leader. 9. The mother will nourish her young ones. 10. Worship God. 11. Do you not love your mother? 12. Build the walls of our city. 13. God created us. 14. Romulus built the walls of the city of Rome. 15. They had written very many letters.

Exercise 11.

THE DOUBLE ACCUSATIVE.

Some Verbs take two Accusatives, especially
a. Those of asking and teaching.
(In the Passive Voice these retain one Accusative.)
b. Those of making, calling, thinking.

1. Nihil me rogavit. 2. Hoc te rogo. 3. Filium suum literas docuit. 4. Pacem te poscimus omnes. 5. Filiam suam Claudiam vocavit. 6. Cur te literas doceam? 7. Rogor sententiam. 8. Te sapientem puto. 9. Primus me auxilium orabit. 10. Nonne nos multa hodie docuisti? 11. Te facimus, Fortuna, Deam. 12. Nunquam divitias deos rogavi. 13. Rogatus sententiam, nihil respondit. 14. Cur hanc artem doceri vis? 15. Milites Caium salutaverunt imperatorem.

1. I shall pray Neptunus for help. 2. Do not teach me letters. 3. Do you call me citizen? 4. The people elected Caesar consul. 5. The king asked the citizens for money. 6. I call you a robber. 7. He called his son Horatius. 8. Being asked for her opinion she said this. 9. Why should you be taught letters to-day? 10. Socrates used to teach philosophy to his disciples. 11. He was asked for advice. 12. Ceres taught the husbandmen useful arts. 13. Will you teach me this? 14. They call Antonius a traitor. 15. He taught me much.

Exercise 12.

PREPOSITIONS WITH ACCUSATIVE.

These Prepositions govern the Accusative :—

ante	cis	iuxta	propter
apud	contra	ob	per
ad	intra	penes	secundum
adversus	erga	pone	supra
circum	extra	post	versus
circa	infra	praeter	ultra
citra	intra	prope	trans

Super, subter, in, sub, implying motion.

1. Apud me vivebat. 2. Quidam coniurationem adversus Caesarem inierunt. 3. Circa urbem erant agri fertilissimi. 4. Arma ob hanc rationem sumpserunt. 5. In urbem se receperunt. 6. Cicero contra

Catilīnam locutus est. 7. Castra extra urbem posuit. 8. Ne hoc attuleris in nostram domum. 9. Urbs penes hostem fuit. 10. Propter hanc caussam in fugam se contulit. 11. Caius ad me venerat. 12. Classis erat ad Actium. 13. Post equitem sedet atra cura. 14. Nihil habeo praeter hoc. 15. Trans Rhenum flumen natabant.

1. I shall return to the city. 2. There was a river beside the city. 3. He made an attack on me. 4. He will be in the power of the enemy. 5. He pitched his camp near the sea. 6. They fled to the woods. ✔7. The emperor sent a long letter to the senate. 8. The girl was pouring wine into a golden cup. 9. Before the door sat a large dog. 10. Among the Lacedaemonians old men used to be greatly honoured. 11. He spoke against us all. 12. The actors were behind the curtain. 13. He was killed on account of this. 14. The camp was pitched outside the city. 15. They fled within the walls.

Exercise 13.

MOTION.

The place whither one goes is put in the Accusative, with the Prepositions *in* or *ad*.

The Preposition is omitted if it is either the name of a town or a small island, or the words domum (*home*), rus (*country*).

1. Regulus Carthaginem rediit. 2. In Africam discesserat. 3. Curio in Africam copias suas transvexerat. 4. Ite domum. 5. Legati in castra Hasdrubalis venerunt. 6. Iter in Galliam longum et difficile erat. 7. Rus ibo. 8. In forum redibimus. 9. Graecorum exercitus Troiam ivit. 10. Ad urbem venerant. 11. Ad Iovis aedem se contulit. 12. Gallorum nonnulli in Asiam pervenerant. 13. Lesbum abiit. 14. Caesar in Italiam rediit. 15. Sextus in Hispaniam solus mox redibit.

1. The chiefs of the senate fled to Africa. 2. They will go quickly to Greece. 3. I shall return home. 4. Will you not go to the country? 5. Don't go to Rome. 6. Did Caesar return to Italy? 7. Who had gone to Asia? 8. The conquered soldiers fled to their camp. 9. The prisoner was led to the forum. 10. Will you go to the city of Athens? 11. Boys go to school daily. 12. He sent gifts to the priest of Jupiter. 13. The head of Hasdrubal was thrown into the camp. 14. Will you go home or not? 15. Why did you return to the country? 16. They fled to Brutus.

✓

Exercise 14.

. TIME AND MEASURE.

The Accusative answers the questions—
1. How long? (of time.)
2. How long? (of space.)
3. How wide?

1. Pericles quadraginta annos rempublicam administravit. 2. Erant muri Babylonis ducenos pedes alti. 3. Aream latam decem pedes facito. 4. Iter unius diei aberat. 5. Triduum ibi manebat. 6. Tria millia passuum progressus erat. 7. Murus viginti pedes altus erat. 8. Num ibi biennium mansisti? 9. Templum iter multorum dierum inde aberat. 10. Navis duodeviginti pedes lata erat. 11. Biduum ibi manebimus. 12. Ne ibi diutius quam sex dies moratus sis. 13. Num ibi biduum an triduum manserat? 14. Turres confecerant quinquaginta pedes altas. 15. Multos annos vixit.

1. Who managed the republic for forty years? 2. Of what city were the walls two hundred feet high? 3. Do not make a threshing-floor nine feet wide. 4. How many days' journey was he distant? 5. He was walking about the city for two days. 6. Did you not remain there two years? 7. The Russians were in vain trying to cross the Danube for two months. 8. Did he live many years? 9. The towers were fifty feet high. 10. Troy was besieged ten years. 11. The river Nile overflows its banks the whole summer. 12. The soldiers made a rampart six feet high. 13. Near Rome the snow lay many feet deep. 14. A wall forty feet high protected our city. 15. He lived all his boyhood near that city.

Exercise 15.

RECAPITULATORY.

1. Tarquinius Superbus, ultimus rex Romanorum, urbem reliquerat. 2. Iam triduum abest. 3. Ver hiemem mox fugaverit. 4. Num libros amisisti, mi fili? 5. Ne pugnam commiseritis. 6. Dux ante castra aciem saepius instruxerat. 7. Frater meus moriens plurimos filios filiasque reliquit. 8. Centurio, vir fortissimus, omnes Gallorum

impetus sustinuit. 9. Croesi filius aprum ingentem venabatur. 10. Nonne vos olim philosophiam docui? 11. Milites coniurationem adversus imperatorem inierunt. 12. Ducem sequamur, comites. 13. Imperator copias suas in Graeciam transduxerat. 14. Ne ocius cucurreris, mi fili. 15. Aegyptii multos deos colebant.

1. The army of Ariovistus, the king of the Germans, had conquered the Gauls. 2. Will you not teach me letters? 3. She will call her daughter Claudia. 4. Paris had carried off Helena, the wife of Menelaus, to Troy. 5. None, except the brave, deserve honours. 6. The fishes were jumping into the net. 7. You set out for Africa before the time. 8. The walls of the city were thirty feet high. 9. Will you not go home quickly? 10. An exile came to Rome to king Numa. 11. Around the house was a green meadow. 12. How many ships did Caesar send to his friend? 13. On account of this reason he will be killed. 14. The Gauls have spears six feet long.

Exercise 16.

RECAPITULATORY.

1. Cur castra ad oppidum posuisti? 2. Numquid vis? 3. Nos pueri patrem Balbum imitabimur. 4. Caesar T. Labienum legatum praemisit. 5. Perfer labores fortiter, amice mi Pompei. 6. Quis te sententiam rogavit? 7. Ne me deceperis. 8. Multos labores passus, domum rediit. 9. Hoc oppidum tridui iter abest. 10. Vir bonus ille bonam hanc uxorem habet. 11. Pueri huius scholae fient docti. 12. Annulum aureum, praeclari artificis opus, in mare coniecerat. 13. Omnes Romani in Italiam se contulerant. 14. Tum hostes fortissime pugnantes ad unum omnes interficiuntur. 15. Nonne alta erat nix tres vel quatuor pedes?

1. O river, why dost thou run so quickly to the sea? 2. Your father Crassus was praising you, my friends. 3. Numa, the king of the Romans, was a very wise man. 4. Both you and I shall be punished. 5. Caesar conquered Ariovistus the king of the Germans. 6. Are your wife and sister dead? 7. I shall soon go to America. 8. Near my house are two large woods. 9. His father taught him the Greek tongue. 10. Is not hope the expectation of good? 11. Do not leave me alone. 12. Are riches and glory placed before our eyes? 13. The Romans have swords two feet long. 14. All the mothers and girls were going home. 15. The man and his wife are well.

The Simple Sentence.

Exercise 17.

The Dative.

Many Adjectives, Adverbs, and Verbs, and more rarely Substantives, take a Dative, when they imply nearness, showing, pleasing, ruling, and their opposites.

1. Est finitimus oratori poeta. 2. Anguis Sullae apparuit immolanti. 3. Patriae sit idoneus, utilis agris. 4. Omnibus supplex est. 5. Caesar captivis pepercerat. 6. Congruenter naturae vivimus. 7. Irae resistamus. 8. Omnibus proeliis eius belli aderat. 9. Sapiens amicorum culpis ignoscet. 10. Venus nupsit Vulcano. 11. Magister pueris ignavis irascetur. 12. Num mihi irasceris ? 13. Hoc nobis utilissimum fuit. 14. Philosophus doctrinae semper vacat. 15. Latrones nobis maledicebant.

1. The enemy did not resist our attack. 2. Do we live agreeably to nature? 3. Do not believe this man. 4. That disaster injured our army greatly. 5. Who envies us? 6. This tree has resisted very many storms. 7. This girl was very like her mother. 8. Our country is very dear to us. 9. Is not the name of Rome dear to all its citizens? 10. This place is suitable for horses and cattle. 11. Many books were given to this good boy. 12. Do not sea and land obey the commands of God? 13. Pompeius would not have spared the soldiers of Caesar. 14. The sun and moon shine for men. 15. Do you believe these words or not?

Exercise 18.

The Nearer and Remoter Object.

Many Verbs govern both a nearer object in the Accusative, and a remoter object in the Dative.

1. Gigantes bellum dis intulerunt. 2. Anatum ova gallinis supponimus. 3. Caesar libertatem populo Romano ademit. 4. Annulum digito detraxit. 5. Quietem aliquot dierum militibus dedit. 6. Num hoc mihi adimes? 7. Multa parentibus debemus. 8. Sabini Romanis bellum indixerant. 9. Caius moriens haec uxori imperavit. 10. Caius, frater meus, optima dona filiis suis dedit. 11. Numa virgines Vestae legit. 12. Aureum pallium deo detraxerat Dionysius, Siciliae tyrannus. 13. Mors crudelis vitam huic optimo viro ademit. 14. Pretiosa munera filiabus dabit. 15. Literas imperatori monstrabimus.

1. Let us give useful gifts to our sons. 2. Give me that book. 3. O Varus, give me back my legions. 4. Tell me your name. 5. The general gave the spoil of the captured city to his soldiers. 6. The death of Decius gave victory to the Romans. 7. Agrippina prepared poison for Claudius. 8. Do you put the eggs of hens under ducks? 9. Do not declare war against the Sabines. 10. Will not death take away everything from us? 11. He surrendered the legions to the enemy. 12. I will show you everything. 13. Cicero read Catiline's letter to the Senate. 14. He preferred death to dishonour.

Exercise 19.

OTHER USES OF THE DATIVE.

I have, etc., may be translated by *est mihi*, etc., instead of *habeo*.

Compounds of *sum* govern a Dative (except *possum*).

A Dative is often used as a complement.

1. Est homini cum Deo similitudo. 2. Erant nobis mitia poma. 3. Dux exercitui non defuit. 4. Exitio est avidum mare nautis. 5. Huic viro nomen Caio datum est. 6. Viri nostri nobis semper absunt. 7. Titum Labienum subsidio urbi miserat. 8. Exemplo est magni formica laboris. 9. Magnus pecudum numerus illis erat. 10. Num militibus nostris virtus deerit? 11. Germanis sunt oculi caerulei, flavi capilli. 12. Hoc nautis illius classis profuit. 13. Nonne hoc nobis multum prodest? 14. Cuinam proelio non affuit? 15. His pueris nomina Caio et Balbo dabuntur.

1. Shall we have apples or not? 2. Whose books are pleasant to us? 3. He had a quantity of slaves. 4. The name of Julia was given to the girl. 5. When will my husband be absent from me? 6. When was Titus Labienus sent as a help to the city? 7. Are not ants an example of industry? 8. He was in command of great forces of cavalry and infantry. 9. He will be in command of the bridge across the Rhine. 10. They will have a great quantity of gold and silver. 11. The Romans generally have black eyes. 12. We were present at the battle. 13. This will benefit us. 14. Do not benefit wicked men. 15. He gave his son the name of Caius.

Exercise 20.

RECAPITULATORY.

1. Equites per urbem fugiebant. 2. Dux Gallorum, vir fortissimus, damnatus est. 3. Moenia urbis viginti pedes alta erant. 4. Ne vitam dedecori anteponamus. 5. Nonne hoc mihi promittes? 6. Multi nobiles cives Catilinae favebant. 7. Haec ne tibi quidem placebant. 8. Num me tuam artem docebis? 9. Milites irati in oppidum impetum fecerunt. 10. Nonne et nos et filius noster diu hic manebimus? 11. Inter Romam Albamque urbes castra posuit. 12. Fossam effodit quinquaginta pedes latam. 13. Ne hoc periculum timueritis, milites Romani. 14. Romam regressus filium ad se vocavit. 15. In Asiam mox abibunt.

1. Have you lost all your money? 2. These boys will sleep the whole night. 3. Was he not walking in my garden? 4. Will he soon have returned to Asia? 5. The slave fears the voice of his master. 6. There are many very high mountains between Gaul and Italy. 7. Sertorius, spare the conquered enemy. 8. The Greeks have taken away the gold from the temple of Apollo. 9. Horatius, a brave soldier, fought against the Albans. 10. Will not Venus marry Vulcan, the god of fire? 11. Summon the cavalry to the camp. 12. Our ancestors fortified this city. 13. He gave many presents to his daughters. 14. Do not pardon these wicked men. 15. Return quickly to Rome.

Exercise 21.

RECAPITULATORY.

1. Hoc tibi iucundissimum erit. 2. Nonne huc redibis, mi fili? 3. Multos annos apud regem nostrum vivebant. 4. Toti exercitui praeerat. 5. Camillus Gallos domum redeuntes devicerat. 6. Totus exercitus fusus fugatusque erat. 7. Exercitum fudit fugavitque. 8. Flumen Tanais est ducentos pedes latum. 9. Aper regis filium vulneravit. 10. Ne amicitias ocius contraxeris. 11. Patriae sint idonei, utiles agris. 12. Venenum uxori suae paraverat. 13. Procella plurimas naves fregerat. 14. Hoc donum nobis proderit. 15. Rex filio suo auream coronam dabit.

1. The virtue of this man is (meet) to be praised. 2. Overcome with thirst, he asked the slave for water. 3. This boy has poured poison into my cup. 4. Did not Romulus call his city Rome? 5. What are you holding, my friend? 6. The French used to prefer victory to peace. 7. She gave many beautiful dresses to her daughters. 8. Will you obey me, or not? 9. Let an ant be to you (for) an ex-

ample of great labour. 10. The fate of her brother also injured Claudia. 11. A wall, many feet high, surrounds the city. 12. Whom did these songs please? 13. They were playing among the boys and girls. 14. I had been taught philosophy. 15. Do not walk across the garden.

Exercise 22.

RECAPITULATORY.

1. Domus ardebat. 2. Uxor tua tibi persuadebit. 3. Capua et otium ipsum Hannibalem corruperant. 4. Maiores vestri universam Italiam vicerunt. 5. Suavissimas literas tuas accepimus. 6. Sapiens semper felix erit. 7. Omne corpus est vel aqua vel aer vel ignis vel terra. 8. Servus totam rem reginae monstravit. 9. Num tibi fratrem tuum anteponebamus? 10. Portas urbis Bruto aperuit, exercitumque tradidit. 11. Nonne maxima multitudo in Capitolium convenerat? 12. Propter hanc caussam condemnati erimus. 13. Ego et Cicero, vir mihi carissimus, valemus. 14. Si rogavero te aliquid, nonne respondebis? 15. Arbor viginti pedes alta erat.

1. The general, a very brave man, gave all the spoils to his soldiers. 2. Whose house was burning? 3. Let not your wife persuade you against your will. 4. He desired to return to Italy. 5. The king and queen died there. 6. They will have given us many useful gifts. 7. Atys was the son of Croesus, king of Lydia. 8. Do not send me to Greece. 9. The king had given many commands to the soldiers. 10. How many feet high is the tree? 11. Are you and your friend Cicero well? 12. On account of this reason I keep you here. 13. He took away all my money from me. 14. Crocodiles are caught very easily. 15. He taught me the art of war.

Exercise 23.

THE ABLATIVE.

The Ablative denotes the cause, instrument, manner, condition, quality (accompanied by an epithet), respect, price, measure.

1. Oderunt scelus boni virtutis amore. 2. Hi iaculis, illi certant defendere saxis. 3. Iniuria fit duobus modis, aut vi aut fraude. 4. Homo mea sententia prudentissimus est. 5. Senex promissa barba, horrenti capillo. 6. Angor animo. 7. Spem pretio non emo. 8. Multo pessimus omnium poeta erat. 9. Hostes veneno interemit. 10. Venator feras sagittis transfixerat. 11. Caesaris naves procellis

fractae erant. 12. Et corde et genibus tremit. 13. Hic liber asse carus est. 14. His conditionibus in Italiam regressus est. 15. Hostium fines ferro et igne vastaverant.

1. He made many friends by his kindness. 2. Virtue is not bought with money. 3. They saved themselves by flight to the woods. 4. She is a foot taller than her mother. 5. Victory was gained by much blood and wounds. 6. Ennius was a poet great in genius. 7. They were slain by the javelins of the enemy. 8. Caesar was brave in war and wise in counsel. 9. Do not kill the birds with stones. 10. In our opinion he is a most eloquent man. 11. They hate theft from fear of punishment. 12. Were you wounded by a javelin? 13. A girl with blue eyes and golden hair. 14. Achilles was wounded by an arrow in the foot. 15. Are you not vexed in mind? 16. At what price did he buy the field?

Exercise 24.

ABLATIVE OF MATTER.

a. These words govern an Ablative :—(1.) The verbs fungor (*perform*), fruor (*enjoy*), utor (*use*), vescor (*eat*), potior (*get possession of*), dignor (*deem worthy*). (2.) The Adjectives dignus (*worthy*), indignus (*unworthy*), contentus (*content*), fretus (*relying on*), praeditus (*endued*). (3.) The Substantives, opus (*need*), usus (*use, need*).

b. Most Adjectives and Verbs *of abounding* or *wanting, enriching* or *depriving*, take an Ablative.

1. Cibus eorum lacte, caseo, carne constat. 2. Ducis munere fungar. 3. Auro et argento utebantur. 4. Rex auro vi potitur. 5. Digna erat laude. 6. Quid opus est verbis? 7. Usus est filio viginti minis. 8. Amor et melle et felle est fecundissimus. 9. Vacare culpa maximum est solatium. 10. Rex servis locuples erat. 11. Nonne victoria uteris? 12. Lacte et carne vescuntur. 13. Nihil opus est ira. 14. Poculum vino erat plenum. 15. Tali supplicio indignus erat.

1. They use copper and iron. 2. There will be need of many words. 3. Is love fruitful in honey or not? 4. He performed the duty of a soldier. 5. He enjoyed a long and happy life. 6. Their food consists of fish. 7. They need water more than food. 8. Relying on his cavalry he drew up his forces. 9. Are you rich in gold and silver? 10. He was endued with great courage. 11. Britain enjoys liberty. 12. Tarquinius got possession of the kingdom by

force. 13. Are you content with these gifts? 14. Do not be contented with silver. 15. The Germans use very long spears. 16. Let us enjoy food and wine. 17. I deem her worthy of great praise.

Exercise 25.

TIME AND PLACE.

The Ablative answers the questions—
 a. When? Within what time? How long before? How long after?
 b. Whence?
 c. By what road?

The question, Where? (of towns), is answered by the old Locative Case, which ends as follows:—

	Singular.	Plural.
First Declension	ae	is
Second ,,	i	is
Third ,,	e (rarely i)	bus

Like these are—humi (*on the ground*), domi (*at home*), belli, militiae (*at the wars*), ruri (*in the country*).

1. Hieme omnia bella conquiescunt. 2. Biduo haec sciemus. 3. Homerus multis annis fuit ante Romulum. 4. Ibam forte Via Sacra. 5. Quid Romae faciam? 6. Is habitat Mileti. 7. Caesaris virtus domi militiaeque cognita est. 8. Demaratus fugit Corintho. 9. Alter Romae, alter Athenis mortuus est. 10. Alii Romae habitant, alii Carthagine. 11. Pax diu Capuae fuit. 12. Iuvenes Romani philosophiae studebant Athenis. 13. Eo anno Carthago deleta est. 14. Postero die adversus Pompeium profecti sunt. 15. Catilina mox Roma fugerit.

1. Do not wars rest in winter? 2. Next day Caesar took the town by storm. 3. At daybreak we shall set out. 4. Within three days we shall fly from Athens. 5. That man always lives in the country. 6. Is Ennius at home? 7. Catiline set out for the camp at midnight. 8. Who was many years before Romulus? 9. We shall go to Rome by the Appian way. 10. Hannibal, being driven from Carthage, betook himself to King Antiochus. 11. Many philosophers used to live at Athens. 12. By this way we came to the citadel. 13. Four years before they used to live at Cadiz. 14. Did he remain at Rome or at Carthage? 15. Do not sleep on the ground.

Exercise 26.

Prepositions with Ablative.

The following Prepositions govern the Ablative :—

a	coram	cum	tenus
ab	de	e	pro
absque	palam	ex	prae
	clam	sine	

Also *super, subter, sub, in,* when they denote rest.

a. Some Prepositions, especially *ab, de, ex,* when compounded with verbs, govern the Ablative.

b. The Ablative of the agent (of living things) takes the Preposition *a, ab.*

' *To be loved* ' can be translated both by 'amari' and 'amandus.' If in doubt which to use, try if you can supply 'fit,' or 'meet,' before ' to be loved,' without injuring the sense. If you can, use the gerundive.

1. Ab urbe profectus ero. 2. Milites nostri in muro stabant. 3. Romam sine mora profecti erunt. 4. Quinctius dictatura se abdicavit. 5. Detrudunt naves scopulo. 6. Laudatur ab his, culpatur ab illis. 7. Cicero multa de natura deorum locutus est. 8. Arma pro communi salute sumpserunt. 9. Dux castra in valle citra montem posuerat. 10. Multa coram iudice locuta est. 11. Cum dolore locuti essemus. 12. Hic puer clam patre suo huc venit. 13. Scythae flumen Istrum in navigiis transibant. 14. Sub terra latet aurum. 15. Remedia doloris a philosophia petenda sunt.

1. He wrote a very pleasant letter to us about his journey. 2. The hunter was killed by a lion. 3. Who resigned the dictatorship? 4. He was stabbed with a sword by the enemy. 5. I have found nothing to be read in this book. 6. Cato betook himself into Africa with his friends. 7. The girls were walking in the garden. 8. Why did the general pitch his camp on the top of the mountain? 9. Do not come to me without the knowledge of your father. 10. By whom was Caesar killed? 11. He left the city with a few companions. 12. I shall ask him for his opinion without any delay. 13. By whom was she blamed? 14. What did they say in the presence of the king? 15. We had gone out of the city of Rome.

Exercise 27.

OTHER USES OF THE ABLATIVE.

Verbs and Participles denoting separation or origin take an Ablative.

The thing compared is often put in the Ablative instead of the Nominative or Accusative with quam (*than*).

The Ablative cannot be used instead of *quam* with the other cases.

1. Cedes domo. 2. Tarquinio natus erat. 3. Nihil est amabilius virtute. 4. Vilius argentum est auro, virtutibus aurum. 5. Puto mortem dedecore leviorem. 6. Neminem Lycurgo utiliorem Sparta genuit. 7. Cupidior sum belli quam pacis. 8. Viri sunt feminis validiores. 9. O, matre pulchra filia pulchrior! 10. Quid est leone fortius? 11. Nemo Romae Crasso fuit ditior. 12. Literae tuae meis sunt suaviores. 13. Dignior erat laude quam culpa. 14. Quis patriae utilior Lycurgo fuit? 15. Nihil tua amicitia iucundius puto. 16. Argento aurum pretiosius est.

1. Will you leave your home? 2. Is he not descended from Tarquinius? 3. What is more loveable than virtue? 4. He is fonder of peace than war. 5. Women are weaker than men. 6. His letters are more pleasant than yours. 7. No animal is more faithful to man than the dog. ✓8. There has never been a greater city than Rome. 9. Porsena was descended from the kings of Etruria. 10. Is gold more valuable than silver or not? 11. They were more worthy of praise than of blame. 12. What is sweeter than honey? 13. Honesty is better than deceit. 14. The rays of the sun are brighter than those of the moon. 15. Do not give better gifts to your daughter than to your son.

Exercise 28

THE ABLATIVE ABSOLUTE.

A Substantive or Pronoun combines with a Participle in the Ablative. This construction is called the Ablative Absolute. It supplies the want of the Perfect Participle Active.

Instead of the Participle we often find another Substantive, Pronoun, or Adjective.

Absolute means *released from agreement;* therefore this construction can only be used when the Substantive is not wanted for the subject or object of its sentence.

1. Regibus exactis consules creati sunt. 2. Natus est Augustus Cicerone et Antonio consulibus. 3. Iamque cinis vivis fratribus Hector erat. 4. Quid dicam hac iuventute? 5. Caesar devictis Gallis Romam rediit. 6. Stricto ense impetum in hostes facit. 7. Mutata militum sententia Brutus haec facere constituit. 8. Occidit, occidit spes omnis et fortuna nostri nominis Hasdrubale interempto. 9. Caesar duobus magnis bellis una aestate confectis exercitum in hiberna deduxit. 10. Omnibus rebus confectis domum redibimus. 11. Tota classis mersa est te aspectante. 12. Tarquiniis Roma expulsis, cives pace fruebantur. 13. Milites strictis ensibus ducem petierunt. 14. Vir bonus ille mortuus est circumstantibus omnibus amicis. 15. Omni spe salutis amissa in arcem se recepit.

1. So two legions having been routed, the army tried to escape. 2. Hasdrubal having been conquered, Carthage soon perished. 3. The enemy returned after taking the city. 4. Who returned to Rome after conquering the Gauls? 5. Cicero defended Milo in the hearing of many (*say*, many hearing). 6. After crossing the Alps, Hannibal will come into Italy. 7. After reading my letter Cicero spoke as follows. 8. Having discovered gold, they remained there. 9. The Romans defeated the Germans under the leadership of Ariovistus (*say*, Ariovistus being leader). 10. Having finished this book, the boy will enjoy rest. 11. Regulus was slain, his enemies looking on. 12. Were consuls elected when the kings had been driven out? 13. Do not do this again, your crime having been found out. 14. I was made quaestor in the consulship of Sulla (*say*, Sulla being consul). 15. Let us fly, all hope of safety having been lost.

Exercise 29.

RECAPITULATORY.

1. Nonne omnes peribimus? 2. Nuntius ad ducem decima fere hora noctis venerat. 3. Romani cum Hannibale multos annos bellum gesserunt. 4. Nonne audetis, me duce, impetum in hostes facere? 5. Magna parte urbis igne consumpta huc veniet. 6. Quot dies hinc abfuisti? 7. Num nos hanc artem docebis? 8. Duo et quadraginta pueri et puellae ab urso interfecti sunt. 9. Duobus horis ante decimam quota hora erit? 10. Immo octava erit. 11. Socrates a populo condemnatus veneno absumptus est. 12. Caius cum uxore sua Athenis habitabat. 13. Caesar a Gallia profectus Rubiconem flumen mox traiiciet. 14. Quid praecipue memorandum videtur? 15. Athenis profecta Romam cum matre sua mox aderit.

Recapitulatory.

1. Having divided the spoil, the soldiers returned to the camp.
2. Do you prefer peace or war? 3. Who married Vulcan, the God of fire? 4. I ask you for bread and meat. 5. She was in the power of a very wicked man. 6. Around the city was a very great wood. 7. He remained many days at Carthage with Hannibal, the general of the Carthaginians. 8. The slave will go away, his work having been finished. 9. On his journey he was killed by a pirate. 10. In her opinion he is a very wise man. 11. From Europe you will go to Africa. 12. A lion, a very fierce beast, was pursuing the terrified huntsman. 13. A man with long hair and a very ugly face was standing before our house. 14. Don't tell him my name. 15. Did he prefer death to dishonour?

Exercise 30.

RECAPITULATORY.

1. Nonne poeta oratori finitimus est? 2. Aurum et argentum ante oculos posita sunt. 3. Ego et filia mea valemus. 4. Fuso hoste, dux cum exercitu in urbem regressus est. 5. Scythae Istrum fluvium ponte iunctum transibant. 6. Non sine timore huc venerant. 7. Erat in exercitu iuvenis quidam eximio vultu. 8. Dato signo, undique in hostes fit impetus. 9. Agrippina, Neronis mater, Romae habitabat. 10. Propter timorem in Asiam me recepi. 11. Ab hoste gladiis interficientur. 12. Ne hanc puellam huic viro tradideris. 13. Nonne philosophiam te docueram? 14. Ille stultus argentum auro anteposuerat. 15. Me iudice, turpissimus es. 16. Mors dedecore non est turpior.

1. Who will marry this woman? 2. Tell me your opinion. 3. Was Sicily once joined to Italy? 4. The foot of Philoctetes was wounded by the bite of a serpent. 5. He preferred your gifts to mine. 6. Having heard these things he left the house. 7. She was descended from Numa, king of Rome. 8. The enemy was standing on the wall. 9. To me she seemed a very eloquent woman. 10. Having taken the city they got possession of the spoil. 11. These husbandmen live on cheese, bread, and milk. 12. About the house was a ditch twelve feet wide. 13. Labienus was put over the cavalry. 14. He returned to Rome next day with his daughters. 15. Catiline fled from the city in the consulship of Cicero.

Exercise 31.

THE GENITIVE.

a. The Genitive is the case of the Possessor.

b. A Genitive sometimes so stands that the words *nature*, *mark*, or *duty* can be supplied.

c. Quality is also denoted by a Genitive with an epithet.

Notice the following Genitives used adverbially, with which the word pretii (*price*), is understood:—

parvi, *of small value*   magni, *of great value*
minoris, *of less value*   pluris, *of more value*
minimi, *of very little value* plurimi, *of very great value*
          tanti, *of so great price*
          quanti, *of what price?*
          maximi, *of very great price.*

d. Words denoting Quantity, or part of a thing, and Neuter Adjectives, takes a Genitive.

After partitive words use the forms nostrum (*of us*), vestrum (*of you*).

1. Cuiusvis hominis est errare. 2. Ingenui vultus puer, ingenuique pudoris. 3. Voluptatem virtus minimi facit. 4. Elephanto beluarum est nulla prudentior. 5. Uterque nostrum hoc cupit. 6. Satis eloquentiae, sapientiae parum est. 7. Stulti est semper ridere. 8. In hoc monte exstiterat aper mirae magnitudinis. 9. Iter viginti mille passuum biduo confecimus. 10. Consul vir erat magnae virtutis. 11. Fortis vir mortem parvi facit. 12. Num magni hoc aestimas? 13. Artis est celare artem. 14. Quanti hunc agrum vendidit? 15. Militis est Romani aut vincere aut mori.

1. Does virtue value pleasure at a high price? 2. Rashness is a mark of youth. 3. We value your gifts very highly. 4. Is not this boar an animal of wonderful size? 5. Claudius was a man of very short slumber. 6. To yield to occasion is held the mark of a wise man. 7. The duty of a young man is to reverence elders. 8. The elder of the Neros soon fought a battle. 9. Of mortals nobody is wise at all hours. 10. Of fishes the females are larger than the males. 11. Is it not the nature of all men to err? 12. It is the mark of a fool to lie. 13. A boy of high-bred countenance was speaking to the master. 14. It is the nature of dogs to bark and bite. 15. Each of you desires ease.

Exercise 32.

RECAPITULATORY.

1. Homini uni animalium luctus est datus. 2. Uter nostrum hoc fecerat? 3. Ne mihi aurum neu argentum dederis. 4. Huic provinciae nomen Achaiae inditum est. 5. Plebs sibi tribunos creavit. 6. In medio oceano sunt insulae quaedam pulcherrimae. 7. Utrum huic viro nupsit annon? 8. Caius inter alios legatos Saguntum venerat. 9. Capta urbe, consulis aedes incensae sunt. 10. In Italiam die quinto, non sine magno navium damno, venit. 11. Darii regis corpore in castra lato, Alexander lacrimas fudit. 12. Ne hoc patri monstraveris. 13. Est mihi multum pecuniae. 14. Romulo oriundi sumus.

1. You are older than I. 2. Sulla lost a hundred and twenty of his men. 3. Being asked for my opinion by Caesar, I said nothing. 4. Having killed the Gaul, Manlius returned to his friends. 5. The Belgae are the bravest of the Gauls. 6. We keep something of our old strength. 7. Who was killed by the bite of a serpent? 8. Do the souls of men after death enter into the bodies of animals? 9. Why did he prefer this girl to her sister? 10. This great poet was born in the consulship of Caesar. 11. What is better than a good man? 12. Hannibal was enjoying the fruits of victory at Capua. 13. They will have gone to Asia. 14. He bought this statue for ten minae. 15. They were defending themselves with stones.

Exercise 33.

THE GENITIVE.

Some Adjectives, Substantives, and Participles, signifying skill, care, desire, or their contraries, take a Genitive.

Verbs and Adjectives signifying power, impotence; guilt, innocence; condemnation and acquittal; memory and forgetfulness, take a Genitive.

The Impersonal Verbs piget (*it irks*), pudet (*it shames*), poenitet (*it repents*), taedet (*it disgusts*), miseret (*it moves pity*), take a Genitive of the thing with an Accusative of the Person.

1. Insitus est menti virtutis amor. 2. Difficilis est cura rerum alienarum. 3. Corpus laborum patiens erat. 4. Imperita morum fuit. 5. Avida est periculi virtus. 6. Labienus belli peritissimus erat. 7. Romani signorum potiti sunt. 8. Fraterni sanguinis est

insons. 9. Servus furti absolutus est. 10. Condemnamus haruspices stultitiae. 11. Mortis memineram. 12. Miseret te aliorum. 13. Hos pueros stultitiae poenitet. 14. Nonne te belli et sanguinis taedet? 15. Patrum memoriae recordati essemus.

1. Did I not condemn the soothsayer of folly? 2. This very wicked man will be condemned to death (*say*, of the head). 3. He is accused of burnings and murder. 4. Will not others be disgusted with you? 5. My mind is conscious of virtue. 6. Do not accuse the slave of theft. ✓7. Death reminds us of religion. 8. All hate a man unmindful of a kindness. 9. He is ashamed of my friendship. 10. Excessive care for riches is disgraceful. 11. Did the Romans gain the standards or not? 12. At last she remembered the words of her dead mother. 13. Catiline was accused of many crimes by Cicero. 14. This boy is very fond of learning. 15. I am not skilled in the art of deceiving.

Exercise 34.

RECAPITULATORY.

1. Galli ab exercitu Romano, Caesare duce, victi sunt. 2. Tu et tua cara soror ad nos venietis. 3. Nonne mors nos relligionis admonet? 4. Avem saxo occidit. 5. Agrum magni emerat. 6. Taedet eum sanguinis et laboris. 7. Utrum in Asiam ibis, annon? 8. Nostra sententia stultissimus est. 9. Quid de Britannis censetis? 10. Nonne Tarquinio, rege Romano, oriunda erat? 11. Ne mihi hoc iterum narraveris, mi care fili. 12. Romam cum ambabus suis filiabus sine mora contendit. 13. In aquam ceciderunt et mersi sunt. 14. Omnibus meis inimicis ignoscam. 15. Haec regio a Roma distat iter quadraginta dierum.

1. The prophet was three days and three nights in the whale's belly. 2. Thou dost not pity thyself. 3. This girl is not fond of writing. 4. All love a man mindful of a kindness. 5. Anger is fond of revenge. 6. This girl was born in the consulship of Crassus. 7. He was bound with chains by the enemy. 8. Our armies were conquered by the forces of the Gauls. 9. The Roman army was sent under the yoke. 10. Being asked for his opinion he answered in these words. 11. We shall remain five days at Carthage. 12. This city was taken and burnt by Sulla. 13. He does not seem wise to me. 14. The people asked the rich for food. 15. He was an old man with a long beard and white hair.

Exercise 35.

The Infinitive.

a. The Infinitive stands as a Substantive for a Nominative or Accusative.

b. In narration it is sometimes put instead of a Finite Verb. (Historic Infinitive.)

c. It also completes the sense of some Verbs, which would not make sense without it. (*Prolate* Infinitive, from *prolatum*, supine of *fero*.)

1. Discere est utile. 2. Invidere non cadit in sapientem. 3. Mori nemo sapiens miserum dixerit. 4. Multi sequi, fugere, occidi, capi. 5. Sapientes diu cogitare solent. 6. Diceris esse pater patriae. 7. Iudices pecunia corrupisse dicitur. 8. Redire non potuerit. 9. Ille improbus patriae legibus parere nolebat. 10. Multa mentiri voluisti. 11. Multa coram iudicibus loqui non audebam. 12. Socrates iuvenes corrupisse dicitur. 13. Nonne discere et docere utilissima sunt? 14. Ne discere inutile dixeris. 15. Capta urbe, passim caedes, incendia, turpissima omnia fieri.

1. I cannot do this. 2. To die for one's country is sweet and glorious. 3. They wish to overthrow our city. 4. They are said to be about to return. 5. All men wish to see the city of Rome. 6. To lie is disgraceful. 7. Pyrrhus did not cease to admire the courage of the Roman troops. 8. Writing is an easy thing. 9. The boys obeyed the orders of their master. 10. Will he be unwilling to obey the laws of his country? 11. Did you wish to tell many lies (say, to lie many things). 12. Socrates is said to have been the wisest of all men. 13. What do you want to do to-day? 14. The first legion having been routed, the enemy began to fly. 15. Who is said to have been the father of his country?

Exercise 36.

The Gerund and Supine.

The Gerunds and Supines supply cases to the Infinitive.

The Supine in *um* expresses a purpose after verbs of motion.

With the Impersonal Infinitive *iri* (a going), it forms the Future Infinitive Passive.

The Supine in *u* is used as an Ablative of respect.

The Infinitive with Gerunds, Supines, and Participles governs the same cases as the Finite Verb.

1. Ad bene vivendum breve tempus satis est. 2. Ars scribendi discitur. 3. Cupidus audiendi est. 4. Par est disserendo. 5. Dat operam legendo. 6. Fugiendo vincimus. 7. De pugnando deliberant. 8. Lusum it Mecenas, dormitum ego. 9. Foedum dictu est. 10. Nefas visu est. 11. Cupio satisfacere reipublicae. 12. Cupidus sum satisfaciendi reipublicae. 13. Non Graecis matribus servitum ibo. 14. Praeda potiti in castra regressi sunt. 15. Bellum Romanis inferens interficitur. 16. Haec puella canendi perita est.

1. There is need of practice for running well. 2. He is skilled in dancing. 3. Are you desirous of satisfying your parents? 4. The art of writing was being learnt by these boys. 5. The Germans excelled our men in running. 6. An iron plough is useful for ploughing. 7. Are they deliberating about fighting or not? 8. I shall go to Rome to see the games. 9. It is difficult to say. 10. I saw an old woman putting the eggs of a duck under a hen. 11. These boys pay no attention to reading well. 12. Having got possession of the city they will divide the spoil. 13. I shall go to Athens to contend in a contest of learning. 14. Do we not conquer by flying? 15. This is horrible to hear.

Exercise 37.

THE GERUNDIVE.

a. In Transitive Gerunds the Object is generally attracted to the Case of the Gerund; the Gerund to the Number and Gender of the object.

b. The Gerundive used impersonally implies necessity. The agent is expressed by the Dative; by the Ablative with *a, ab*, when the Verb governs the Dative, to avoid confusion.

c. The Gerundive used in agreement with a Substantive implies necessity.

1. Brutus in liberanda patria est interfectus. 2. Hi Septemviri fuerunt agris dividendis. 3. Bibendum est. 4. Eundum erit. 5. Bibendum est nobis. 6. Vobis eundum erit. 7. Civibus est a vobis consulendum. 8. Suo cuique iudicio est utendum. 9. Chaldaeis minime credendum est. 10. Deus et diligendus est nobis et timendus. 11. Non tangenda rates transiliunt vada. 12. Omnia parata sunt ad bellum gerendum 13. Platonis audiendi studiosus erat. 14. Opus muri aedificandi difficillimum erat. 15. Num huc venisti spe videndi Caesaris?

1. Brutus was killed in freeing Rome. 2. One must not drink often. 3. One had to go to Rome. 4. He must not drink. 5. Will you not have to go? 6. The bravery of this soldier is to be admired. 7. The Gauls are to be feared by us. 8. The pleasure of reading good books is very great. 9. This sword is not to be touched. 10. He must consult for us. 11. This wicked man should not be pardoned. 12. These words must be answered. 13. Are you fond of seeing the sea? 14. They must get possession of the gold. 15. Must we not drink?

Exercise 38.

RECAPITULATORY.

1. Morte mea reipublicae satisfaciam. 2. Nonne maxima praemia forti huic militi dabuntur? 3. Samnites magnum auri pondus ad Curium ad focum sedentem tulerunt. 4. Rogata sententiam respondere noluit. 5. Persae, Dario duce, flumen Istrum transiere. 6. Caesaris literas apud senatum cum magno omnium plausu recitavi. 7. Semper studiosus erat huius philosophi audiendi. 8. Aemilius, consul Romanus, in praelio Cannensi periit. 9. Hunc oratorem disserentem audicram. 10. Nonne hoc consilium omnibus optimum videbatur? 11. Mortuo duce, in acie peribimus. 12. Sulla Romanis timendus erat. 13. Filium suum filiabus anteposuit. 14. Non sum canendi peritus. 15. Lepus a cane mox capietur.

1. The Roman army was captured at the Caudine Forks. 2. Outside the city of Rome stood the troops of the enemy. 3. Wild beasts defend themselves with their teeth, horns, and claws. 4. Bound with chains he was given up to the accuser. 5. He seems to us a very good citizen. 6. Do not try to deceive us by the appearance of friendship. 7. Did this counsel seem best to all? 8. The work of building the city is finished. 9. Is this girl skilled in dancing? 10. I am descended from Porsena, king of the Etrurians. 11. He will be punished by the good judge. 12. You and I, my dear friend, are well. 13. He will return to Asia without the knowledge of the consul. 14. Tell me your opinion about this thing. 15. He will be punished within three days.

Exercise 39.

RECAPITULATORY.

1. Filius meus omnium artium peritissimus erat. 2. Quando urbs Roma a Gallis capta est? 3. Iudices pecunia donisque corrupisse dicor. 4. Cives cum coniugibus et liberis in muro stabant. 5. Num quis tibi credet? 6. Galli a Romanis devicti sunt, Caesare et Labieno ducibus. 7. In Asiam redire nolueramus. 8. Non ausa est multa mentiri. 9. Regulus Carthaginem in Africam rediit. 10. Hac de caussa tibi irascor. 11. Discendo doctiores fiemus. 12. Multi sequi, capere, occidere inimicos. 13. Pericula non timebit, nam fortissimus est. 14. Haec dona sorori tuae sunt idonea 15. Parati erimus pro patria pugnare.

1. My daughter is skilled in no art. 2. The city will be taken within three days. 3. He will go with us to Egypt. 4. By learning the girls became more learned. 5. Let us hasten home. 6. Writing is an easy thing. 7. I shall not fear danger, for I am guarded by you. 8. This horse is fit for a bold rider. 9. She was ready to die for her husband. 10. Who prefers dishonour to honour? 11. Claudius, the son of Caius, is thought wise. 12. The sheep was torn in pieces by a wolf. 13. Don't sin. 14. He killed a wolf with sharp teeth and claws. 15. They are grieved in mind. 16. This shall happen, under your leadership.

Exercise 40.

RECAPITULATORY.

1. Orpheus arbores et saxa canendo trahebat. 2. Num multos libros adhuc scripsisti? 3. Nonne in Asiam redire parati sumus? 4. Totumne opus confecisti? 5. Magister pueri culpis ignoscit. 6. Prima luce Sulla aciem instruxit. 7. Iter facturus haec coniugi mandaverat. 8. Strictis gladiis in hostem impetum fecimus. 9. Urbs nostra a duce peritissimo munita erat. 10. Currentes aquas carmine tenuisse dicitur. 11. Rex ab armigero suo confossus periit. 12. Utrum amicos an inimicos vis habere? 13. Amicus regi forma praestabat. 14. Mulier captiva regem veniam oravit. 15. Devicto hominum universo genere, cum omnibus aliis rebus bellum vis gerere.

1. He could not return to Athens. 2. A civil war was being waged by the citizens. 3. The courage of our troops is to be praised. 4. We see the light of the rising sun. 5. Are you not vexed in mind? 6. He was unwilling to marry the general's daughter. 7. The general's daughter was unwilling to marry him. 8. Do not cross the river. 9. He preferred the friendship of the philosopher Socrates to riches. 10. These beasts were killed with arrows. 11. The love of drinking

wine has become excessive. 12. They will go from Europe to Asia. 13. Does he not live at Miletus? 14. These boys will repent of their folly. 15. He will perish together with his sons and daughters.

Exercise 41.

RECAPITULATORY.

1. Libris optimis legendis fit doctus. 2. Num barbari legiones nostras vincere poterunt? 3. Postridie legiones magnam victoriam adeptae sunt. 4. Triduum in urbe manserat. 5. Troia capta, Ulysses donum ad coniugem suam redire constituit. 6. Nonne in meo horto ambulabas? 7. Legiones cum cohortibus redierunt. 8. Nonne haec Romano exercitui nocebunt? 9. Venturo Caesare, magnum gaudium in urbe erat. 10. Nihil tibi auferre volumus. 11. Hi septemviri fuerunt urbi aedificandae. 12. Humi iacebat tristi voltu. 13. Ab Aegypto in Asiam magnis itineribus contendebat. 14. Haec domus ab oppido iter unius diei abest. 15. Carthagine in Hispaniam profecti sumus.

1. The name of Brutus was given to the youth. 2. Lead is heavier than iron. 3. I could wish to have leisure for books. 4. The younger of the Scipios fought a battle with the Carthaginians. 5. Was not Romulus many years after Homer? 6. Will this girl marry the old man? 7. The walls of this city were fifty feet high. 8. I shall have taught my son letters. 9. You and I shall have been wounded. 10. They burn with a great desire of collecting riches. 11. When Troy was taken the Greeks went home. 12. Even my enemies pity me. 13. He was condemned to death. 14. A lion of great size was killed. 15. Crocodiles are found in the river Nile. 16. Do not be ruled.

Exercise 42.

RECAPITULATORY.

1. Philippus suis civibus semper favebat. 2. Atticae caput, urbs praeclara, igne consumitur. 3. Pecuniam pauperibus ne invideamus. 4. Urbs a nostris vallo et fossa munita est. 5. Cupidus erat satisfaciendi civibus. 6. Amor doctrinae laudandus est. 7. Pelope natus est, Peloponnesi rege. 8. Puellae, ne senibus nupseritis. 9. Mercatores a latrone interfecti sunt. 10. Genibus et pedibus angor. 11. Pompeius a Caesare victus in Aegyptum se contulit. 12. Pacem

posceris, dux fortissime. 13. Puella ingenuo pudore coram iudice constituitur. 14. Circa Cereris templum erat murus decem pedes altus. 15. Nonne voluptatem virtus parvi facit ?

1. The work is nearly finished. 2. The shepherd was feeding his sheep in a fertile valley. 3. A great hail and wind have injured the corn. 4. Will you not dare to fight for your country ? 5. He was unwilling to go to Greece, for he feared the pirates. 6. She was accused of theft. 7. These men are willing to give gold for iron. 8. Caesar was stabbed by his friend Brutus. 9. She was desirous of hearing my voice. 10. Go quickly to Rome. 11. Sleep is pleasant to the weary. 12. Spare the conquered. 13. In my opinion she is very beautiful. 14. The city having been burnt we fled. 15. The fish were swimming on the top of the water.

✓ *Exercise* 43.

RECAPITULATORY.

1. Ego et uxor mea canendi sumus studiosissimi. 2. Mea sententia vita est somnium. 3. Divitias gloriae non anteposuere. 4. Salute frui sine sapientia non possumus. 5. Naturae legibus parendum est. 6. Hostem fugientem cum toto exercitu sequebatur. 7. Gallinarum ova anatibus quis supponet ? 8. Scipioni cognomen Africano datur. 9. Hic centurio exemplo erat magnae virtutis. 10. Nonne filius simillimus est patri ? 11. Hieme mare ventis turbatur. 12. Multa huiusmodi scelera clam amicis admiserat. 13. Nonne te mei pudet ? 14. Num Gallorum fortissimi sunt Belgae ? 15. Iter mox facturus haec mihi dedit.

1. In summer the sea is not troubled with many storms. 2. Then I was informed of Caesar's death. 3. Thebes, the capital of Boeotia, was destroyed by fire. 4. Are you desirous of hearing Socrates ? 5. Many ships having been wrecked, he determined to make others. 6. Having been accused of theft, he escaped punishment by the help of the orator. 7. He was pouring poison into my cup. 8. That storm wrecked two hundred ships. 9. Return to Rome within eighteen days. 10. Venus wished to marry Mars. 11. Is not the girl very like her mother ? 12. We must not believe liars. 13. I am fond of bathing. 14. Why did he call his city Rome ? 15. The camp was pitched at the foot of the mountain.

Exercise 44.

RECAPITULATORY.

1. Nuntius Tarquinium regem in horto ambulantem invenerat. 2. Te iudice, non condemnabor capitis. 3. Nonne Sicilia quondam Italiae adhaesit ? 4. Num vis mecum in horto ambulare ? 5. Devicto Hannibale, Poeni de salute desperabant. 6. Philosophus divitias minimi faciet. 7. Ob hanc victoriam praeclarus fies. 8. Dedecus morte turpius est, me iudice. 9. Acie ita ordinata fortissime pugnatum est. 10. Huic stulto homini minime credendum est. 11. Ducis virtus laudanda videbatur. 12. Diu Athenis praeerat Pericles. 13. Hos equos maximo pretio emam. 14. Ne captivos securi percusseris. 15. Avis ab accipitre capietur.

1. Do you not pity this poor man ? 2. Don't cross the Aegean sea, my son. 3. Having held a levy the consuls returned to the camp 4. Let us go to Asia with you. 5. A treaty was made on these conditions. 6. A lion of great size was killed by our weapons. 7. This robber took away our money from us. 8. For this reason the name of Corvus was given to the soldier. 9. Scaevola killed the secretary of Porsena, king of the Etrurians, with a dagger. 10. The soothsayer was accused of folly. 11. The hail will have injured the crops. 12. Will you not teach your daughters the art of singing ? 13. I saw the light of the rising sun. 14. One must fight for one's country. 15. You will be answered by us.

Exercise 45.

RECAPITULATORY.

1. Equites Romani barbarorum copias fudisse dicuntur. 2. Centurio vir fortissimus, omnes Gallorum impetus sustinuit. 3. T. Labienum legatum cum duabus legionibus omnique equitatu praemittit. 4. Nonne nos pueri felicissimi sumus ? 5. Hae literae tibi proderunt. 6. Pastores lupum saxis interficiebant. 7. Cupida erat satisfaciendi parentibus. 8. Labienus ab equitatu hostium lacessitus nuntios ad Caesarem mittit. 9. Devicti Galli, obsidibus datis, pacem petierunt. 10. Nulla pars urbis muro munita erat. 11. His verbis Ariovisto responsum est. 12. Quis fugientem hostem timebit ? 13. Otium deos rogat nauta. 14. Opus urbis aedificandae militibus profuit. 15. Boni viri suis culpis non ignoscent.

1. This work will be very easy to a brave soldier. 2. Our soldiers will kill many enemies with their swords. 3. Juno married Jupiter. 4. The consul praises the centurion, a very brave man. 5. Let us fly from Corinth to Rome. 6. Ariovistus must be answered in these words. 7. Having been expelled from the city, the king fled to our enemies. 8. We are not ashamed of this brave deed. 9. This work having been finished, we shall go to Gaul. 10. It is not always easy to catch fish with a hook. 11. The Gauls were overcome by the valour and counsel of Labienus our general. 12. Numa, the king of the Romans, is said to have been a very wise man. 13. We heard the birds singing in the garden. 14. He taught his son the art of singing. 15. I have sent the letter of Cicero the consul to your father.

Exercise 46.

RECAPITULATORY.

1. Consules bina castra muniunt. 2. Diu a nostris pugnabitur. 3. Multi utrinque cadere, plures vulnera accipere. 4. Prima luce summus mons a Labieno tenebatur. 5. Trecenti sex periere, unus relictus est. 6. Uxor deinde eum ac liberi amplexi sunt. 7. Cerere nati Liber et Libera appellati sunt. 8. Tres validissimae urbes, Etruriae capita, pacem petebant. 9. Urbem ditissimam, caput eius gentis, expugnat diripitque. 10. Nostrae patriae a nobis consulendum est. 11. Iucundiorem faciet libertatem servitutis memoria. 12. Castra promovit, et sub monte considit. 13. Progrediuntur et sub montem succedunt. 14. Ad bene pugnandum breve tempus non est satis. 15. Caesar milites cohortatus aciem commisit.

1. Cincinnatus named Atratinus master of the horsemen. 2. I am a Roman citizen, I am called Brutus. 3. He found his wife sitting alone in the house. 4. One of the legions was given to Fabius to be led against the enemy. 5. I asked this of you very often. 6. Ennius the poet was walking in the garden with me. 7. Do you wish to cross the river in this boat or not? 8. Our horsemen having followed the flying enemy killed a great number of them. 9. We have seen a serpent of great size. 10. This town is distant from Rome a journey of many days. 11. Do not beat your sister. 12. After this victory he got possession of the city of Athens. 13. Having received this news he determined to pitch the camp. 14 Fish often swim at the top of the water. 15. I shall remain here two days.

Exercise 47.

RECAPITULATORY.

1. Murus et porta fulmine icta sunt. 2. Nobis nec deus nec quisquam homo invidet. 3. Mors pro patria praeclara videtur. 4. Iterum tribunus plebis fieri voluit. 5. Cincinnatum dictatorem creaverunt. 6. Aedui victi Sequanis obsides dare coacti sunt. 7. Nos caussa belli, nos vulnerum ac caedium viris ac parentibus sumus. 8. Huic deo nomem Mercurio est. 9. Flumen transire conati, telorum multitudine repulsi sunt. 10. Captivi pane nigro in carcere vescebantur. 11. Mea sententia doctissimus est. 12. Romani non viam tantum, sed tecta etiam proxima portae occupaverant. 13. Helvetii copias suas per fines Sequanorum transduxerant. 14. Filiis et filiabus a nobis consulendum est. 15. Utrum Romae habitat, an Corinthi? 16. Ego et tu, viri fortissimi, capitis condemnabimur.

1. About the fourth hour of the day he saw a lion. 2. He demanded of the magistrates the keys of the gates. 3. Some were standing on shore, others were rushing into the water. 4. We are all skilled in singing. 5. I heard the young men singing outside the walls of the town. 6. I was born in the consulship of Cicero. 7. I am thirty-one years old. 8. Crassus will be made consul by the Roman people. 9. He took away the arms from all the cavalry. 10. The ship having been wrecked, twenty men were drowned. 11. I saw the slaves going and returning. 12. Are you unwilling to return to Italy with me? 13. She wishes to be first of all. 14. They live on eggs and milk. 15. We have bought a statue of the goddess for a large price.

Exercise 48.

RECAPITULATORY.

1. Extra urbem multi vinci, capi, vinciri. 2. Illud semper proderat, hoc semper proderit civitati. 3. Caesar apud Sequanos multos dies moratus est. 4. Agricola anguem paene frigore confectum reperit. 5. Multi flumen frustra transire conati, hostium telis repelluntur. 6. Medicus artis suae erat peritissimus. 7. Brutus in liberanda patria interfectus esse dicitur. 8. Aliis terrori, aliis praesidio erat. 9. Fortis viri est in periculis non timere. 10. Erat inter Labienum atque hostes difficili transitu flumen. 11. Uterque nostrum idem faciet. 12. Gallia civium Romanorum eo tempore plena erat. 13. Pane et lacte contentus erat. 14. Capta urbe, magnus captivorum numerus in potestatem victorum venerat. 15. Nonne pax bello erit melior?

1. Caesar said this to Brutus in my hearing. 2. Then Tarquinius became king, the children of Ancus being still alive. 3. The legion set out in the middle of the night. 4. Clodius was killed by the slaves of Milo on the Appian road. 5. Dionysius, having been expelled from Syracuse, used to teach boys at Corinth. 6. Do not go to Pompeius in Greece. 7. The people withdrew to the Sacred Mountain, three miles from the city. 8. Is it not a sin to betray one's country? 9. Why am I called a robber? 10. She will marry a man of great courage and wisdom. 11. This country is fit for rearing sheep. 12. She was not content with these gifts. 13. Relying on his cavalry, he determined to attack the Gauls next day. 14. Do not use deceit. 15. In my opinion he is not worthy of such honour.

Exercise 49.

RECAPITULATORY.

1. Temeritas nostra non solum nobis, sed etiam reipublicae nocuit. 2. Caesar Sequanis ab Ariovisto oppressis auxilium tulit. 3. Equitatum secuti nostri, magnum numerum sine ullo periculo interfecerunt. 4. Omni aetati mors est communis. 5. Vulpes corvum ob dulcem vocem laudabat. 6. Huic uxor ad portam occurrit. 7. Num perita est canendi? 8. Castra et urbem vobis praedae dabo. 9. Barbarorum est in dies vivere. 10. Consulum alter exercitum perdidit, alter vendidit. 11. Nonne tibi multum pecuniae a nobis datum est? 12. Quaedam bestiae alius generis bestiis vescuntur. 13. Magnis copiis ad hoc bellum opus erat. 14. Num bellum pace melius est? 15. Romulus patre Marte natus est.

1. The Carthaginians, Hannibal being their leader, waged war with the Roman people for many years. 2. In my garden are most beautiful flowers at all times. 3. She was eighteen years old at that time. 4. The Spartans, under the leadership of Leonidas, fought with the Persians near Thermopylae. 5. In the second watch of the following night he sets out for Rome. 6. Pompeius set out from Greece for Alexandria in Egypt. 7. This city is distant a mile from the sea. 8. Who is desirous of reading this book? 9. I saw these soldiers carrying heavy burdens. 10. On the road a serpent of huge size attacked the Roman army. 11. Is anything more precious than gold? 12. The danger of attacking the city is great. 13. This satisfies us. 14. Is not this girl meet to be loved? 15. They built a wall eighteen feet high.

Exercise 50.

RECAPITULATORY.

1. Num vis consul fieri? 2. Dux dolorem tulisse aequo animo dicitur. 3. Caesaris legati haec coram Ariovisto locuti sunt. 4. Agricola lupum secutus ad antrum venerat. 5. Brutum adolescentem copiis praefecimus. 6. Tertia hora exploratores ad castra redierunt. 7. E ducentis navibus vix quadraginta incolumes fuerunt. 8. Centum boves militibus dono dedit. 9. Catella eo nomine mortua erat. 10. Britanni sunt capillo promisso et corpore raso. 11. Gallorum ducenti a nostris interfecti sunt. 12. Alii eum capitis damnare, alii pecunia multare volebant. 13. Hunc agrum maximi emerat. 14. Multa Romae passus in Asiam se contulit. 15. Quis unquam Themistocle clarior fuit?

1. He was again created consul during my consulship. 2. It is the nature of a fool to do this. 3. The war was finished within twenty days. 4. Meanwhile Caesar was remaining in Gaul. 5. Did he not come to you in Italy? 6. Then the Greeks returned to the island of Samos. 7. A signal being given the fleet sailed about four miles. 8. We must retire from this province immediately. 9. Do not call me a robber. 10. Did you prefer silver to gold? 11. Courage is valued very highly by all. 12. The name of Britain was given to this island. 13. He sent two thousand soldiers for a help to the citizens. 14. The city, having been taken by the Germans, was burnt. 15. He defended himself against the attacks of the enemy with his sword.

THE SIMPLE SENTENCE

CONTINUED.

A Simple Sentence is either—

(*a.*) A STATEMENT,—Verb in the Indicative :—
   Ex. Caesar vicit Gallos, *Caesar conquered the Gauls.*

   Sometimes in the Conjunctive :—
   Ex. Caesar hoc fecisset, *Caesar would have done this.*

(*b.*) A COMMAND,—Verb in the Imperative or Present Conjunctive :—
   Ex. Fac hoc, *or* facias hoc, *do this.*

In commands with a negative use (*a*) the Present Conjunctive with First and Third Persons ; (*b*) the Perfect Conjunctive with the Second Person :—
   Ex. (*a*) Ne hoc faciam, *let me not do this.*
   Ne hoc faciat, *let him not do this.*
   (*b*) Ne hoc feceris, *don't do this.*

(*c.*) A QUESTION,—Verb in the Indicative, with an Interrogative word.

Interrogative words are,—
   Quantus, uter, qualis, quis, quot, quotus, unde, ubi, quando.
   Cur, quoties, quare, quam, quomodo, num, nĕ, ut, an, utrum.

Translate *whether—or*, by *utrum—an*.
   Ex. Utrum Gallus es an Romanus? (*whether*) *are you a Gaul or a Roman?*

Exercise 51.

The Athenians were building the walls of their city. The Lacedaemonians bore this ill ; but Themistocles deceived them *in this way*. He went to Sparta (as) an ambassador, and spoke thus : 'My citizens are not building the walls. You seem not to believe *me*. Send therefore trusty men ; they will inspect the city ; meanwhile do ye detain me.' The Lacedaemonians did this.

   in this way, *ablative of manner.* me, *dative.*

Exercise 52.

Themistocles at the same time secretly sent a messenger to the Athenians, saying, 'Build the walls of the city quickly. Do *not* abandon the enterprise—detain the Lacedaemonian ambassadors.' The Athenians did this. Therefore Themistocles returned to Athens; the Lacedaemonian ambassadors were dismissed, and Athens was fortified. By the help of Themistocles Athens became the most splendid city of Greece.

      not, *ne.*

Exercise 53.

Many pelicans arrive annually from the Black Sea; with them also come swans, cranes, and geese. They ascend the river Don, and in autumn return by the same way. The pelicans make their nests with rushes; within they place soft grass. They lay two eggs like *the eggs* of the swan. Seeing danger, they hide their eggs in the water; afterwards they take them out with their bill. They feed on fish. Pelicans and cormorants together pursue fish in this way. The pelican extends its wings and troubles the water; the cormorant diving into the water then catches the terrified fish. They then share the booty equally.

     the eggs, *dative.*

Exercise 54.

Seagulls *by flying* from the sea to the shore, and crows and swallows by flying to the sea, foretell rain and wind. I shall now tell *you* the reason of this thing. All birds *are fond of* a moist air. Seagulls especially love an air like to water, and birds from the land also delight *in bathing.* On account of this reason geese utter cries, and crows seem to summon rain, *for* they are refreshed by the mildness of the air.

by flying, *volando.* you, *dative;* the remoter object of *tell, reason* being the nearer object. are fond of, *love.* in bathing, *lavando.* for, *enim.*

Exercise 55.

A husbandman found a snake almost dead with cold. Moved with pity he cherished it in his bosom, and placed it under his garment. Soon the snake, being refreshed, recovered its strength, and inflicted a deadly wound *on the husbandman* (in return) *for* his kindness.

 on the husbandman, *dative;* the remoter object of *inflicted.*
 (in return) for, *pro.*

Exercise 56.

Once upon a time a dolphin is said to have contracted a friendship with the son of a poor man. The boy *used to feed* him with crumbs of bread. Every day the dolphin, being called by the boy, swam to *the top of the water;* and, having been fed by his hand, carried the boy on his back from the shore to a school in another place, and brought him back in the same way. At last the boy died, and the dolphin is said to have died *from* grief.

used to feed, *imperfect.* the top of the water, *the highest water.*
from, *on account of.*

Exercise 57.

Among the ancient Greeks and Romans quails were taught to fight *with each other.* The quail is a bird of great courage, and prefers to die than to be conquered. Once there was a very celebrated quail, for it had conquered all its adversaries. A certain mayor wishing to honour the Emperor Augustus, served it up *at table.* Augustus, angry on account of the death of *so* brave a bird, exclaimed: 'Kill this mayor; to have slain so brave a bird is disgraceful.'

with each other, *among themselves.* at table, *dative.* so, *tam.*

Exercise 58.

Mars, the god of war, was worshipped *by* the Romans with great honours. The wolf and the horse were sacred to him. He was represented as a warrior, generally standing in a car, or sitting on a horse, armed with a spear and a whip. *His* sister Bellona used to perform the duty of charioteer in his car. Mars is said to have been the father of Romulus, the founder of Rome.

by, translate *by,* with living creatures, by *a* or *ab.* his, *of him.*

Exercise 59.

Bacchus was the god of wine. He is represented as a naked youth, long-haired and beautiful. He is crowned with ivy, and carries in his hand a thyrsus, that is, a spear surrounded either with ivy or vine leaves. His car is drawn by tigers or lions. The companions of Bacchus were the nymphs and goat-footed satyrs. Once Silenus had been his master; he also follows Bacchus, and is represented as a fat old man, with naked body, crowned with leaves. A he-goat *used to be sacrificed* to Bacchus, for this animal is wont to injure the vines.

used to be sacrificed, *imperfect.*

Exercise 60.

Two dogs, mother and son, were hunting in a wood. A servant of the lord of the wood killed the mother. The son, being frightened, ran away, but soon returned to the place. *Having found her body*, he lay down beside her, and was afterwards found by his master. He was then brought home, together with the body of his mother. *For a long time* this affectionate animal refused all food, and at length died, worn out with grief.

    having found her body, *her body having been found*.
    for a long time, *diu*.

Exercise 61.

A boy once met an old woman driving asses. '*Good morning, mother of asses*,' said he; 'Good-morning, my son,' she replied.

    good-morning, *hail*.

Exercise 62.

A quarrel once arose between a philosopher and a soldier. The soldier beat the philosopher with a stick, but the philosopher bore the blows quietly, *without being angry*. One of his friends then said, 'Why do you endure this quietly? Such things are not *to be endured* by a brave man.' The philosopher replied, 'These things, my friend, happen behind my back; they do not disturb me.'

    without being angry, *neither was he angry*.
    to be endured, *gerundive*.

Exercise 63.

Rome had sent ambassadors to *the city of Tarentum in Italy*. The ambassadors were going to the assembly. On the road a wretched fellow spat *on the dress* of one of the ambassadors. The citizens began to laugh. 'You laugh,' said the Roman, 'but my dress shall be washed with your blood.' War was declared, and the city of Tarentum lost many of its citizens. Thus the dress of the ambassador was washed with blood.

    the city of Tarentum, *the city Tarentum*. in Italy, *into Italy*.
    on the dress, *in with acc*.

Exercise 64.

Before a battle a certain soldier came to the General and said, 'My father is ill, and will soon die: I wish to see him; will you give me permission *to go?*' 'Go,' said the General; 'you honour your father and your mother: *your days will be long* in the land.'

    to go, *of going*. your days will be long, *you will live long*.

Exercise 65.

The Greeks had sent an expedition against Troy. Agamemnon, the leader of the Grecian army, had wounded a doe sacred to Diana. An adverse wind sent by the goddess detained the expedition. Therefore Agamemnon consulted the augurs. These answered, 'Sacrifice your daughter to Diana; thus you will appease the anger of the goddess.' Ulysses was sent to Clytemnestra, the mother of Iphigenia, the daughter of Agamemnon, and said to her, 'Give me your daughter: Agamemnon has promised her *in marriage* to Achilles.' The girl was therefore given to him. Agamemnon was *going to sacrifice* her, but Diana, pitying the girl, put a doe in her *place*. Then she carried off Iphigenia, and made her the priestess of her temple.

    in marriage, *in matrimonium* (acc.).   going to sacrifice, *fut. part.*
                    place, *acc.*

Exercise 66.

The quadrupeds once declared war *against the birds*. The lion was chosen general. He began to review his forces. The ass and the hare passed by. The bull said, 'What will these be able to do?' The lion answered, 'I shall use the ass *as* a trumpeter, and the hare *as* an orderly.'

    against the birds, *dative, of remote object.*   as, *pro.*

Exercise 67.

Alexander, king of Macedon, examined *his* portrait at Ephesus. Apelles, the most celebrated painter of that time, had painted it. Alexander did not praise it enough. But the horse of Alexander having been brought in neighed at *the horse* in the picture. Then said Apelles, 'O king, this horse seems to be more skilled *in the art of painting* than you.'

    his, *of himself.*   the horse, *dative.*   in the art, *genitive.*
              of painting, *gerund.*

Exercise 68.

A widow woman once had a hen. This hen used to lay an egg every day. But the woman wished to receive *two* or *three* eggs daily from the hen, therefore she began to feed and fatten it more abundantly. Then the hen became fat, and immediately ceased to lay eggs.

    two, three, *use the distributive numerals.*

Exercise 69.

Zeuxis, the most celebrated of painters, had painted a boy carrying grapes. A bird tried to eat the grapes. Then Zeuxis said: 'I painted the grapes better than the boy, otherwise the bird *would have feared* the boy.'

would have feared, *pluperf.-conjunctive.*

Exercise 70.

The crocodile *from being* very small becomes very large. It lives a long time, and inhabits water and land alike. It has no tongue, nor can it move its lower jaw. It eats not only fish and cattle, but also human beings. The Egyptians hold it sacred. Many crocodiles are said to be kept in their temples. The priests adorn them with golden rings and bracelets.

from being, *from.*

Exercise 71.

Some one once said to a funny *fellow*, 'The sun is wont to set towards the west: why does it rise from the east?' The other replied, 'The sun always returns by the same way after *sunset*, but cannot be seen (while) returning; for the darkness of night hides it.'

fellow, *quidam.* sunset, *the setting of the sun.*

Exercise 72.

A *lady* once visited Cornelia, the mother of the Gracchi, and showed *her* all her most beautiful ornaments. Cornelia delayed her with conversation for a long time. At last her boys returned from school. Then she said, 'These are my ornaments.'

lady, *woman.* her, *dative of remote object.*

Exercise 73.

A swallow wishing to build a nest flew to a sheep and began to pluck wool from its back. The sheep feeling pain from the plucking, began to jump and complain. 'What!' said the swallow, 'do you grudge *me* a little tuft of wool? Men shear (off) all your wool, and you say nothing.' The sheep answered, 'Men indeed shear (off) all my wool, but they treat me more gently.'

me, *to me.*

Exercise 74.

A magpie and a dove visited a peacock. (While) returning the ill-tongued magpie said, 'I do not love the peacock. He utters ugly sounds. Why is he not silent? Why does he not hide his ugly feet?' But the innocent dove replied, 'I did not notice his defects, but I admired the beauty of his body and the splendour of his tail. I cannot enough *praise* him.'

praise, *infinitive, carrying on the meaning of 'I cannot.'*

Exercise 75.

Once (upon a time) a doctor said to Pausanias, the king of the Spartans, 'You have become an old man.' Pausanias answered, 'I truly am old; I never *employed* you as a doctor.' The doctor went away *without saying anything*.

employed, *used*. without saying, see 62, Note.
anything, *quidquam* (only to be used with negatives).

Exercise 76.

Many wonderful stories are told about the animals of Egypt. There are found many winged snakes. There is a kind of bird by name the ibis. The ibis catches these snakes and lives on their flesh. In the temples crocodiles are kept; these wear golden rings on their arms, and are *held* sacred by the Egyptians. The priests give *them* food daily. Cats and dogs are also held sacred by the Egyptians. Dead cats are pickled in salt and myrrh and other perfumes. The priests guard them in the temples.

held, *habeo*. them, *to them*.

Exercise 77.

Phocion the Athenian was a poor man. Once *when Alexander sent him a large sum* of money, he asked, 'Why does he give me this money?' The messenger replied, 'Alexander thinks you the only good man among the Athenians.' Then said Phocion, 'Take away the money, I prefer to be good.'

when—sent, *abl. abs.* him, *to him.* a large sum, *much.*

Exercise 78.

Once (upon a time) some one said to Alexander, king of Macedonia, 'Darius, the king of the Persians, is leading an immense army to battle.' Alexander replied, 'One butcher *is not afraid of* many sheep.'

is not afraid of, *does not fear*.

Exercise 79.

Once upon a time some one laughed at a Spartan, saying, 'You are lame, how will you be able to fight?' The Spartan answered, '*I want* to fight, not to run away.'

I want, *I desire*.

Exercise 80.

There exist in the ocean huge animals. These are called whales. They are considered fishes by some, but really they are animals, for their blood is warm. They have arms; they have not legs. The whale produces young, *two at a time*. They are said to fly from danger, holding their young in their arms. Sailors pursue them and kill them with spears. They give a great quantity of oil.

two at a time, *use the distributive numeral.*

Exercise 81.

Caesar saw many wonderful animals in Gaul. Among these was an ox with the shape of a stag; from the *middle of the forehead* a long horn projects between the ears, longer and straighter than the horns of our oxen. From the end of this horn branches are spread out *in* the likeness of palms. The nature of the female and the male is the same the shape and size of the horns is also the same.

the middle of the forehead, *the middle forehead*. in, *into*.

Exercise 82.

There are also other wonderful animals; these the inhabitants call elks. They are like roe-deer in shape and colour, but excel them in size. They have legs without joints; hence they never lie down *for the sake* of repose, nor can they (while) lying on the ground raise themselves. They use trees instead of a couch; *against* these they recline themselves, and so enjoy repose. These trees having been discovered, the hunters nearly cut them down. Then the elks recline themselves against the trees, and break them down with their weight, and are thus easily taken.

for the sake, *caussa (abl.)*. against, *in, with acc.*

Exercise 83.

There is also a third kind; these animals are called bisons. In size they are a little smaller than elephants; in shape and colour they are like bulls. Their strength and swiftness are very great: they spare neither *man* nor wild beast. Not even (when) captured *very small* can they be tamed. The size and shape of their horns differ much from the horns of our oxen. The Gauls use the horns of these animals instead of cups.

   man, *dative.*   very small, *the emphatic word is put between* ne *and* quidem (*not—even*).

Exercise 84.

The nation of the Suevi is *by far* the greatest and most warlike of all the Germans. The Suevi are said to possess a hundred cantons. They are said to lead out every year from their territory *one* thousand of armed men for the sake of waging war. *The remainder* stay at home and cultivate the fields; these in turn are in arms the year after. Thus neither farming nor war is neglected. No one possesses *any private land,* nor is it lawful to remain longer than a year in one place. Their food consists chiefly of milk and flesh; they also hunt often. Their daily exercise and this kind of food makes them men of great stature, and increases their strength. They are clothed only with skins, and bathe in the coldest rivers.

   by far, *longe.*   one, *use the distributive numeral.*   The remainder, *the rest.*   any private land, *anything* (quidquam) *of private land.*

Exercise 85.

Their horsemen often in battle leap down from their horses and fight *on foot.* The horses meanwhile stand in the same place. Nothing is held more disgraceful than to use saddles. Therefore a small number of them dare to attack any number of horsemen provided with saddles. Their horses are small and ugly, but they train them with great care. They never use wine, for wine is thought to weaken their bodies.

   on foot, *pedibus.*

Exercise 86.

Leonidas, king of the Spartans, heard a man saying, 'The Persians are very numerous; their arrows will darken the sun.' '*So much* the better,' said Leonidas, 'we shall fight in the shade.' A herald from Xerxes, the king of the Persians, came to him and said, 'Surrender your arms.' Leonidas answered, 'Come and take them.'

   so much, *tanto.*

Exercise 87.

A certain nobleman *was very fond of* wine. The king once said to him, 'You are fond of *a glass* of wine; your friends tell me so.' 'They are unjust to me, O king,' replied the other; 'I am fond of a bottle of wine.'

was very fond of, *greatly loved.* a glass, *a cup.*

Exercise 88.

A certain fellow had been relating many incredible things. Wishing to repress his impertinence, an old man remarked, 'These things are indeed wonderful; but I will tell you something even more wonderful. One of my friends, a flute-player, once imitated thunder very well, and immediately all the milk in the house *turned* sour.'

turned, *became.*

Exercise 89.

Venus, the goddess of love and beauty, was born from the foam of the sea. She is represented sitting in a car drawn by swans or doves. *Of* trees the myrtle was sacred to her. Her son Cupid accompanies her, a winged boy, equipped with a bow and arrows. Besides him she has the Graces, the goddesses of beauty, as companions. These are generally represented naked, and with hands joined.

of, *out of.*

Exercise 90.

Vulcan, the ugliest of all the gods, was the husband of Venus, the most beautiful of all the goddesses. On account of his ugliness he was thrown from heaven by Jupiter, and fell into the island of Lemnos. This fall made him lame. He was the god of fire and of smiths. He had a workshop in Mount Aetna. His servants were the Cyclopes, giants having one eye *in the middle of the forehead.*

in the middle of the forehead, *in the middle forehead.*

Exercise 91.

The Scythians neither cultivate the fields nor have fixed dwellings, but, feeding oxen and sheep, are wont to wander through uncultivated wastes. They bring *with them* their wives and children in waggons. They feed on milk, honey, and flesh; they despise gold and silver, nor do they use money. Their bodies are clothed with skins.

with them, *secum;* cum is written after me, te, se, nobis, vobis, quo, qua, quibus, quis.

Exercise 92.

In India there are many elephants. This animal excels all others in docility. They learn to use weapons, to fight, to dance, to walk along a tight rope, and to do many other wonderful things. Elephants always go *in herds*. The oldest leads *the line of march*; another old elephant walks behind the rest. (When) about to cross a river they send on the smallest. They are caught in pitfalls by the natives, and are easily tamed.

in herds, *gregatim.* the line of march, *agmen.*

Exercise 93.

The Chinese are very skilful workmen. They can imitate *anything you please*. Once a sailor gave a garment and a cloth to a Chinese, and said, 'Out of this cloth make for me a garment like to this.' But the garment was worn out and torn. So the Chinese made the garment, and then tore it. Then he brought it to the sailor, and said, 'Here is the new garment; I have made it like the old one.' The sailor was angry, but could say nothing, for he had said, 'Make a garment like to the old one.'

anything you please, *quilibet.*

Exercise 94.

Mercurius, the son of Jupiter and Maia, was the messenger of the gods. He was the god of eloquence, of merchants, and also of thieves. He was besides the inventor of the lyre. He *used to escort* the souls of the dead to the gods below. He was represented as a handsome youth, *with winged feet*, carrying a wand in his hand surrounded with two snakes. Mercurius also performed the office of a herald, and was the god of peace. He was worshipped by the Romans with great honour.

used to escort, *imperfect.* with winged feet, *abl. of quality.*

Exercise 95.

Ostriches equal the height of a horseman sitting on a horse. They are swifter than all other animals. Their wings assist them (while) tunning; they cannot use their wings *for flying*. They have hoofs like the feet of deer; with these they are said to seize stones in their flight, and throw them *at* their *pursuers*. They are also said to be able to digest iron and stones. Their feathers are sought *for* ornaments. They are stupid animals, for they hide their heads in a bush, and then seem to themselves to be well hidden.

for flying, *ad, with gerund.* at, *in, with acc.*
pursuers, *those-pursuing (pres. part.).* for, *ad.*

Exercise 96.

Africa breeds snakes twenty feet long. In India also there are immense snakes; some are said to be able to swallow stags and oxen whole. Others are able to kill them at once with their bite, for their teeth are full of poison. There is no remedy *for the bite* of these snakes. The Indians do not use shoes, and the greater part of their body is naked; they are therefore often killed by the snakes.

for the bite, *of the bite*.

Exercise 97.

Ducks are often caught by fowlers in this way. The fowlers place nets near a lake, and then hide themselves in the bushes. Tame ducks are then liberated. These swim on the lake and attract the wild ducks. Then they swim towards the nets; the wild ducks follow them and are easily caught. Tame ducks taught to do this are sold *for a large price*, and are *highly* valued by the fowlers.

for a large price, *abl.* highly, *magni (pretii, price, being understood).*

Exercise 98.

The Indians in America are very swift; they are said to equal horses in swiftness. There is also a race of frogs in the marshes of America. These frogs can leap nine feet in one leap. *Some fellows* once said to an Indian, 'Will you contend in a race with a frog? We will give you much *money*.' The Indian agreed. They then caught a frog in a marsh. Then they attached a lighted stick to its tail. The animal leaped in a wonderful way, and escaped to the pond, nor could the Indian equal its swiftness.

some fellows, *quidam.* money, *of money.*

Exercise 99.

A certain rich merchant had lost all his money. Soon afterwards one of his friends met him and said, '*How are you?*' 'Tolerably well,' replied the merchant; 'I can use my legs in walking better than formerly.' Then said his friend, 'I do not understand your words; will you explain them to me?' 'Certainly,' answered the other; 'I have been obliged to sell my horses, and I am now compelled to walk.'

how are you? *how do you hold (habeo) yourself?*

Exercise 100.

A certain man once had a celebrated frog. This frog could jump very well. A stranger once said to him, 'Give *me* a frog also ; then let both jump : here are ten pence : do thou also lay down ten pence ; the owner of the victorious frog shall have all the money.' The other joyfully agreed, and went out. Soon he returned carrying another frog. The frogs were placed on the ground, but the celebrated jumper could not jump at all, and was easily defeated. The stranger took the money and went away. Then the other examined his frog ; he found it full of lead. The stranger had filled it with the lead *in his absence.*

me, *dative.* in his absence, *he (being) absent.*

Exercise 101.

We left our ship, and began to walk about. There stood not far off a vast palace, well built, *with a gate of ebony.* This gate having been opened, we saw before us a large hall ; there lay two huge heaps, the one of human bones, the other of spits. Seeing this spectacle we began to tremble. Suddenly the door opened with a loud crash, and there came out an ugly man of immense stature. He had one eye only, in the middle of his forehead : his teeth were very long and sharp ; his lips hung down *to* his breast : his ears were like the ears of an elephant. From fear we became immediately like dead men.

with a gate of ebony, *abl. of quality (with epithet).* to, *as far as.*

Exercise 102.

At last we collected our minds, and saw him sitting in the hall and looking at us. Then he advanced and took me by my neck, and examined me. I was very thin, therefore he let me go. He then took up the rest *one by one,* examined them, and at last chose the pilot. *Now* the pilot was a very fat man. Then he thrust a spit through his body. This being done, he kindled a great fire. Then he cooked and ate him. Then he fell asleep.

one by one, *use the distributive numeral.* now, *autem (put it after the first word in the sentence).*

Exercise 103.

We were all-nearly dead *from* fear. At last I determined to try to save myself and my companions. Therefore I addressed them with these words: 'My friends, the giant will soon awake; then he will kill another man; thus shall we all perish. Let us try to do something. Do not fear, but perform my commands. Harden a stake with fire; let us pierce his eye with this; thus we shall escape death!' All *joyfully* agreed. The stake was hardened with fire. Then we pierced the eye of the sleeping giant with it. He awoke, uttering terrible cries, but could not see us. Then we ran away, and escaped death.

from, on account of.   joyfully, adjective.

Exercise 104.

The Chinese *are very fond of* the flesh of pigs. Formerly they used to eat the flesh raw, for they were ignorant of the use of fire in *cooking*. Once a house in a certain city was burnt, and the pigs perished in the flames. Their flesh gave (forth) a very pleasant smell. A boy tasted the flesh, and then said to his friends, 'The fire has made the pigs sweeter.' Then all the inhabitants burned their houses, and ate the flesh of the roasted pigs. At length a certain philosopher said to the citizens, 'My friends, I have an idea in my mind. Cease to burn your houses for the sake of roasted flesh. Perhaps pigs can be roasted without a house. Let us try.' The citizens joyfully roasted a pig without a house; its flesh was very sweet: therefore, from that time, they began to cook the flesh with fire, and ceased to burn their houses together with the pigs.

are very fond of, love much.   cooking, gerund.

Exercise 105.

The mountains in Scythia are said to be inhabited by goat-footed men. There is also in those regions another wonderful race of men. These sleep for six months *every* year. Another race is said to cook and eat the bodies of their dead relations. These men clean the heads of the dead, and gild them. Then they use them instead of cups. There are other wonderful men in these mountains; these have only one eye in the middle of the forehead. There are also said to be treasures, guarded by monsters.

every, singuli.

Exercise 106.

Augustus used often to walk through the city of Rome, and receive all men with great kindness. Once a poor man, wishing to ask a favour, *kept holding out* his hand, and then drawing it back from fear. Augustus, laughing, said to him : 'Are you giving a penny to an elephant? Do not fear; what do you desire?' An old soldier, being summoned before the judges, said to Augustus, 'Plead my cause.' Augustus then said to one of his companions, 'Plead the cause of this soldier.' Then the soldier exclaimed, 'I did not seek a substitute; I fought for you myself; see my scars; I received these wounds *while fighting* in your army.' Augustus blushed, and pleaded the cause of the soldier himself.

kept holding out, *imperfect*. while fighting, *inter, with gerund*.

Exercise 107.

A brave soldier had been sent with a message written on paper to one of the generals of his army. *While making the journey* the enemy attacked him. He was severely wounded with a javelin, and by the same blow his companion was killed. Leaving the dead man he fled swiftly. At last, worn out by fatigue and wounds, he fell on the ground. Fearing the approach of the enemy, *and not* forgetful of his duty, he concealed the paper in the wound. He was found next day by his friends. He showed the paper hidden in the wound, and then died with a joyful countenance. The general built a monument to this brave soldier. On the monument were these words, 'Here lies a brave soldier. He died, faithful to the last, *in the discharge of* his duty.'

while making the journey, *on the road*. and not, *neither*.
to, *of*. in the discharge of, *discharging*.

Exercise 108.

War had broken out between the French and the Germans. A celebrated general of the French was severely wounded in the leg. The surgeons being consulted said, 'The leg *must be cut off*.' The general received the news with a calm countenance. There were many men around him in the tent; among these he saw a faithful servant shedding tears. Then the general said, smiling, 'Why do you shed tears, my friend? This accident will lighten your labour. Now you will clean one boot only.'

must be cut off, *gerundive*.

Exercise 109.

Once a French pirate attacked the ship of *some* merchants. The merchants determined to resist the enemy, for there was *much gold* in their ship. Among them was a certain priest. He said, 'I shall not fight: it is not (the duty) of a priest to fight.' The pirates attacked the merchants. These for a long time repelled the enemy. At length the pirates attempted to board the merchantman. Then the priest seized the leader of the pirates, and said, 'My friend, there is no need of thee in this vessel.' Having said these words with a calm countenance, he threw him into the sea. The pirates, terrified by the loss of their leader, were easily defeated.

some, *certain (quidam)*. much gold, *much of gold*.

Exercise 110.

A brave centurion with a few soldiers was trying to storm a fort. Three hundred Gauls were defending the fort. For a long time they were not able to get possession of it, for the enemy fought very bravely. At last one of the Gauls tried to pierce the centurion with a spear. But he seized the spear with both hands, and held it. The Gauls then drew him into the fort. But the centurion having drawn his sword, attacked the enemy bravely. They retreated; and the rest of the soldiers, having followed their brave leader, soon got possession of the fort, and killed all the Gauls.

A, *quidam*.

Exercise 111.

A certain man had taught *his dog many things*, and among others to fetch his food from the cook in a basket. Once the dog was returning to his master thus laden. Two other dogs, attracted by the smell of the food, determined to attack him. The dog put the basket on the ground, and fought bravely against *one* of them, but meanwhile the other ran to the basket and began to eat. At length, seeing no hope of victory, he threw himself between his two opponents, and quickly devoured the food himself. Then he returned to his master with the empty basket.

his dog many things, *both in the acc. after 'taught.'*
one (*alter*), one of *two*.

Exercise 112.

A philosopher wishing to test the ingenuity of the spider, often used to place one on a small stick stuck in the ground, and surrounded the stick with water. The spider, seeing no means of escape, ascends the stick, and then ejects its web. The wind carries the web to some stick or stone. Then the wise spider escapes by this, but it always *beforehand* tests the strength of the web.

beforehand, *ante*.

Exercise 113.

The Russian army was once crossing the Alps. The soldiers, overwhelmed with fatigue and overcome with want, no longer obeyed the command of their general, or observed their usual discipline. Then the general with a loud voice exclaimed, 'Dig a ditch, and cover me with earth; your general desires to be interred here, for you desert him.' Overwhelmed with shame, the soldiers are said to have thrown themselves *at* his feet, and to have demanded pardon.

at, *ante*.

Exercise 114.

The laws of Draco, the Athenian, were very severe; he punished almost all crimes with death. Hence the orator Demades used to say, 'The laws of Draco are written with blood.' He used to punish thieves *as* severely *as* parricides. Once being asked by a friend, 'Why do you punish little crimes with death?' he replied, 'Even the smallest crimes are worthy of death: there is no greater punishment for greater ones.'

as—as, *tam—quam*.

Exercise 115.

Phocion, the Athenian general, never allowed domestic or private things to interfere with the republic. He often refused to ask for anything even for his own friends and relations. Once his son-in-law was summoned *before* the judges. The accuser said, 'He has taken the money of the republic for himself.' Then Phocion addressed him in these glorious words, 'I have made you my son-in-law, but only *for* just and honourable things.'

before, *apud*. for, *ob*.

Exercise 116.

Diocles proclaimed to the Syracusans, 'Let *no one* dare to enter, armed, into an assembly of the people; death will be the punishment of this crime.' Once an alarm was given of an enemy approaching, and Diocles hastened with his soldiers girt with a sword. On the way he entered armed into the assembly of the people. Some one immediately exclaimed, 'Diocles, armed among the people, has broken his own law.' Diocles then replied with a loud voice, 'Thou speakest the truth, nor *shall Diocles be the last to sanction* his own laws.' Then, having drawn his sword, he killed himself.

    Let no one, *ne quis.* shall Diocles be the last to sanction,
                          shall Diocles last sanction.

Exercise 117.

A general had taken a well-fortified city. Soon afterwards a woman of low rank approached him, and complained with these words, 'One of thy soldiers has taken my cattle, my sole wealth.' 'Didst thou not hear the robbers?' replied the general; 'thy sleep was very sound.' 'Certainly,' answered she, 'my sleep was sound, for I trusted thy authority.' *The general pitied the poor woman*, and *much money* was given to her instead of the cattle.

    the general pitied the poor woman, *it pitied the general of
      the poor woman.* much money, *much of money.*

Exercise 118.

Once a certain man had beaten one *of* his companions. Being placed *before* the judge he said, 'I cannot pay the fine, for I have *no money*.' *Now* he had a long beard. His accuser then said, 'The defendant has a long beard, but no money : let his beard be shaved; he has nothing else; thus he will be *sufficiently* punished.' The judge replied, 'Certainly; let his beard be shaved.' The defendant, being terrified, then exclaimed, 'Do not shave my beard; I shall pay the fine.'

    of, *e.* before, *coram.* no money, *nothing of money.*
             now, *autem.* sufficiently, *enough.*

Exercise 119.

Arion was a celebrated harper. He lived for a long time *at the court of* Periander, king of Corinth. He once went to the city of Tarentum, and there acquired great riches. Afterwards he wished to return home. Therefore he embarked *on board* the vessel of *some* Corinthian sailors. These wished to kill him on account of his wealth. Then Arion took his harp, and sang a beautiful song. Then he leaped into the sea. A dolphin, charmed by the song, placed him on its back, and swam with him to land. Thence he went to Corinth, to king Periander. Meanwhile the sailors had reached Corinth, and had said to the king, 'Arion is dead.' But Arion accused them *before* the king, and they were condemned *to death*.

at the court of, *apud*.   on board, *in, with acc.*   some, *nonnullus*.
before, *coram*.   to death, *of the head*.

Exercise 120.

The hero Hercules formerly lived in Greece. He killed his children *through* madness, and was therefore compelled to serve Eurystheus, king of Tiryns, in Argolis. *By* his command he performed many wonderful labours. Greece was then devastated by some fierce beasts. These Hercules destroyed with his club and arrows. He was afterwards freed *from slavery* by Eurystheus. He then married Deianira. Once a centaur, Nessus by name, tried to carry her off, but Hercules slew him with an arrow. The dying Nessus gave his shirt stained with his poisonous blood to Deianira, and said, 'This shirt will preserve to you the love of your husband.' Afterwards Deianira gave the shirt to Hercules. But the garment stuck to his limbs, and he was killed by the poison. Thus Nessus avenged his death.

through, *propter*.   by, *ex*.   from slavery, *abl*.

Exercise 121.

Anacharsis, the Scythian, was a very wise man. He is *an example* of frugality. There exists a letter of his nearly in these words:—
'Anacharsis *sends* greeting to Hanno. My clothing is the skin of a wild beast; my couch is the ground; my sauce is hunger; I live on milk, cheese, and flesh. Therefore give these gifts either to your own citizens, or to the immortal gods.' He is said to have refused the gifts of a rich man with these words.

an example, *for an example*.   sends, *says*.

Exercise 122.

In the Gallic war, a certain Gaul of great stature *came forward* and said, '*Will any* Roman fight with me ?' Marcus Valerius, a young military tribune, obtained permission from the consul. He took his arms and *advanced* towards the Gaul. Then a wonderful thing is said to have happened. A raven perched on his helmet. They began to fight. Then the raven attacked the face and eyes of the Gaul with its beak and wings. Valerius then easily slew the Gaul with his sword. The raven then flew away. Afterwards Valerius was called Corvus on account of this wonderful *circumstance*.

came forward, *advanced*. will any, *numquis?* circumstance, *thing*.

Exercise 123.

Hannibal, the general of the Carthaginians, had arrived in Apulia. The two consuls, Aemilius and Varro, went out against him. They pitched their camp near the village of Cannae. Varro, *against the will of his colleague*, formed line of battle, and gave the signal *for* battle. The Roman army was conquered. Never was the republic afflicted by a more severe wound. Aemilius fell, overwhelmed with darts. A soldier, seeing him covered with blood, said, 'Take this horse, Aemilius, and fly.' Aemilius replied, 'Do thou rather fly, and say to the senators, "Fortify the city;" I shall perish here with my soldiers.'

against the will of his colleague, *his colleague (being) unwilling*.
for, *of*.

Exercise 124.

Titus Manlius had been sent away by his father to his farm, on account of the sluggishness of his intellect and tongue. Pomponius, a tribune of the people, summoned his father *before* the judges. The youth, hearing this, *formed* a plan. Armed with a knife, he went in the morning to the city, and entered the house of Pomponius. There, standing above the bed of Pomponius, he said, 'Desist from your accusation, otherwise I shall slay you.' The terrified tribune said, 'I shall desist from the accusation.' The youth was greatly honoured on account of his love for his father, and in the same year was made military tribune.

before, *apud*. formed, *entered into* (*ineo*).

Exercise 125.

The tyrant Dionysius once was supping *with* the Lacedaemonians. They said to him, 'Have you supped well?' He answered, 'I am not at all delighted with that black soup.' Now the black soup was the *principal dish* of the supper. Then said the cook, 'It is not at all wonderful, for the sauces were wanting.' 'What were they, *pray?*' said he. The cook answered, 'Labour in hunting, sweat, running, hunger, thirst,—with these things the feasts of the Lacedaemonians are seasoned.'

with, *apud.* principal dish, *caput.* pray, *tandem,* lit. *at length.*

Exercise 126.

The Romans used to be annoyed by the forays of the Veientes. Then the Fabian family approaches the senate. The consul Fabius speaks *for* his family,—'Do you take care of other wars; give the Fabii as enemies to the Veientes; we wish to wage the war at our own private cost.' Great thanks were *given* to him. The consul going out from the senate-house, returns home *accompanied by all the Fabii.* The Fabii are greatly praised by all the citizens. Next day they take their arms. Never did an army, either smaller in number or more distinguished in reputation, march through the city,—306 soldiers set out, all patricians, all of one family.

for, *pro.* given, *agere.* accompanied by all the Fabii, *all the Fabii accompanying.*

Exercise 127.

They arrive at the river Cremera. The enemy were routed in several battles, and asked for peace. Soon *the Veientes repented* of peace. Therefore war having been recommenced, they formed a plan for destroying their warlike enemy by an ambush. The Fabii were laying waste the fields; cattle were driven by the Fabii towards them. The Fabii having advanced, fell into an ambush and were all killed. The day of this slaughter was reckoned among the unlucky days. The Fabii had marched out of one the gates of the city. This gate was called Wicked. One boy alone remained *of* the whole family. He had been left at home on account of his youthful age. He became father of an illustrious family of Fabii.

the Veientes repented, *it repented the Veientes.* of, *e.*

Exercise 128.

Porsena, the king of the Etrurians, determined to restore the Tarquins ; therefore he came with a large army to Rome. With his first assault he took the hill Janiculum. Never before did so great fear seize the Romans; they leave their fields; they fly into the city; they surround the city itself with forts. One part of the city seemed safe, on account of its walls, another part on account of the Tiber. A bridge nearly gave a road to the enemy. There was a man, Horatius Cocles by name. He had received this name on account of an eye lost in battle. He stood before the bridge, and alone resisted the enemy. Meanwhile the citizens were cutting down the bridge behind him. The bridge being cut,-he leapt into the Tiber, and swam across safe to his friends. The state was grateful towards so great valour. *Much land* was given to him, and his statue was placed in the city.

much land, *much of land.*

Exercise 129.

Porsena was besieging the city of Rome. Mucius Scaevola, a brave man, went to the senate and said, 'I will go to the camp of the enemy and kill their king.' Permission having been given, he went to the camp of Porsena. There he stood, in a great crowd, near the king. Pay was then being given to the soldiers, and a clerk in a splendid dress was sitting there. Mucius being deceived by his dress slew him instead of the king. Being placed *before* the king he thrust his right hand into the fire, saying, 'Perish, right hand ; thou didst not perform thy duty.' The king being astonished liberated him. Then Mucius said, 'O king, three hundred men like me have conspired against thee.' Porsena terrified by these words ceased to fight against the Romans, having received hostages.

before, *coram.*

Exercise 130.

Porsena received Cloelia, a noble virgin, among the hostages. His camp was not far from the bank of the Tiber ; therefore Cloelia, *having eluded the guards* by night, seized a horse, and swam across the Tiber. This was told to king Porsena, and so being angry he sent ambassadors to Rome, saying, 'Restore Cloelia the hostage.' The Romans restored her. Then the king, wondering at the valour of the girl, praised her, and said, 'I will give you part of the hostages.' The hostages having been brought in, Cloelia chose some little girls, and returned with them to her country.

having eluded the guards, *the guards having been eluded.*

Exercise 131.

Orpheus used to be able to draw along rocks and trees *by singing*. His wife Eurydice having been killed by the bite of a snake, he descended to the infernal regions, wishing to bring her back. He said to Pluto, 'Restore to me, I pray, my wife Eurydice.' Pluto answered, 'I will do so; do not look back (while) returning; you will at length reach home, and there you can look at your wife.' But Orpheus (while) returning looked back at his wife; immediately she was snatched away.

by singing, *gerund*.

Exercise 132.

Procas, king of the Albans, *had* two sons, Numitor and Amulius. He left the kingdom to Numitor, for he was the elder; but Amulius drove away his brother, and reigned. He determined to deprive Numitor *of offspring;* and so he made his daughter, Rhea Sylvia, priestess of Vesta. She, however, gave birth to Romulus and Remus. Amulius threw her into chains, and cast the little boys, placed on a raft, into the Tiber. The stream subsiding left them on dry ground. They relate this story about the boys. A she-wolf, hearing them crying, ran up and licked them with her tongue, and discharged the duty of a mother towards them.

Procas had, *to Procas were.* of offspring, *ablative.*

Exercise 133.

The wolf used often to come to the boys as if to her cubs, and so Faustulus, the king's shepherd, perceiving this, took them to his cottage, and gave them to Acca Laurentia, his wife, *to be brought up.* The boys, growing up among the shepherds, increased their strength by games, and then began to roam over the valleys and mountains, hunting wild beasts, and afterwards to drive away robbers from the herds. Therefore the robbers lay in wait for them. Remus was taken; but Romulus defended himself. Then Faustulus said to Romulus, 'Numitor is your grandfather, Rhea Silvia your mother.' Romulus at once armed the shepherds and hastened to Alba.

to be brought up, *gerundive.*

Exercise 134.

Meanwhile the robbers brought Remus to king Amulius, and accused him with these words, 'This youth, O king, plunders the herds of Numitor.' Therefore Remus was surrendered to Numitor *for* punishment; but Numitor seeing the youth's face, nearly recognised him. For Remus was very like his mother, and his age agreed with the time of their exposure. Meanwhile Romulus arrived suddenly, liberated his brother, and restored Numitor to the throne *after killing Amulius.*

    for, *ad.* after killing Amulius, *Amulius having been killed.*

Exercise 135.

Then Romulus and Remus founded a city in the place of their exposure. But soon a quarrel arose between them. For they said, 'Whether of the two shall give a name to the new city, and be king?' so they used augury. Romulus first saw six vultures, afterwards Remus saw twelve. So Romulus called the city Rome. He wished to rule it by laws, so he said, '*Let no one* cross the rampart.' Remus, laughing, leaped over it. Romulus being enraged slew him, saying these words, '*Every one* attempting this shall thus perish: my walls are not *to be crossed.*' So Romulus alone got possession of the throne.

    let no one, *ne quis.* every one, *all.* to be crossed, *gerundive.*

Exercise 136.

Romulus had made rather the outline of a city than a city,—inhabitants were wanting. There was a wood near; this he made a refuge. Thither immediately a number of robbers and shepherds betook themselves. He and his people had no wives. So he sent ambassadors to the neighbouring peoples, saying, 'Give us wives.' The ambassadors were nowhere well received; jests also were added— 'Why don't you also open a refuge for women? Such women would be a fit alliance for you.' Romulus dissembling his anger prepared games. Many of the neighbouring people came *from* the desire *of seeing* the new city, and especially the Sabines with their children and wives. Suddenly, a signal having been given, the girls were carried off. This at once was the cause of war.

    from, *propter.* of seeing, *gerundive.*

Exercise 137.

The Sabines took up arms against the Romans on account of the carried-off girls. They found a girl, Tarpeia by name. She had left the city *for the sake of* drawing water. Her father *was in command of* the Roman citadel. Titus Tatius, the leader of the Sabines, offered the girl her choice of reward, saying, 'Lead my army into the citadel.' She asked the Sabines for the ornaments of their left hands, that is (to say), their rings and bracelets. These having been promised, Tarpeia led the Sabines into the citadel; then Tatius said to his soldiers, 'Throw your shields on her,' for they had their shields also in their left hands. Thus her wicked treachery was visited by a prompt punishment.

for the sake, *caussa*. was in command of, *commanded*.

Exercise 138.

Romulus marched against Tatius, and fought with his army. At the first charge, a distinguished man among the Romans, Hostilius by name, fell fighting most bravely. The Romans, terrified by his death, began to fly. Already the Sabines began to shout, 'We have conquered our treacherous hosts, our unwarlike enemies. It is one *thing* to carry off girls, *another* to fight with men.' Then Romulus raising his arms to heaven vowed a temple to Jupiter; and his army, either by chance or by the help of the god, halted. And so the battle was renewed, but the carried-off women, with dishevelled hair, dared to come between the flying darts, and, imploring *at one time* their fathers, *at another* their husbands, brought about peace.

one thing—another, *aliud—aliud*. at one time—at another, *nunc—nunc*.

Exercise 139.

Romulus made peace with the Sabines, and received them into the city. He chose out of the older men one hundred counsellors. These on account of their old age were called the Senate. He appointed three centuries of horsemen; he distributed the people into thirty curiae. These things having been thus appointed, he was *one day* reviewing his army, near the Goat's pool. Suddenly there arose a storm with loud thunder, and Romulus was carried off out of sight. A nobleman, Proculus by name, said, and affirmed with an oath, 'I have seen Romulus and talked with him.' He said, 'Let the Romans *refrain* from dissension and *worship* virtue.' So Romulus was worshipped as a god, and called Quirinus.

one day, *olim*. refrain, worship, *future imperat.*

Exercise 140.

In the reign of Tullus Hostilius war broke out between the Romans and the Albans. It seemed good to Hostilius, the king of the Romans, and Fuffetius, the general of the Albans, to intrust the destinies of *either* people to the hands of a few chosen men. There were three brothers among the Romans, by name Horatii, and also three brothers among the Albans, Curiatii by name. The kings said to them, 'Are you willing to fight for your country?' 'We are willing,' answered they. Then said the kings, 'The conquerors in this combat shall give victory and rule to their own country.' So the brothers take their arms, and advance into the middle between the two armies. The two armies sat down on either side.

In the reign of Tullus Hostilius, *Tullus Hostilius reigning.*
either, *uterque.*

Exercise 141.

The signal is given. The youths rush together with drawn swords. Soon two Romans fell dying, one over the other—the three Albans were wounded. The Alban armies shouted with joy *at* the misfortune of the Horatii. Hope was already abandoning the Romans. The three Curiatii had surrounded the remaining Horatius. He, though untouched, pretended flight. At length, looking back he saw one of the Curiatii near. He returns against him with a fierce rush and slays him. Then he slays the second. Now one on each side remained, but the body of one was untouched by the sword, and his courage increased by his success. The other was weary *from running* and from his wounds. The Roman kills him, holding his arms with difficulty, and spoils him *as he lies.*

at, *ad.* from running, *gerund.* as he lies, *lying.*

Exercise 142.

The Romans triumphing escort Horatius home. First marched Horatius bearing before him the spoils of the three brothers. His sister met him. She had been betrothed to one of the Curiatii, and seeing his cloak on her brother's shoulders, she began to weep and tear her hair. The fierce youth was enraged on account of the tears of his sister, and so, drawing his sword *he ran her through*, upbraiding her with these words, '*Be off* from hence to your lover, forgetful of your brothers, forgetful of your country! Roman women mourning a foe shall perish thus.'

he ran her through, *pierced her.* be off, *go away.*

B.L.W.   H

Exercise 143.

This seemed a horrible deed to the senators and the people; and so Horatius was condemned to death before the judges. Then Horatius appealed to the people. Meanwhile the father of Horatius *kept exclaiming*, 'My daughter was rightly slain : look at the spoils of the Curiatii, do not deprive me of the last of my children.' The people could not endure the father's tears, and liberated the youth, more from admiration of his valour than from the right of his cause. However, the father resolved to expiate the crime ; and so he sent his son under a yoke, *after completing some sacrifices. Now* to go under the yoke was a sign of disgrace.

    kept exclaiming, *imperfect*. after completing some sacrifices, *some sacrifices having been completed*. Now, *autem* (*second word in the sentence*).

Exercise 144.

Peace did not *last* long, for Fuffetius roused the Veientes against the Romans. Tullus Hostilius drew up his forces. They fought for a long time. Fuffetius being summoned by Tullus *to his assistance* drew off his forces to a neighbouring hill. Tullus seeing this exclaimed with a loud voice, 'Fuffetius is doing this by my order ; he will surround the enemy.' The Veientes hearing this were terrified and easily conquered. Next day Fuffetius came to the Roman camp. Tullus exclaimed with a loud voice, 'Seize the traitor ; bind him to two four-horsed chariots, and tear him asunder.' This was at once done. Then Tullus destroyed Alba on account of the treachery of its general, and took the Albans with him to Rome.

    last, *remain*. to his assistance, *for an assistance* (*dat.*).

Exercise 145.

Tarquinius the Proud had been made king at Rome. For a long time he fought with the neighbouring nations. He took the city of Gabii by the treachery of his son Sextus. Sextus went to Gabii complaining of his father's cruelty towards him. He was kindly received by the citizens, and soon was chosen their leader. Then he sent a messenger to his father, asking, *What must I do?* His father did not answer the messenger, but went into the garden, and (while) walking there, *followed by the messenger*, kept cutting down the heads of the tallest poppies with his stick. At last the messenger being weary returned to Gabii. Sextus understood the matter at once. He slew the chief men of the state, and surrendered the city to his father without any *fighting*.

    what must I do ? *what does it behove me to do ?* followed by the messenger, *the messenger following*. fighting, *battle*.

Exercise 146.

A certain funny fellow was once travelling through France. On the road he was seized with a severe illness, nor could he obtain the assistance of a skilful doctor. One of his friends said to him, 'A skilled doctor lives not far off; shall I send for him?' The sick man replied, 'He is *too* great a man for me; send for the doctor of the village; perhaps he will not dare to kill me.'

too, *nimis*.

Exercise 147.

A certain celebrated senator was walking through a village. On the road he saw a fellow beating an ass. 'At *what* price will you sell your ass?' asked he *of* the man. '*I am willing* to sell it for a hundred pence,' replied the other. 'I give you the money,' said the senator. Then the money having been paid, he said to the peasant, 'Why do you dare to beat my ass, you rascal?' *With these words* he began to beat the peasant with his stick, and drove him from the place, uttering loud lamentations. The peasant used afterwards to say, 'Seeing an ass I always remember that senator.'

what, *quantus*. of, *ex*. I am willing, *I wish*.
with these words, *having spoken these (words)*.

Exercise 148.

Three robbers attacked a Scotch traveller on the road. He defended himself bravely for a long time, but was at last conquered and bound. The robbers then said, 'This man has defended himself very bravely; there is much money in his purse.' But *having examined* the purse they only found one penny. The Scotchman had defended this penny *at* the risk of his life. The astonished robbers said, 'He has only one penny; having tenpence *he would have killed* us all.'

having examined, *having been examined*. at, *cum*.
he would have killed, *pluperf.-conjunctive*.

Exercise 149.

Two soldiers, *one* an Irishman, the other a Scotchman, were walking along the street in a certain town. They saw a pretty girl working with her needle in a shop. The Irishman wishing to behold the face of the girl again, said to his companion, 'Let us go into the shop and buy something.' The Scotchman replied, 'Do not waste your money; let us rather go into the shop and ask for the change of a penny.'

one, *the one*.

Exercise 150.

A nobleman once met a schoolmaster on the road. He asked him, 'Who are you, and how do you support yourself?' The schoolmaster replied, 'I am the master of this town.' The nobleman being astonished again asked him, 'How are you the master of this town?' The other replied, 'I am the master of the boys ; the boys are masters of their mothers ; the mothers rule the fathers ; therefore I am master of the whole town.' The nobleman being greatly pleased with this wise answer said to the schoolmaster, 'I have never met a wiser man than you.'

Distinguish carefully between *magister*, a (school) master, and *dominus*, a master.

THE COMPOUND SENTENCE.

(*a.*) The Compound Sentence consists of a Principal Sentence with Dependent Clauses.

(*b.*) Dependent Clauses are called Substantival, Adjectival, or Adverbial, according as they take the place of a Substantive, Adjective, or Adverb.

ADJECTIVAL CLAUSES.

Verb in the Indicative with Relative words:

Ex. Caesar, qui Gallos vicit, dux fortissimus erat.
Caesar, who conquered the Gauls, was a very brave general.

The Adjectival clause, *qui Gallos vicit*, takes the place of an adjective, describing Caesar.

Rule for the agreement of the Relative.—The Relative agrees with the Substantive it describes in Number, Gender, and Person; in Case it agrees with its own clause.

If *since, although, in order that, such that,* is understood in the Relative, the Verb will be in the Subjunctive.

Ex. Legatos misit, qui pacem peterent.
He sent ambassadors who (= in order that they) *should ask for peace.*

Exercise 151.

Once (when) travelling through Germany I saw a very wonderful thing in an inn. After supper the landlord placed on the floor a large dish of soup. Then with a loud voice he summoned a dog, a cat, an old raven, and a very large rat, *who had a bell hung from its neck.* These four animals approached the dish and devoured the soup *which was in the dish,* nor did they disturb each other. Then the dog, the cat, and the rat, lay before the fire, but the raven walked *about* the room.

who had a bell hung from its neck, *adjectival clause qualifying the word 'rat.'* which was in the dish, *adjectival clause qualifying 'soup.'* about, *per.*

Exercise 152.

A bone had stuck in the throat of a wolf. Therefore he hired a crane with a reward, *who, having inserted his beak* into the throat, *pulled out the bone,* which he was easily able to do *by* the length of his neck. Then he asked for his reward. The wolf, for whom he had done so great a service, replied, 'You have extracted your head safe from my jaws : is not that *enough reward* for you ?'

    who pulled out the bone, *adjectival clause qualifying ' crane.'*
    having inserted his beak, *his beak having been inserted.*
    by, *on account of.* enough reward, *enough of reward.*

Exercise 153.

King Porus, in a battle against Alexander, king of Macedon, being severely wounded, fell from the back of his elephant. The enemies, who had seen his fall, advanced, for they desired to deprive him of his rich clothing and arms ; but the faithful elephant standing over the body of his master bravely repelled all who dared to approach, and taking up Porus with his trunk, placed him again on his back. At length the soldiers of Porus came up and the king was saved : but the elephant died *of the wounds* which he had received.

    of the wounds, *abl. of cause.*

Exercise 154.

A certain peasant, who was lying in his bed, sent his daughter into the garden, saying, ' Look at the sun-dial.' The girl soon returned. Her father said, ' *What o'clock is it ?*' She said, 'I don't know.' The peasant sent her again. The girl, who was ignorant of numbers, took the sun-dial, and brought it to her father, saying, ' Behold ! see (for) yourself.'

    what o'clock is it ? *what (quotus) hour is it ?*

Exercise 155.

In India they hunt tigers in this way : A large number of men are sent armed with sticks. These beat the bushes, in which the tiger is thought to be hid, uttering loud cries. Meanwhile the hunters lie in ambush ; the tiger *hearing the noise* runs away, and is received by the hunters, who kill it with their weapons. Sometimes the hunters ride on elephants, which advance through the bushes. Sometimes the hunters lie in ambush near the carcass of an ox which has been killed by the tiger.

    hearing the noise, *the noise having been heard.*

Exercise 156.

In Ireland are found the snipe and the woodcock. These by night feed on small worms in the marshes, but by day lie hid in the grass and among bushes. The fowler pursues them with dogs, who perceive them by their smell. The dogs, being well taught, stand still. The fowler then approaches. (On) perceiving his approach the birds fly away, but are often struck down by the weapons of the fowler, who at once sends on a dog *to bring them* to him in his mouth. In this way a great number of these birds is often taken.

to bring them, *who may bring them (subj.).*

Exercise 157.

The Gauls were once besieging Rome. They determined to attack the citadel. They first sent a soldier, who should seek a path. Then by night, dragging *each other* (up), they arrived at *the top of the hill* on which the citadel stood. Not even *the dogs* heard their approach. Geese, birds sacred to Juno, from which the Romans had abstained in their great want of provisions, were kept in the citadel. The Gauls did not escape the notice of the geese. Manlius, a brave soldier, roused by the cries of the geese, and the flapping of their wings, summoning the rest of the soldiers, hurled down the ascending Gauls.

each other, *alius—alium.* the top of the hill, *the highest hill.* the dogs, put '*dogs,*' *which is the emphatic word, between* ne *and* quidem.

Exercise 158.

Lysimachus was one of Alexander's generals ; a man of noble birth, but by far more distinguished by virtue than by race. Once upon a time Alexander mutilated Callisthenes, a philosopher, in all his limbs, and besides shut him up with a dog in a cage. Lysimachus, who had been wont *to listen to* the philosopher, and receive from his mouth the precepts of virtue and wisdom, gave him poison as a remedy *for* his misfortunes. Alexander *took this very ill,* and said to his soldiers, 'Expose Lysimachus to a lion.' The lion rushed at Lysimachus, who thrust his hand, wrapped in a cloth, into its mouth, and slew the beast *by tearing out its tongue.* This having been told to the king, astonishment succeeded anger, and he held Lysimachus dearer than before on account of his courage.

to listen to, *to hear.* for, *of.* took this very ill, *bore this very ill.* by tearing out its tongue, *its tongue having been torn out.*

Exercise 159.

There is in Egypt an animal *with a small body* and long head, which is called the ichneumon. It kills and eats snakes. (When) wounded by the bite of a snake, it runs away into the woods. Soon it returns unhurt. It is said to find a plant whose juice keeps off the poison of the snake. There is a great quantity of snakes in Egypt. They enter into *any* house where there is not an ichneumon, and live there. Men and animals are often killed by their bite.

    with a small body, *abl. of quality.*   any, *quilibet.*

Exercise 160.

The town of Platea in Boeotia was besieged by Archidamus, the Spartan king, with a large army. The inhabitants, who fought very bravely, were able to repel their enemies for two years. Archidamus at length compelled them to surrender themselves, all the food which they had prepared being consumed. The inhabitants were then placed before the judges, who questioned them *as follows*—'Have you assisted the Lacedaemonians in this war?' They were compelled to reply, '*Not at all.*' Then they were all killed by the order of the cruel king. The town of Platea was given to the Thebans, by whom it was destroyed.

    as follow, *thus.*   not at all, *minime.*

Exercise 161.

The frogs are said formerly to have asked a king for themselves from Jupiter. Overcome by their prayers, the god threw down a huge log into the water. The frogs, who were greatly terrified, long remained quiet; but at last, seeing the nature of the new king, they begged for another; but soon, a water-snake having been sent, who killed very many, *they repented* of their folly. All said, 'The first king whom we had was better than this one.'

    they repented, *it repented them.*

Exercise 162.

Once Alexander, king of Macedon, invaded Egypt, which had long been subject to the Persians. He remained there a long time, and founded the city of Alexandria, which to this day bears his name. He said, 'This city which I have founded shall be the capital of my empire.' Elated with success, he now *laid claim to* divine honours. Among the *very* priests were found base persons who flattered him, and said, 'Thou art the son of Jupiter Ammon.' He marched to the temple of this god, which was distant a journey of seven days from Alexandria, but many of his soldiers were killed by fatigue and thirst on the road.

    laid claim to, *claimed.*   very, *ipse.*

Exercise 163.

The birds were waging war with the quadrupeds, and the fortune of war for a long time was doubtful, *at one time* the former, *at another* time the latter carrying off the victory. The bat, who preferred safety to honour, used to betake himself to those who had conquered. Among the birds he used to say, 'I am a bird;' among the quadrupeds he used to say, 'I am a mouse.' When the birds and quadrupeds had made peace the deceit *was evident* to both. Therefore, being condemned by both, he escaped, and from that time used only to fly by night.

at one time—at another, *nunc—nunc*. was evident, *appeared*.

Exercise 164.

Octavianus brought assistance to Brutus, who was being besieged by Antonius at Mutina. He was not able to approach the city, for Antonius held all the approaches. Therefore, wishing to inform Brutus *of* everything, he at first sent letters written on leaden plates, which were carried by a diver under the water of the river; he afterwards used pigeons *for* this (purpose), which he used to keep for a long time without food; then he used to tie letters to their necks, and let them go from a place near the walls. The pigeons, eager for food, used *to make for* the highest buildings, and were then taken by Brutus.

of, *de*. for, *ad*. to make for, *to seek*.

Exercise 165.

Once there was a man at Athens, by name Timon, who had conceived a hatred towards the whole race of men. He one day came into the assembly, which he was not wont to do. Therefore there was great expectation of all men. Then said he from the platform, on to which he had ascended, 'Athenians, I have a fig-tree, from which many men have already hanged themselves. I am *going to build* a house on the place where it grows. Does any one wish to hang himself? Let him *make haste*, the tree will soon be cut down.'

going to build, *about to build*. make haste, *hasten*.

Exercise 166.

Socrates once met Xenophon. Seeing the honest and modest countenance of the youth, he stretched out his stick and said, 'Do not pass on.' The youth stopped. Socrates asked him, 'Where are the things sold which are necessary for the various *requirements* of men?' Xenophon at once answered. Then Socrates asked him, 'Where do men become honest and good?' The youth replied, 'I do not know.' Then said Socrates, 'Follow me, and learn.' From that time Xenophon began to be a hearer of Socrates, and became good and honest.

requirements, *uses*.

Exercise 167.

A certain man was cutting logs beside a river. By chance his axe slipped from his hands and fell into the river. Then he, sitting on the bank, began to lament his misfortune, and weep piteously. But Mercurius, who had heard his complaints, having pitied the man, brought to him an axe—not indeed that which he had lost, but *one made of gold*, and said, 'Is this the axe which you have lost?' The man said, 'That is not my axe.' Then Mercurius brought another made of silver; the woodman, however, again *made the same answer*. Then at last he brought one made of iron, which the woodman joyfully received. The god, being delighted with such honesty, gave all the axes to the man.

one made of gold, *golden (adj.)*.
made the same answer, *answered the same (thing)*.

Exercise 168.

A woman had a bird which she used to allow to come out of its cage daily. Once the bird was eating crumbs of bread. Her cat, who always before had shown great kindness towards the bird, suddenly seized it, and jumped, holding it in its mouth, on to a table. The woman was greatly frightened on account of this, but soon saw the cause of the deed. Another cat had just come into the room through the door, which was open. She drove the stranger away, and her own cat then *came down* from the table, and replaced the bird *in safety*.

came down, *descended*. in safety, *safe*.

Exercise 169.

A few years *ago* an elephant in India killed its master with a blow of its trunk. The man's wife, who had seen this dreadful thing, took her two children, and threw them before the feet of the enraged animal, saying, 'Thou hast slain my husband ; kill me also, and my children.' The elephant at once stopped, and as if moved with remorse, took up the eldest boy with its trunk, and placed him on its neck. The animal, which had killed its master, adopted the boy in his place, and never afterwards allowed *any* other person to mount it.

ago, *ante.* any, *quisquam* (only used with a negative).

Exercise 170.

A young man, who wished to kill his dog, took it *with him* to a river. He then hired a boat, and began to cross the river. After a short time he threw the animal into the water. The miserable dog attempted to *climb up* the side of the boat, but his master, who wished to kill him, often *pushed* him *back* with the oar. Doing this he fell himself into the water, and nearly was drowned ; but the dog seeing his master struggling in the river, allowed the boat to go away, and held him (up) above water. At length some men came in a boat, and his life was saved.

with him, *secum ; cum* is written after me, te, se, nobis, vobis, quo, qua, quibus. climb up, *ascend.* pushed back, *repelled.*

Exercise 171.

A dog, who owed more to the kindness of a neighbour than to his master, was once left by accident in the *well-stored* pantry of his benefactor, where there was a great quantity of milk, cheese, bread, (and) meat. At length the maid returned to the pantry, who seeing the dog, feared punishment *for* her negligence. But the honest animal, who loved his benefactor, had tasted nothing ; but it was hungry, for it devoured a bone which they then gave him. All were greatly *astonished at* the honesty of the dog, who preferred to be hungry than to eat the food of his friend.

well-stored, *rich.* for, *on account of.* astonished at, *wondered at.*

Exercise 172.

Hannibal, who had been appointed general by the Carthaginians, came into Italy, *after crossing the Pyrenees and the Alps*. Three Roman generals who were sent against him were conquered with great slaughter. At length Q. Fabius, who had been appointed dictator, checked the attack of Hannibal by delay. He used to lead his troops over the hills, and never trusted any (thing) to fortune. The troops were kept in camp. He used to follow Hannibal (when) marching, and cut off the stragglers. Thus he conquered him in skirmishes, and the Romans began to fear the enemy less.

after crossing the Pyrenees and the Alps, *the Pyrenees and the Alps having been crossed*. any, *quisquam* (only used with negatives).

Exercise 173.

Hannibal was once besieging a Roman city. The inhabitants had no food; therefore a Roman general who was not far distant filled many jars with corn, and threw them into the river, which flowed beside the city. He also sent a messenger *to say*, 'Take up the jars which the river is bringing down.' The following night the jars were brought down by the river. The corn was equally divided among all the inhabitants; the same thing was done next day. Hannibal, having detected *the affair*, threw chains across the river, and intercepted the jars. Then the Romans threw nuts into the river, which were carried down to the city, and taken up by the inhabitants with baskets. By this provision their want was lessened.

to say, *who should say*. the affair, *the thing*.

Exercise 174.

M. Regulus, who had been made consul, *was the first* Roman general *to cross over* into Africa. He took the city of Clypea and many forts; and he fought not only with men but also with beasts. A snake which lived near a river attacked the Roman army; it seized many soldiers with its huge mouth; it crushed others with blows of its tail, and slew some with its pestilential breath. Nor could it be pierced by the darts which the Romans used. At length it was destroyed by stones, which the Romans hurled with huge catapults. It infected the river and the neighbouring country with its blood. Regulus was obliged to move his camp. He sent its skin, which was 120 feet *in length*, to Rome.

was the first to cross over, *first crossed over*. in length, *long*.

Exercise 175.

A certain doctor who was lying on his bed *on board* a ship once saw a wonderful thing of this kind. A rat appeared, which examined *everything* with the greatest care, and then went away. Soon it returned, leading a second rat, whose ear it was holding, and which it left near a hole. Then a third rat also came. They then collected crumbs of bread, which they gave to the second rat, which seemed to be blind, and which remained in the place where they had left it. It then devoured the food which its friends had brought.

   everything, *omnia.* on board, *in.*

ADVERBIAL CLAUSES.

Adverbial Clauses take the place of Adverbs; that is to say, they show *when, why,* or *how* a thing is done.

They are introduced by Conjunctions.

(*a.*) Some of these require the Subjunctive; as, ut (*that*), quin, ne, quo (= ut when there is a comparative in the sentence), quominus (*by which the less*), quum (*since*), dum (*provided that*), licet, quamvis, ut (*although*), tanquam, velut, ceu, quasi (*as if*).

(*b.*) All others usually require the Indicative.

The following require the Subjunctive, if the action is not completed:—

Dum, donec, quoad (*until*); antequam, priusquam, si, nisi, etsi, etiamsi.

Ex. Hoc faciam priusquam huc veniam.
I shall do this before I come hither.

Quum (*when*) takes the Subjunctive of the Imperfect and Pluperfect tenses; the Indicative of the other tenses.

(*c.*) The following Conjunctions do not introduce Adverbial Clauses; they merely join words or sentences without influencing Mood:

et, que, ac, atque, aut, vel, ve, sed, autem, nam, enim.

SEQUENCE OF TENSES.

In Dependent Clauses, the Tense of the Subjunctive is regulated by the Tense of the Verb on which it depends.

RULE.—Primary Tenses are followed by Primary,
Historic Tenses are followed by Historic.
So—

Primary { Present / Perfect / Future } are followed by { Present (of same time). / Perfect (of time before). }

Historic { Imperfect / Aorist / Pluperfect } are followed by { Imperfect (of same time). / Pluperfect (of time before). }

Ex. Venio ut te videam, *I come to see you.*
Veni ut te viderem, *I came to see you.*

As there is no Future Subjunctive in Latin, the want of it is supplied by the Future Participle of the Verb conjugated with

Sim after Primary Tenses.
Essem after Historic Tenses.

Exercise 176.

There were once two very celebrated painters, one of whom was called Zeuxis, the other Parrhasius. Zeuxis had painted grapes, and had so imitated nature *that birds flew to the picture, as if the grapes were real.* Then Parrhasius brought a picture on which he had painted a cloth. *Since* Parrhasius seemed to delay, Zeuxis being deceived said, 'Take away the cloth, that I may see the picture.' Then when he understood his mistake, he conferred the prize *on* Parrhasius, saying, 'I have deceived birds : thou hast deceived me.'

that birds flew to the picture, *adverbial clause introduced by* '*ut,*' *showing* how *the grapes were imitated. Ut=that, always takes the subj.*
as if the grapes were real, *adverbial clause introduced by* '*tanquam,*' *showing* how *the birds flew to the picture.*
since, *quum = since, takes the subj.* on, *in (c. acc.).*

Exercise 177.

A certain poor slave is said to have dared a glorious deed *in order to save* his master, whom he loved greatly. When his master, whose name was Urbinius, had been proscribed, and was being sought by the soldiers, who had arrived at the house where Urbinius *was hiding,* the slave took his master's dress and ring, and sent him away secretly. He then betook himself to his master's bedchamber, and allowed himself to be slain instead of his master.

in order to save, *in order that he might save.*
was hiding, *was lying hid.*

Exercise 178.

Curius, *after triumphing over* the Samnites, the Sabines, and Pyrrhus, spent the last days of his life in rustic labours. When the Samnites had brought a great weight of gold to him sitting near the hearth, they were dismissed by him, for, he said, 'I do not think it glorious to have gold, but to command those who have gold.'

after triumphing over, *when he had triumphed over (de).*

Exercise 179.

In Africa there is a race of men who pursue elephants with wonderful skill. They hunt in the *following way*. One of them mounts a swift horse, and when he has found an elephant provokes it to combat *by riding* near it and shaking his spear. Then the elephant pursues him, uttering terrible screams. Then another hunter lying hid in the long grass wounds the leg of the elephant with a sharp sword. The elephant can no longer pursue the enemy, and is easily despatched by darts. When they have killed the elephant they extract its teeth, which consist *of* ivory. These they sell to the merchants, and feed on the flesh themselves.

following way, *this way.* by riding, *gerund.* of, *ex.*

Exercise 180.

Scipio, while still a youth, saved his father by his great courage. For when he had been severely wounded in a battle (fought) against Hannibal, and was almost in the hands of the enemy, his son opposed himself to the advancing Carthaginians, and saved his father from danger. This dutiful deed won the favour of the people for Scipio *when a candidate for* the aedileship. When the tribunes of the people said, 'The youth has not yet reached the lawful age,' Scipio replied, 'If the Romans wish to make me aedile, *I am old enough.*' He was received with so great applause that the tribune desisted from their attempt.

when a candidate for, *seeking (peto).*
I am old enough, *I have enough of years.*

Exercise 181.

Appius Claudius, *a foolish and rash man*, set out as consul against the Carthaginians. He used openly to blame the plans of the former generals, and say, 'I shall finish the war *as soon as I have seen* the enemy.' *Before fighting* a naval engagement he took the auspices; and when the keeper of the fowls had announced evil omens, saying, 'The fowls do not come out of their coops nor feed,' Claudius, laughing, said, 'Throw them into the sea, that they may at any rate drink, since they do not wish to eat.' Soon afterwards the Romans were defeated with great slaughter—8000 men were slain, and 20,000 captured. Wherefore Claudius was condemned by the people.

a foolish and rash man, *a man of foolish rashness.*
as soon as I have seen, *as soon as I shall have seen.*
before fighting, *before he fought (subj.).*

Exercise 182.

Rashness also ruined Claudia, the sister of the consul Appius Claudius. For when she was pressed by the crowd (while) returning from the public games, she said, 'Would that my brother *were* alive, and again *in command of* a fleet!' This seemed to the Romans to be the same *as* if she had said, 'Would that the excessive number of the citizens were diminished!' On account of this wicked speech Claudia was also condemned *to death.*

were, *conj. expressing a wish, not a fact.* in command of, *commanded (praesum).* as, ac. to death, *of the head.*

Exercise 183.

M. Tullius Cicero was born of knightly rank at Arpinum, which is a city of the Volsci. One of his ancestors had a wart *on the end of his nose* like to a pea; hence the surname of Cicero was given to the family. When some one laughed at M. Tullius on account of this, he replied, 'I shall take care that this surname *shall surpass* the splendour of the most noble names.' He excelled all other youths of that time in learning, and became the most eloquent man of the Roman senate. (When) consul he saved his country, for he crushed the conspiracy which Sergius Catilina had made.

on the end of his nose, *summo naso.*
shall surpass, *may surpass.*

Exercise 184.

When Cicero had seen his son-in-law Lentulus, a man of small stature, girt with a long sword, he said, 'Who has tied my son-in-law to the sword?' A certain lady used often to say, '*I am only thirty years of age.*' Cicero remarked, 'It is true, for *I have been hearing* it thirty years.' When Caesar's colleague died on the last day of the year Caninius was made consul *for the rest of the day.* When many went to salute him according to custom, Cicero remarked, 'Let us make haste before his (term of) *office* expires.' Cicero wrote *of* the same man, 'Caninius was a man of wonderful vigilance, since he did not sleep once during his consulate.'

I am only thirty years of age, *I am born only thirty years.*
I have been hearing, *present tense.*
for the rest of the day, *for (in) the remaining day (acc.).*
office, *magistratus.* of, *concerning.*

Exercise 185.

M. Brutus, descended from the man who had expelled the Tarquins from Rome, learned oratory at Rhodes. He was distinguished on account of his virtue. His father had been put to death by the order of Pompeius; yet in the civil war he followed Pompeius because his cause seemed the juster, and preferred the advantage of the republic to his own grief. When Pompeius was defeated, Caesar pardoned Brutus, and even made him praetor. Afterwards, when Caesar seemed to despise the authority of the city, and to wish to be king, the people desired a champion of liberty. Some one wrote under the statue of the first Brutus, 'Would that you *were* alive!' Also under the statue of Caesar was written, 'Brutus was made the first consul because he expelled the kings; this man was made king because he expelled the consuls.' There was also written on the tribunal of M. Brutus, 'Thou sleepest, O Brutus.'

were, *conj.*

Exercise 186.

When Caesar had been slain, Antonius, showing his blood-stained garment,-excited the people against the conspirators. Therefore Brutus *retired* to Macedonia, and there fought near the town of Philippi against Antonius and Octavianus. Being defeated, he said to one of his companions, 'Slay me with your sword, lest I fall into the hands of the enemy.' Antonius seeing the body of Brutus, threw over it his purple cloak. Octavianus, on the contrary, said to his soldiers, 'Cut off the head of Brutus and bring it to Rome, that it may be placed under the statue of Caesar.'

retired, *betook himself.*

Exercise 187.

Demosthenes wonderfully assisted a woman, who had received a sum of money from two men, *on condition* that she should give it up to both at the same time. After some time, one of the two came dressed in *mourning*, and deceived her, saying, 'My friend is dead.' So she gave him all the money. Then the other came and began to ask for the money. The unhappy woman hesitated from want of money or excuse, and was already thinking *of* hanging. But Demosthenes came to them and said, 'The woman is ready to pay the money, but cannot do so unless you bring your partner, since the money *must be paid* to both at the same time.

on condition, *on that* (*is*) *condition.* mourning, *dark* (*pullus*) *dress.*
of, *de.* must be paid, *is to be paid* (*gerundive*).

Exercise 188.

A quarrel had arisen among the sons of a certain peasant. *For a long time* their father exhorted them in vain, saying, 'Be agreed.' At length he said to his sons, 'Bring me fifty sticks and sit down.' Then he bound together all the sticks into one bundle and gave them to his sons, in order that they should break them. But they, though they used all their strength, laboured in vain, nor were they able to break them. Then the father cut the knot, and gave them the sticks *one by one*, which they broke easily. When this had been done, he addressed his sons as follows: 'Let this be *an example* to you. You will be safe from your enemies, as long as you remain agreed. But as soon as quarrels shall have arisen among you, your enemies will attack you safely.'

for a long time, *long.* one by one, *use the distributive numeral.*
an example, *for an example* (*dat.*).

Exercise 189.

A king *one day* on the road met a dog, which was guarding the body of a slain man. Some soldiers said, 'This dog *has been sitting* near the body for three days, without food, and will not leave the body.' The king said, 'Bury the body, and take care of the dog.' A few days after the king reviews his army. The soldiers pass by *one at a time.* The dog is present. He, though he had been quiet before, as soon as he saw the murderers of his master, rushed forward, and attacked them with such fury *as to excite* the suspicion of the king and of all who were present. Therefore they were seized and questioned, and some having *turned* informers, were condemned to death.

one day, *olim.* has been sitting, *sits.* one at a time, *use the distributive numeral.* as to excite, *that he excited.* turned, *become.*

Exercise 190.

A certain fellow having returned to his country, *from which* he had been absent some years, used to boast in all the assemblies, and brag of his glorious exploits. Among other things he used to say, 'In the island of Rhodes, I conquered in leaping all the best leapers.' He used also to show the length of the leap, saying, 'I have all the Rhodians (as) witnesses of this leap.' Then one of those who were standing by exclaimed, 'If you tell *the truth*, there is no need of these witnesses ; let Rhodes be here ; leap here.'

from which, *whence*. the truth, *true things*.

Exercise 191.

Two friends were travelling. When they arrived at a certain town, one went to an inn, the other stayed *with* a friend. By night *the former* appeared to *the latter* in a dream, and seemed to say, 'Assist me ; the innkeeper wishes to kill me.' His friend arose terrified, but *on collecting* himself, lay down again. Again his friend appeared to him, saying, 'Since you have not helped me (while) alive, do not leave me unavenged (when) dead. I have been slain by the innkeeper, my body is in a cart, covered with manure. Stop the cart before it *leaves* the city.' The spectre then disappeared. In the morning they seized the cart, and found the body. The innkeeper was taken and condemned to death.

with, *apud*. the former—the latter, *ille—hic*.
on collecting, *when he had collected*. leaves, *subj*.

Exercise 192.

Another wonderful dream is thus related. Simonides having seen a dead body exposed, buried it. Not long after, when he *intended* to embark *on board* a ship, he was warned in a dream by the man whom he had buried, who said, 'If you go you will perish by shipwreck.' Therefore Simonides is said to have gone home. The others who went in the ship perished by shipwreck.

intended, *wished*. on board, *into*.

Exercise 193.

War had been declared against the Tarentines, who had offered an insult to the Roman ambassador. Pyrrhus, king of Epirus, came *to their assistance.* The consul Laevinus was sent against Pyrrhus. When he had taken some of the king's scouts, he led them round the Roman camp, and then dismissed them *in safety,* (in order) that they might tell Pyrrhus everything which they had seen. The battle soon began. When his troops were already retreating, Pyrrhus led his elephants against the Romans ; then the fortune of the battle was changed. The bulk of their huge bodies terrified the Romans ; the horses also, terrified at the sight and smell of the beasts, betook themselves to flight. Night made an end of the battle.

to their assistance, *for an assistance to them.* in safety, *safe.*

Exercise 194.

Pyrrhus held the Roman prisoners in the highest honour ; and seeing the slain lying with their wounds in front and with faces fierce even in death, he is said to have used these words—' With such men I should have conquered the whole world in a short time.' Then he hastens towards the city of Rome by *forced* marches ; he lays waste all things with fire and sword ; he pitches his camp near the twentieth milestone from the city. Laevinus came to meet Pyrrhus with a new army. Seeing this, the king said, ' I have the same luck against the Romans which Hercules had against the Hydra, to whom as many heads arose *as* had been cut off.' Then he retired into Campania. He dismissed the Roman prisoners without a ransom, in order that the Romans, already knowing his courage, might also recognise his generosity.

forced, *great.* as, *quot.*

Exercise 195.

C. Fabricius was one of the ambassadors who had come to Pyrrhus *to speak* about the captives. When Pyrrhus heard his name praised among the Romans as of a good and brave but poor man, he honoured him greatly, and sent him gifts and gold. Fabricius refused *everything.* Next day Pyrrhus, wishing to frighten him by a sudden sight of an elephant, said to his servants, ' Let the beast be placed close to Fabricius behind a curtain.' When this was done, at a given signal, the curtain being removed, the beast suddenly uttered a fearful scream, and hung its trunk over Fabricius' head. But he smiled gently, and said to Pyrrhus, ' Your beast does not move me to-day more than your gold did yesterday.'

to speak, *in order that he might speak.* everything, *all things.*

Exercise 196.

Pyrrhus, admiring the courage of Fabricius, addressed him in these words—'Desert your country and live with me; if you *are willing* to do this, I will give you a fourth part of my kingdom.' Fabricius replied, 'If you consider me a good man, why do you wish to corrupt me? but if a bad one, why do you want to have me?' Next year, all hope of peace having been taken away, Fabricius was made consul, and sent against Pyrrhus. Since the camps were near each other, the king's physician came by night to Fabricius, and said, 'If you are willing to give me a reward, I am prepared to kill Pyrrhus by poison.' Fabricius immediately sent him bound to the king, with a letter *to tell of* his baseness. Then the king is said to have remarked, 'It is easier to move the sun from his course than Fabricius from honour.'

are willing, *wish*. to tell of, *which might tell*.

Exercise 197.

They fought for a long time. At last Manius Curius, who had been made consul, defeated the army of Pyrrhus, and triumphed *over* that king. Four elephants, with their howdahs, then seen at Rome for the first time, rendered his triumph remarkable. The conquered king returned to Epirus, leaving a garrison at Tarentum. Therefore, since he was thought *sure to renew* the war, Curius was again made consul; but the unexpected death of the king freed the Romans from fear. For Pyrrhus, while besieging the city of Argos, was slain by a woman, who hurled a tile from the roof of the house on which she was standing on to his head.

they fought, *it was fought*. over, *de*. sure to renew, *fut. participle*.

Exercise 198.

War was declared against the French by Edward III., king of England. Therefore, when he had landed a large army in France, he marched against the king of the French. The two armies pitched their camps near *a* village. Next day the French drew up their line of battle, nor did the English refuse the contest. The son of Edward, who was called the Black Prince, commanded part of the army. Suddenly a storm arose, which injured the French greatly, for the rain softened their bows. The English had covered their bows, and received *no* injury. The French archers could not use their bows well, and were routed by the English, who, having discharged their arrows from a distance, then attacked them at close quarters. Edward, who was unwilling to assist his son, lest he should lose the glory of the victory, said, 'Let my son finish what he has so well begun.' The French were defeated with great slaughter, and their king was taken.

a, *quidam*. no, *nothing of*.

Exercise 199.

Hannibal got possession of the city of Tarentum by treachery. Thirteen young nobles among the Tarentines conspired against their country. They *having gone out* of the city by night, under *pretence* of hunting, came to Hannibal, whose camp *was not far distant*. Hannibal praised them, and said, '(When) returning to the city, drive the cattle of the Carthaginians towards the gates, and give part of the spoil to the guards.' This was often done; and soon the gates used to be opened whenever the youths *gave* the signal. Then Hannibal with ten thousand men followed them by night. When they approached the gate the youths aroused the guards. The gates were opened; the youths entered, bringing with them a wild boar of huge size. The unsuspecting sentinel, (while) admiring the huge beast, was slain. Then the Carthaginians rushed in, and *after slaying* the remaining guards, got possession of the city.

having gone out, *when they had gone out.* pretence, *acc.*
was not far distant, *was not absent far.*
gave, *subj., because indefinite; no particular time being mentioned.*
after slaying, *when they had slain.*

Exercise 200.

Lucius Aemilius Paullus (when) consul, obtained by lot the province of Macedonia, in which Perseus the son of Philippus had renewed war against the Romans. When he was *on the point of setting out* against Perseus, and was returning home *towards* night, he saw his daughter Tertia, who was then *quite* little, crying. Kissing her, he said, 'What is it, Tertia? why are you sad?' 'Father,' replied she, 'Perse is dead.' *Now* Perse was a puppy which the girl had loved greatly. Then he, embracing the girl more closely, said, 'I accept the omen, my dear daughter.' So from a chance saying he conceived a certain hope of victory. He then set out *for* Macedonia, and marched at once against the enemy.

on the point of setting out, *about to set out.* towards, *sub.*
quite, *admodum.* now, *autem.* for, *into.*

SUBSTANTIVAL CLAUSES.

Substantival Clauses (Oratio Obliqua, Indirect Speech) take the place of a Substantive, either as subject of an Impersonal Verb, or object of a Transitive Verb.

They are divided into—

(1.) INDIRECT STATEMENT,—Accusative with Infinitive, after Verbs of saying, perceiving, thinking, hoping, promising :—

> *Ex.* Dixit se civem Romanum esse.
> *He said that he was a Roman citizen.*

This is the usual construction; there are some exceptions.

(2.) INDIRECT COMMAND,—Ut, ne, with Subjunctive, after Verbs of commanding, forbidding, entreating, persuading :—

> *Ex.* Imperavit ei ut abiret.
> *He ordered him to depart.*

Iubeo (*order*), veto (*forbid*), prefer the Infinitive Construction.

(3.) INDIRECT QUESTION,—Interrogative Words, with Subjunctive, after Verbs of asking, doubting, and telling :—

> *Ex.* Quaerit ex nobis quid agamus
> *He asks us what we are doing.*

Observe that the Simple Sentences become Substantival Clauses when made to depend on another Verb.

Adjectival and Adverbial Clauses, qualifying words in Substantival Clauses, take the Subjunctive, unless they are introduced as explanatory notes by the author.

Exercise 201.

A very wise man was reading in his room, when his servant came to him greatly alarmed, and said *that* the house *was on fire*. 'Go,' said his master, 'and tell my wife. This does not concern me, for I never *take any notice* of domestic affairs.'

    that, *not translated, being the sign of the acc. with infinitive*.
    was on fire, *was burning* (ardeo); 'that the house was on fire' *is a substantival clause, acting as object to* '*said*.'
    take any notice, *ullam rationem habeo*.

Exercise 202.

A Lacedaemonian woman had five sons, who had gone *to fight* in a battle near the city of Sparta. Seeing a soldier returning from the battle, she asked how affairs *went on*. 'Your five sons have been slain,' replied he. 'This only concerns my sons,' said the woman; 'tell me the things which concern my country.' 'We have conquered our enemies,' said the soldier. 'Then,' said she, 'I am happy,—my country has conquered her enemies.' It is well known *that the Lacedaemonians preferred death to dishonour*.

    to fight, *use the supine*. went on, *had themselves (indirect question)*;
    'how affairs went on' *is a substantival clause, acting as object to asked*.
    that—dishonour *is the subject to* '*it is well known*.'

Exercise 203.

A soldier had painted a fly on his shield *as a* crest. His friends began to laugh, and asked him why he used so small a crest. He replied 'that it was big *enough*, for he would go very close to the enemy.' A battle was soon fought, and this soldier surpassed all his companions in bravery. It is well known that true courage is always modest.

    as, *pro*. enough, *satis*.

Exercise 204.

A certain soldier had been ordered to perform the duty of a sentinel in a certain place. The duty was not altogether without danger, so soon the soldier begged the general *to remove him*. 'On account of what reason?' asked the general. The soldier answered 'that it did not seem to him that he was brave enough *for* the duty.'

    to remove him, *indirect command*. for, *ad*.

Exercise 205.

A quarrel arose between a hedgehog and a hare. It was agreed *that they should contend in a race*, and that a prize should be given to the conqueror. The hare ran very swiftly, but when he had arrived at the goal, he found the hedgehog sitting there. Being greatly astonished, he said to the hedgehog next day, 'Tell me how you defeated me, and I will give you another prize.' The hedgehog replied, 'My wife is very like me, so I placed her at the goal; I myself remained at the starting-post. You thought that she was your opponent. Neither of us ran at all.'

    that they should contend in a race, *substantival clause acting as subject to* 'it was agreed.'
    that, *ut.* Here '*ut*' *with subj. takes the place of the usual acc. with inf.*

Exercise 206.

One of his friends once said to a philosopher who was *going to make* a journey across the sea, 'Do you not fear lest, your ship having been wrecked, you should become food for the fishes?' 'Not at all,' replied the philosopher; 'it is well known that I have eaten many fishes; therefore I do not wish to seem ungrateful *by not being willing* to be eaten in turn by the fishes.'

    going to make, *future participle.* by not being willing, *nolendo.*

Exercise 207.

When some one was *one day* praising the wisdom of a very foolish man, a lady who was present said, 'I do not wonder that he has a great quantity of wisdom, for he never uses any wisdom *at all.*'

    one day, *olim.* at all, *omnino.*

Exercise 208.

A citizen, walking one day in his garden, found one of his servants sleeping in the shade. He rebuked his laziness severely, and said that he was so lazy *that* he was not worthy of the light of the sun. '*It was for this reason,*' replied the servant, '*that* I was sleeping in the shade.'

    that, etc., *adverbial clause introduced by* ut.
    It was for this reason that, *ideo.*

Exercise 209.

Once upon a time the mice assembled a council, in order that they might discover *how they might escape from the cat*. An old mouse addressed the rest thus: 'Let us hang a bell from the neck of the cat; being warned by the sound, we shall be able to escape.' All praised the plan, but no one was willing to hang the bell from the cat's neck.

how they might escape from the cat, *indirect question.*

Exercise 210.

A widow woman, who used to support life *by weaving*, was accustomed to summon her maids to work when she heard the first crow of the cock. At last the maids, worn out by labour, killed the cock. This being done, their condition became worse than before; for their mistress, who did not know *what o'clock it was*, used often to rouse them even *in the middle of the night*.

by weaving, *use the gerund.* what o'clock it was, *quota hora; indirect question.* in the middle of the night, *in the middle night.*

Exercise 211.

Croesus, king of Lydia, had a son, by name Atys, whom he loved greatly. He saw in a dream this son pierced by an iron weapon, therefore he determined always to keep him at home, *and not to expose him to danger in war*. At this time a wild boar of huge size appeared and began to ravage the fields. The husbandmen begged the king *to send* his son with men and dogs *to kill* the monster. At length Croesus allowed him to go, thinking that weapons, not the teeth of a boar, were *to be feared*. While they were pursuing the boar, a spear thrown by one of the husbandmen killed Atys. Thus the dream of Croesus was fulfilled.

and not, *neque.* to send, *indirect command.* to kill, *adverbial clause,* ut, *etc.* to be feared, *gerundive.*

Exercise 212.

It is well known that Salinator, who, *after losing the city*, had fled into the citadel, boasted and said, 'By my help, Quintus Fabius, you have recovered Tarentum.' 'Certainly,' replied Fabius, laughing, 'for unless you had lost it, I should never have retaken it.'

after losing the city, *abl. abs.*

Exercise 213.

The father of a boy came one day to Aristippus the philosopher, and begged him *to teach* his son. The philosopher demanding much money, the father, who was very avaricious, was frightened by the price, and said to the philosopher, that he could buy a slave *for less*. 'Do so,' said Aristippus, 'thus you will have two slaves.'

to teach, *indirect command.* for less, *minoris.*

Exercise 214.

Xenophon was sacrificing to the gods, when he heard that his eldest son had been slain in battle. He only laid down his crown and asked how he had died. Being informed that his son had died fighting bravely for his country, he placed the crown again on his head. Then he called the gods to witness that he received *more pleasure* from the courage of his son than *pain* from his death.

more pleasure—pain, *more of pleasure, of pain.*

Exercise 215.

A certain king, who had been expelled by his citizens, betook himself to the country, where he contracted a friendship with a certain man, by name Conon, *at whose house* he used often to eat turnips. Afterwards, when the king had recovered his kingdom, Conon sent to him a turnip of great size. The king received the gift kindly, and ordered *a large sum of money* to be given to him. A certain man seeing this, gave a horse to the king. The king, however, knowing that his liberality towards Conon was the cause of this gift, presented him with the turnip, which he said *had cost him more* than a horse.

at whose house, *apud quem.* a large sum of money, *much of money.*
had cost him more, *had stood to him of more value.*

Exercise 216.

Augustus *used* not *to sleep* more than seven hours, and often awoke three or four times during the night. If *he was unable* to sleep, he used to call one of his servants *to read* to him till sleep should return. Having heard that a certain senator, although involved in debt, was wont to sleep long and soundly, he bought his pillow at a large price. He then remarked to his wondering friends, 'the pillow on which a man, who owed so much, could sleep, is a most invaluable thing.'

used to sleep, *imperfect.* he was unable, *subj. because of the uncertainty.* to read, *who should read.*

Exercise 217.

Piso the orator, lest he should be interrupted, had ordered his servants to answer questions only, and not to say anything else. Once he told them to invite a certain Clodius to supper. Already all the other guests were present. Clodius alone was absent. Piso sent the servant, who used to invite the guests, *several times to see if he was coming*. At last when his arrival was despaired of Piso said to the servant, 'Did you invite Clodius?' 'I did invite him,' replied the servant. 'Why then does he not come?' 'Because he said that he would not come.' 'Why did you not say so at once?' 'Because you did not ask me.'

> several times, *saepius*. to see, *supine*. if, *num*.

Exercise 218.

The Romans used to think Jupiter the first and greatest of all the gods. He was born and brought up in the island of Crete. But when he had grown up, he expelled his father Saturnus from his kingdom, which he divided between himself and his brothers. He obtained the empire of the sky and earth, Neptunus (that) of the sea, and Pluto (that) of the infernal regions. But Neptunus and Pluto *used to obey* him. He was represented sitting on a throne, holding a thunderbolt in his right hand. Beside him stood an eagle. The Romans used to think that the fig-tree was sacred to him.

> used to obey, *imperfect*.

Exercise 219.

Thetis knowing that her son Achilles *would* quickly perish, if he followed the Grecian army to Troy, sent him to the island of Scyros. There the king kept him among his daughters dressed in female apparel. But Ulysses, when he had heard that Achilles was hidden there, placed ornaments and beautiful apparel in the hall of the royal palace, and also a shield and spear. Then he ordered the girls to be summoned. While they were examining the gifts, suddenly a trumpet *sounded*, which sound being heard, Achilles seized the arms, whence it was understood that he was a man. He was afterwards killed near Troy.

> would; *after a past tense* would *is the sign of the future*
> sounded, *cano*.

Exercise 220.

Troy was taken by the Greeks *under the command of Agamemnon*. Then the Greeks wished to return home, but were prevented by a wind *from setting out*. A spectre is said to have appeared on the tomb of Achilles. At last a voice from the tomb was heard, which warned the Greeks *not to leave* their bravest soldier without honour. So the Greeks sacrificed Polyxena, the daughter of Priam, king of Troy, near the tomb. Then they were able to depart.

    under the command of Agamemnon, *Agamemnon being leader*.
    from setting out, *lest they should set out*.
    not to leave, *indirect command*.

Exercise 221.

It is well known that cattle can foretell the arrival of rain. A traveller relates that he once saw a herd of oxen, who *had been without* water for a long time. The owner of the oxen sent his servants *to look for* water. Meanwhile the cattle began to stretch out their necks and look towards the west. After a short time clouds began to appear, and soon so great a quantity of rain fell to the earth, that the cattle were able to drink as much as *they wished*. They also say that pigs can foretell rain or wind.

    had been without, *had lacked*. to look for, *supine*.
    they wished, *subjunctive*.

Exercise 222.

An old writer relates that a raven, perceiving fourteen chickens with a hen in a garden, seized one in his claws; but that, *on a girl opening* a window and making a noise, the robber flew away. After a short time the raven is said to have returned with thirteen other ravens; then each (one) seized a chicken and flew away.

    on a girl opening, *abl. abs.*

Exercise 223.

At Smyrna there are many cranes, who build their nests on *the tops of the houses*. The inhabitants sometimes, *to amuse* themselves, put the eggs of a hen into the nest of a crane. When the eggs are hatched, the male crane, seeing that the young are unlike other cranes, utters loud cries. Then a great number of cranes come to the place and kill the female crane, for they think that she has disgraced her race. Meanwhile the male crane laments his misfortune with loud cries.

    the tops of the houses, *the top houses*. to amuse, *that they may amuse*.

Exercise 224.

Once upon a time there was a very strong man in Greece, Glaucus by name. (When) a youth he used to cultivate the ground, but *while ploughing* one day the ploughshare fell from the plough. The youth put back the ploughshare into its place, (a thing) which no one else could do without a mallet. He went to the Olympic games as a boxer, but being unskilled in the art of fighting, he was so severely wounded that *every one* thought that he would soon be conquered. Then his father exclaimed, 'My son, do you not remember the ploughshare?' They say that the youth, roused by these words, slew his adversary with one blow.

while ploughing, *inter arandum.* every one, *all.*

Exercise 225.

They say that the goddess Latona, after long wanderings and flight, arrived at the island of Delos, and there gave birth to Apollo and Diana. *From this belief* this island is thought sacred to these deities; and so great is and has always been the sanctity of the island, that not even the Persians (*after declaring* war against the whole of Greece, and men and gods, and after touching at Delos with a fleet of a thousand vessels), dared to injure *anything.*

from this belief, *hence.* after declaring, *when they had declared.*
anything, *quidquam.*

Exercise 226.

To a certain man, who had learned to stand for a long time on one foot, *on saying* to a certain Lacedaemonian that he did not think that any one of the Lacedaemonians could do the same so long, the latter answered, '*Well,* geese can stand on one foot longer than you.'

on saying, *when he had said.* well, *at.*

Exercise 227.

The poets relate that Perseus was sent by Minerva *to kill* Medusa, who alone of the Gorgons was mortal. *Now* the Gorgons were malignant monsters *in* female form. This Medusa had snakes for hair. If *any one* looked at her he *was* immediately *turned into* a stone. To destroy this monster, Perseus received arms from the gods. Thus equipped he went to the relations of Medusa, *some* old women, who had only one eye among them. They foolishly intrusted this eye to him, and he *said he would not* restore it until they had said where Medusa lived. Then Perseus went to the place, and having found Medusa sleeping, cut off her head at one blow.

to kill, *who should kill (subj.).* now, *autem.*
in, of, *gen. of quality.* any one, *quis.* was turned into, *became.*
some, *nonnullus.* said he would not, *denied that he would.*

Exercise 228.

A certain man once lost a large sum of money. Thinking that one of his slaves had taken it he ordered them to assemble, and then addressed them thus, 'My friends, a great snake appeared to me in a dream and said that the man who had *taken* the money would have a feather on *the end of his nose*.' The thief at once touched his nose with his hand *to see if* the feather was there. 'Thou art the thief,' exclaimed his master. The foolish slave confessed his crime, and the master recovered his money.

    taken, *subj.*, *adjectival clause dependent on a substantival clause.*
    the end of his nose, *end* (extremus) *nose.* to see, *that he might see.*
    if, *num.*

Exercise 229.

The poets who have written about Philoctetes have said that he was the armour-bearer of Hercules, and received from him the arrows which *had been dipped* in the poisonous blood of the Hydra. *Now* the Hydra was a great snake which Hercules had killed. The foot of Philoctetes was wounded by the fall of one of these arrows. The wound caused so unpleasant an odour that the Greeks, with whom he was going to Troy, removed him from them, and left him on the island of Lemnos. At last it was found that Troy could not be taken without his arrows, so Ulysses was sent *to bring* him to the Grecian camp. With the greatest difficulty *he was persuaded to go*, for he had not forgotten that they had deserted him. Troy, which had been besieged for ten years in vain, was taken by the help of his arrows.

    had been dipped, *subj.*, *adjectival clause dependent on the substantival clause.*
    now, *autem.* to bring, *who should bring ; who = in order that he.*
    he was persuaded, *it was persuaded to him.* to go, *indirect command.*

Exercise 230.

The god Mercurius, wishing to know *at what price he was valued* by men, went to the house of a sculptor. Seeing the statue of Jupiter, he asked *what was the price.* The sculptor informed him. Then he asked about a statue of Juno. The sculptor told him that her statue was more valuable than the statue of Jupiter. Mercurius, thinking that his own statue would be the most valuable of all, asked the price. 'If you will buy the other two,' replied the sculptor, 'I will give you this one also.'

    at what price, *quanti.* he was valued, *indirect question.*
    what was the price, *at what price it was.*

Exercise 231.

C. Duilius *was the first to conquer* the Carthaginians in a *sea* fight. He, seeing that the Roman vessels were excelled by the Carthaginians in swiftness, prepared iron grapnels. These machines were *of great use* to the Romans, for they grappled with the hostile vessels, and then fought with the sword as if in a land fight. The Romans, who excelled the Carthaginians in strength, easily conquered them. Thirty of the enemy's ships were taken and thirteen sunk. Duilius returned to Rome, and was the first to lead a naval triumph. No victory was more acceptable to the Romans, for they were able to say that they had conquered all their enemies *by sea and land.*

was the first to conquer, *first (adj.) conquered.* sea, *naval.* of great use, *for great use.* by sea and land, *by land and sea.*

Exercise 232.

Herodotus relates that crocodiles are taken by the Egyptians in this way; that the fisherman lowers into the water of the river a young pig attached to a hook for a bait; that he then beats a young pig while standing on the shore; that the crocodile *hearing the sounds,* which the young pig utters, hastens to the spot and swallows the bait; that the fisherman, when he with his companions has drawn the crocodile out of the water, plasters its eyes with mud, *so that* he may the more easily kill it. I have heard that crocodiles are taken in this way in other countries also.

hearing the sounds, *the sounds being heard.*
so that, *quo = ut eo, used instead of ut after comparatives.*

Exercise 233.

When the Romans were *going to fight* against the Macedonians, Gallus, a military tribune, freed the Roman army from a great fear. For he, since he knew that an eclipse of the moon *would take place* the following night, summoned the troops and addressed them thus: 'There will be an eclipse of the moon next night. Do not fear this. It happens at fixed times, and can be known and foretold beforehand. Therefore, *just as* no one wonders when the moon shines at one time with full orb, at another with a small crescent, so it is not wonderful that it is obscured, when it is concealed by the shadow of the earth.' Accordingly the Romans were not terrified by the eclipse, but the Macedonians, thinking it a gloomy portent, were greatly terrified.

going to fight, *fut.-part.* would take place, *would be.* '*would*' *is the sign of the future after a past tense.* just as, sicut.

Exercise 234.

Marcus Aemilius Scaurus was born *of a noble* but poor family. He was a most eloquent man, and by his eloquence gained glory and wealth. (When) appointed consul he *shewed* himself severe in *maintaining* military discipline: of which discipline he himself used to tell an instance worthy of admiration, in the books which he had written concerning his own life. Though there was a tree laden with ripe fruit on the spot where he had pitched his camp, when the army went away in the morning the tree was left with the fruit untouched. He also punished the praetor Publius Decius *for sitting* while he was passing by, *and not* obeying (when) ordered to rise.

    of a noble, *abl. of origin.* shewed, *praebeo.* maintaining, *gerund.*
        for sitting, *because he had sat.* and not, *neque.*

Exercise 235.

Rutilius Rufus was distinguished on account of his virtues and the innocence of his life. Since there was no one more honest than him in the state, he was held worthy of every honour, and made consul. When one of his friends kept asking him *to do* some unjust act, and Rutilius steadily refused, his friend having become angry said: '*What use* is your friendship to me, if you do not do what I ask?' 'Nay,' replied Rutilius, 'What use is your friendship to me, if on account of you it behoves me to do an unjust act?' For Rutilius well knew that religion and honesty *should be preferred* to friendship.

    to do, *indirect command.* what use, *for what use.*
        should be preferred, *gerundive.*

Exercise 236.

Formerly *women were not allowed* to act in a theatre, but young men dressed in female costume used to act female parts. One day the king came earlier *than usual* to the theatre, and found that the actors were not ready. So he sent one of his servants *to ask* what was the cause of the delay. The manager, knowing that it would be wisest to tell the truth, went to the king and told him, that the queen was not yet shaved. The king laughed, and waited till the queen was shaved and the curtain *drawn*.

    women were not allowed, *it was not lawful for women.*
    than usual, *than he was wont.* to ask, *supine.* drawn, *removed.*

Exercise 237.

Sertorius had a white doe of extraordinary beauty, which was *of great use* to him, in *making* the troops more obedient. Sertorius had taught her to follow him and obey his words. He persuaded *the army* that she was a gift of Diana, and that she told him what ought to be done. If he wished to order *anything difficult*, he used to say that he had been warned by the doe, and all used at once to obey. Once the doe was lost, and believed to have perished, which vexed Sertorius greatly. Many days after she was found by a certain man. Sertorius hid her near the place where he was wont to dispense justice, and then told the troops that the doe had appeared to him in a dream. When they approached the tribunal the doe leaped forth, and ran to Sertorius. The whole army was greatly astonished.

     of great use, *for great use.* making, *gerund.*
the army, *dat. of remoter object.* anything, *quid.* difficult, *comparative.*

Exercise 238.

A certain judge used to relate a story about a fellow who had claimed his friendship in a strange way. The judge one day while walking could not find the house where he was going to sleep, so he asked a man whom he met to show him the way. The other answered, 'I will do this willingly, my lord; *I had the honour of being accused* before you *of stealing* sheep.' The judge replied, 'I remember you perfectly; *how is your wife?* she too had the honour also of appearing before me. She had received the sheep which you had stolen.' 'She is well, *your lordship;* we were acquitted of the theft: I still am a butcher.' 'Then,' replied the judge, 'perhaps I shall meet you again.'

I had the honour of being accused, *it happened to me that I was accused*
  (ut *with subj.*). of stealing, *because I had stolen (subj.).*
  how is your wife? *How does your wife hold herself?*
    your lordship, *my lord.*

Exercise 239.

Jupiter had spoken in a dream to a certain man, Titus by name, and said, 'Go and order the consuls to repeat the games, for some one danced lately in the games whom I liked not, therefore great danger awaits this city.' But Titus feared lest *every one* would laugh at him, if he should go to the consuls with such a message, and so he did not obey the god. A few days after his son died, and again a voice said to him, 'Dost thou still despise my orders? Thy son is already dead, and if thou *wilt not* obey, worse disaster awaits thee.'

    every one, *all.* wilt not, *nolo.*

Exercise 240.

But Titus still lingered, so he was himself seized with a sudden weakness; neither could he walk, but his friends carried him in a litter. Then he delayed *no* longer, but ordered his relations to carry him to the consuls. Then he told the consuls the orders of the god, and all the things *that* had happened to him. When they had heard this, the consuls remembered that on the first day of the games a citizen had beaten his slave with a whip *in the midst of the circus;* and the citizens noticed *it* not, but Jupiter saw it and was angry; for it was a holy day, and a day suited for mirth, but not for tears and pain.

    no, *haud, used often with adverbs instead of* non.   that, *relative.*
    in the midst of the circus, *in the middle circus.* and it, *which.*

Exercise 241.

The Helvetii, whom Orgetorix had persuaded to seek more fertile regions, *on hearing* that Caesar had suddenly arrived at Geneva, asked him *to allow* them to pass through the Roman province, promising *to do* no injury. Caesar, who as yet had only a small army, said that he would soon be able to reply; *let* the ambassadors of the Helvetii *return* to him after a few days. Meanwhile Caesar, having collected a great army, said that he would not allow them to pass; (and) that, if they attempted to go, he would prevent them by force.

    on hearing, *when they had heard.* to allow, *indirect command.*
    to do, *that they would do. Verbs of hoping and promising take
    the fut. inf.* let—return, *indirect command.*

Exercise 242.

Hannibal being conquered by Scipio, fled to Antiochus, king of Syria. Ambassadors were sent from Rome to Antiochus, among whom was Scipio, who asked Hannibal whom *he thought* to be the greatest general. Hannibal replied, that Alexander king of Macedon seemed to him to have been the greatest, because with small forces *he had routed* innumerable armies. Then Scipio asked whom he placed second. 'Pyrrhus,' said he, 'because he first taught (how) to measure (out) a camp, *and no one* could better choose *ground*, or place guards.' Again, when Scipio asked whom he placed third, he replied, 'Myself.' Then Scipio, smiling, said, 'What then would you say if you had conquered me?' 'I should have placed myself before Alexander and Pyrrhus and all others.'

    he thought, *indirect question.* he had routed, *subjunctive, because of the
    oratio obliqua.* and no one, *neque quisquam—more elegant
    than 'et nemo.'* ground, *a place.*

Exercise 243.

Two men were once brought *before* a judge; the one seemed to be a tailor, with his shears in his hand, the other a peasant. Then the tailor spoke as follows: 'This man came to me yesterday and showed me a cloth, asking *whether* there was enough *to make him a cap*. "There is enough," said I. Then he asked was there enough for two. Seeing his meanness I said, "Certainly." So at last he ordered five caps to be made, which I finished according to his order. To-day, he will not pay me the money.' 'Thou speakest the truth,' said the peasant, 'but show the caps to the judge.' Then the tailor drew forth his hand from his bosom, and showed his four fingers and thumb, from each of which hung a very little cap. 'Here are the five caps,' said he, 'which the man ordered; nothing remains over of the cloth.' All began to laugh, but the judge said, 'Let the tailor lose his trouble, the peasant his cloth, and let the caps be given to the poor.'

    before, *apud.* whether, *num.* to make him a cap, *for* (ad)
        a cap to be made (*gerundive*).

Exercise 244.

After the battle of Cannae, when his troops were congratulating Hannibal, and advising him to take *some rest* himself, and give some to his weary troops, one of his officers, by name Maharbal, urged him *to start* for Rome at once, since he was *sure to feast* in the Capitol as victor within five days. When Hannibal rejected this advice, Maharbal said, 'You know (how) to conquer, Hannibal, but you do not know how to use victory.' The delay of this day is believed to have saved the city.

    some rest, *something of rest.* to start, *indirect command.*
        sure to feast, *future participle.*

Exercise 245.

Next day, at dawn, the Carthaginians began to collect the spoil. So many thousands of the Romans lay on the field, that three bushels of the rings which had been taken from the fingers of the knights and senators were sent to Carthage. Then Hannibal led his troops into Campania, where he himself and his troops, given up to ease, became less fit for war. It is well known that *he ought* to have gone to Rome at once, for meanwhile the Romans enrolled fresh forces, and fortified the city.

    at dawn, *at first light.* ought, *it behoved him, perf. inf.*

Exercise 246.

Regulus was conquered by the Carthaginians *under the leadership of Xanthippus*. Only two thousand men remained out of the whole Roman army. Regulus himself was captured and thrown into prison. Afterwards he was sent to Rome *to* consult about *an exchange* of prisoners, after giving an oath that he would return to Carthage if he did not effect *his object*. When he had arrived at Rome, he explained his orders before the senate, but said that he was no longer a senator, since he had fallen into the power of the enemy. Being ordered however to give his opinion, he said that the Carthaginian prisoners ought not to be restored, since they were youths, but he himself was worn out with old age. The captives were therefore, *on his recommendation*, retained. Then Regulus returned to Carthage, although he knew that he was going to a most cruel enemy and dreadful punishment, for he thought his oath should be kept. It is well known that he was put to death at Carthage with every kind of torment.

    under the leadership of Xanthippus, *Xanthippus being leader.*
    to, *in order to.* an exchange, *exchanging, gerundive.*
    his object, *what he wished (subj.).*
    on his recommendation, *he being the proposer (auctor).*

Exercise 247.

Marcus Brutus, knowing the wish of the Roman people, conspired against Caesar. Porcia, his wife, being aware of his plan, wounded herself with a knife, as if by accident. Brutus was summoned to his wife's chamber by the shrieks of the maids. Porcia said to him secretly, 'I did not wound myself by accident, but on purpose, my dear Brutus; for I wished to try whether I had enough courage *to meet* death, if your plan did not succeed.' *Hearing these words*, Brutus is said to have raised his hands and eyes to heaven, and to have exclaimed, 'Would that I could seem worthy of such a wife!'

    to meet, *that I might meet.*
    hearing these words, *these words having been heard.*

Exercise 248.

Octavianus fought in a naval battle with Antonius off Actium, *which* is a place in Epirus ; he conquered Antonius and pursued him to Egypt, and having besieged Alexandria, whither Antonius and Cleopatra had betaken themselves, he got possession of it in a short time. Then Antonius, *having taken his seat* on the royal throne crowned with the diadem, killed himself with his sword. But Cleopatra, whom Octavianus greatly desired to be taken alive, and kept for his triumph, ordered a snake to be brought to her in a basket among some figs, and with her own hand applied it to her arm. When Octavianus heard this, he ordered the physicians to apply remedies to the wound. The physicians used all their arts in vain ; Cleopatra soon died. She was then buried together with Antonius.

which, *to agree with* '*a place*,' *instead of with Actium, its antecedent; this is called attraction.* having taken his seat, *when he had sat.*

Exercise 249.

When Augustus was entering Rome, after the war with Antonius, a certain artisan met him, among those who were congratulating him, carrying a raven, which he had taught to say these words : 'Hail, victorious Caesar, Emperor.' Augustus wondering at the bird bought it for a large price. The companion of the artisan, who had received nothing, told Augustus, that *the latter* had also another raven, which he begged *might be produced.* The raven being brought, uttered the words which it had learnt, 'Hail, victorious Antonius, Emperor.' Augustus only laughed, and ordered the teacher of the ravens to divide his reward with his companion. He is also said to have bought a parrot, which had in like manner saluted him.

the latter, *hic.* might be produced, *indirect command.*

Exercise 250.

Incited by this example, a certain cobbler trained a raven to a like salutation, but since it learned slowly, he used often to say to the bird, 'My trouble and expense is lost.' At length the raven began to produce the desired salutation, hearing which, while *passing* by, Augustus replied, 'I have enough of such saluters at home.' Then the raven added those words, with which it was wont to hear its master complaining, 'My trouble and expense is lost.' At this Augustus laughed, and ordered the bird to be bought at a very great price.

passing, *he passes by.*

Exercise 251.

The brother of a very celebrated actor used to ask daily, '*Did my dear brother want* me?' At last the actor died. Soon afterwards his brother died also. Some asked why he had died so soon after the death of his brother. It was answered, 'that his brother wanted him.'

  did my brother want? *was there need* (opus) *to my brother?*

Exercise 252.

They say that bears use wonderful stratagems in order *to catch* deer, for they are not able to catch them by running, since they are much swifter. The deer love to feed *at the bottom of mountains*. The bear pursues them by scent until he sees them. They say that he then ascends the rocks cautiously, and when he has arrived at the summit, that he pushes down rocks *at them*. Sometimes one of the deer is wounded by the rock, and then the bear descends and seizes it.

  to catch, *that they may catch.* at the bottom of mountains,
   at the bottom mountains. at, *in.*

Exercise 253.

Greece was saved by one man—Themistocles. The generals of the other Grecian states admitted this, when they assembled *to* assign the prizes of wisdom and valour. Upon the altar of Poseidon at Corinth each general placed a ticket, on which was written the names of those whom he considered worthy of the first and second prizes. But vanity and love *of self* were defeated in this. Each commander had written that he was worthy of the first prize; but the greater part had said that Themistocles was worthy of the second. Themistocles also received from the Spartans splendid prizes. He was presented with a crown, and the *most splendid* chariot which the city could afford.

  to, *ad, followed by gerundive.* of self, *sui.* most splendid, *to go in the adjectival clause in agreement with the relative.*

Exercise 254.

Quintus Fabius, *in his old age*, was an officer in the army of his son, who had been made consul. When he was coming into camp his son went out to meet him; twelve lictors, according to custom, preceded him. The old man was riding on horseback, nor did he dismount from his horse *at the approach of the consul*. Already eleven lictors had passed by *in silence*. When the consul had perceived this, he ordered the last lictor to call to his father Fabius, *to dismount* from his horse. Fabius, then dismounting, said, 'I did not despise your authority, my son, but I wished to see *if* you knew (how) to act the consul.'

 in his old age, *an old man*. at the approach of the consul, *the consul approaching*. in silence, *silently*. to dismount, *indirect command*.
  if, *num*.

Exercise 255.

Menenius Agrippa restored concord between the patricians and the people. For when the people revolted from the patricians, Agrippa, an eloquent man, was sent to the people. Being brought into their camp, he is said to have spoken thus: 'Once upon a time the limbs, since they saw the belly idle, revolted from it, and conspired *that* the hands should *not* bring food to the mouth, *and that* the teeth should *not* chew the food. But, while they tried to overcome the belly, they themselves became weak, and the whole body became ill. Hence it appeared that the belly was *of use*, and that it sent the food through all the limbs; therefore the revolt ceased.' The senate and the people then made peace, and returned to the city.

 that—not, *ne*. and that not, *neu*. of use, *for a use*.

Exercise 256.

Hannibal, the *admiral* of the Carthaginian fleet, leaped into a boat and escaped from the hands of the Romans. Fearing, however, lest he should *suffer* punishment for the loss of the fleet, he sent one of his friends to Carthage before the news of the disaster had reached home. He, entering the senate-house, said, 'Hannibal asks you, *should he fight* with the Romans?' The whole senate exclaimed, 'There is no doubt *but that* he should fight!' Then said he, 'He did *so*, and was conquered.' So they were not able to condemn him, because they had ordered him to fight. Thus Hannibal escaped the penalty of the gallows, for with this kind of punishment a defeated general was visited among the Carthaginians.

 admiral, *leader*. suffer, *give*. should he fight, *indirect question introduced by* '*num*.' but that, *quin, with subj*. so, *this*.

Exercise 257.

Antisthenes *used to exhort* his disciples *to pay* attention to wisdom. Few obeyed him ; therefore he dismissed them all. Among these was Diogenes ; and when he, stirred with great desire *for learning*, used to keep coming to Antisthenes, *and* would *not* go away, Antisthenes at length threatened that he would beat his head with the stick which he used to carry in his hand. Diogenes did not go away, but said, 'Strike if you wish ; I will offer you my head. You will not find a stick so hard *as to drive* me away from your school.' It is well known that Antisthenes at length admitted a pupil so desirous of learning, and loved him greatly.

used to exhort, *imperfect.* to pay, to give. for learning, *of learning, gerund.* and—not, *neque.* as to drive, *which may drive; which = that it.*

Exercise 258.

Phocion, when condemned *to death*, bore himself bravely. When some wretched man spat on him while *going* to prison, 'Will no one,' said he, 'check this fellow's indecency?' To one who asked him *whether* he had any message to leave to his son Phocus, he answered, 'Let him not be angry with the Athenians.' And when the hemlock which had been prepared seemed to be insufficient for all the con-. demned, and the jailer *said that he would not give* more unless money was paid to him ; 'Give the man his money,' said Phocion to one of his friends, 'since at Athens *one cannot even die* without money.'

to death, *of the head.* going, *he was going.* whether, *num.*
said that he would not give, *denied that he would give.*
one cannot even die, *it is not lawful even to die ;—the emphatic word to go between* 'ne' *and* 'quidem.'

Exercise 259.

The king prepared a large fleet, for he had determined to prevent the enemy *from assisting* the city which he intended to besiege. Then he ordered a fort to be built, by which he hoped to guard the approaches of the harbour. *After losing* much money and time, the fort seemed to be so badly built that he was obliged to abandon it ; and though he had collected a large army, he was not able to effect anything great. He indeed made an incursion into the region which used to give supplies to the garrison of the city, and laid it waste with fire and sword. One of his knights was wounded in a wonderful way. A lance struck his head between his eye and nose ; and although the lance was broken and the head of it remained in the wound, he was not thrown from his horse by so violent a wound, and the head of the lance being extracted by a skilful surgeon, he afterwards was cured.

from assisting, *lest they should assist.* after losing, *when he had lost.*

Exercise 260.

As Polycarp stood in the theatre at Smyrna, the multitude around him crying out that he despised the gods, the Roman proconsul, pitying his old age, begged him to pronounce the words which should show that he trusted the old gods and abhorred the Christian faith. 'Swear by the fortune of Caesar; cry, Death to those who do not believe that there are gods.' Those who tell the story of his death say that Polycarp, on hearing this, looked with a severe countenance at the crowd who were filling the theatre with their voices, and *casting up* his eyes to heaven, said, 'Death to those who do not believe there is a God.' Thus he said the one thing but omitted the other. The Romans *took* it ill, and he was burnt.

    as, *when.* casting up, *raising.* took, *bore.*

Exercise 261.

A peasant *on the point of death*, since he was not able to leave riches to his sons, desired to rouse their minds to the desire of diligent cultivation of the fields and to earnest labour. He therefore summoned them to him and addressed them thus, ' My sons, you see how my property *stands ;* but *you must seek* in my vineyard the money which I have saved *during* my life.' *After saying this* the old man died. The sons, thinking that their father had hidden a treasure in the vineyard, take their spades, and dig up the whole soil of the vineyard. They indeed find no treasure, but *by digging* the soil they made it so fertile that the vines bore fruit most abundantly.

    on the point of death, *about to die.*
    stands, *has itself; indirect question.* you must seek, *fut. imp.*
    during, *per.* after saying this, *these things having been said.*
    by digging, *gerund.*

Exercise 262.

Tyler, having ordered his companions to retire until he should give them a signal, dared to come into the midst of the king's attendants. He then *behaved in such a way* that the mayor of the city was not able to bear his impertinence. He drew his sword and struck him so heavily that he fell on the ground, where he was immediately despatched by the soldiers. The conspirators, seeing the death of their leader, determined to revenge themselves; and the soldiers with the king *would have been* killed immediately, unless the king had seen *what ought* to be done. He ordered his companions to stop; he advanced alone towards the angry crowd, and addressing them with a kind and fearless countenance, asked them why they had made such a tumult. 'Are you angry, my friends,' said he, 'because you have lost your leader? I am your king: I will be your leader.'

    behaved, *bore himself.* in such a way, *ita.*
    would have been, *it would have been that (futurum fuisset ut).*
    what ought, *indirect question.*

Exercise 263.

When the Gauls had pitched their camp near the river, the Roman army set out from the city and halted on the near side of the river. A Gaul of huge stature advanced to *the middle of the bridge*, and exclaimed with a loud voice, Will any Roman fight with me, that the result may show which nation *is best* in war? For a long time there was silence among the Roman chiefs. Then Titus Manlius approached the general and said, 'If you allow me, I wish to show *this beast* that I am descended from the family which hurled the Gauls from the Tarpeian rock.' To whom the general replied, 'I give you permission; advance and fight bravely for your country.'

the middle of the bridge, *the middle bridge.* is best, *indirect question.*
this beast, *dative of remoter object.*

Exercise 264.

Then his companions arm the youth. He takes his shield and sword. The Gaul awaited him joyfully, sticking out his tongue *in* mockery. When they stood between the two lines of battle the Gaul struck the shield of Manlius with his sword with a loud noise. But Manlius thrust himself between the arms and body of the Gaul, and pierced him with his sword. From him as he lay he took his collar, which he put round *his own neck*. The Romans joyfully received their soldier, and brought him to the general. It is well known that Manlius received the name of Torquatus on account of this exploit.

in, *per.* his own neck, *dative of remoter object.*

Exercise 265.

The same Manlius, being afterwards made consul, in the Latin war, in order to restore military discipline, ordered *that no one* should leave his station *to fight*. By chance his son had approached the camp of the enemy; he who commanded the Latin cavalry, when he recognised the consul's son, said, 'Will you fight with me, that the result may show *how much* a Latin horseman *excels* a Roman?' Forgetful of the general's order, the youth rushes to the conflict, and slays the Latin. Having collected the spoils, he returns to his father. The consul at once summons the troops with the trumpet; then he addresses his son as follows: 'Since thou, my son, hast not obeyed the order of the consul, it behoves you to restore discipline by punishment. Go, lictor, bind him to the stake.' His head was then cut off by the lictor with an axe. It is well known that only the old men went out to meet Manlius when he was returning home; he was always afterwards hated by the youth.

at no one, *ne quis,* lit. *lest any one.* to, *ut.* how much, *quantum.*
excels, *indirect question.*

Exercise 266.

There was at Corinth a great quantity of statues and valuable pictures, with which Mummius, the Roman general, *after the capture of Corinth*, filled Rome and the *whole of* Italy, but took nothing to his own house. Mummius, however, was so ignorant of these things, that when he sent the pictures to Rome he warned the sailors *that, if they lost them, they would have* to restore new ones. One of the pictures, the work of a celebrated painter, was used by some soldiers who were playing *hazard, for* a board. This picture, when the plunder was being sold, was bought by king Attalus for a large price. Mummius wondering at the price, ordered it to be sent to Rome.

    after the capture of Corinth, *after Corinth taken.* whole of, *totus.*
    that they would have, *that it behoved them.*
    was used by some soldiers, *some soldiers used.*
    hazard, *accusative, used adverbially ; to play, being intransitive, does not govern any case.* for, *pro.*

Exercise 267.

When the two armies stood ready, and were just *going to begin* the battle, a hind came running down from the mountains between the lines of battle, *with a she-wolf in chase of her.* She ran in among the ranks of the Gauls, who transfixed her with their javelins. But the she-wolf ran towards the Romans, who immediately made way for her, thinking that this was the beast which had fed with its milk the founder of their city, and whose image they had set up the year before under the *very* fig-tree where, as it had been related, the miracle had been. 'See,' cried one of the soldiers, 'the barbarians have slain Diana's sacred hind, and she will punish them ; but the Roman she-wolf, unhurt by spear or sword, gives us a good omen of victory, and orders us to remember Mars and our founder Romulus.' So the Roman soldiers, encouraged as if by a sign from the gods, attacked the enemy joyfully.

    going to begin, *fut. part.* with a she-wolf in chase of her, *whom a she-wolf was pursuing.* very, *ipse.*

Exercise 268.

In Italy there was a physician who used to receive lunatics into his house, and in order to cure them used to order them to stand in a pond, some *up to* the knees, others up to the chin, *in proportion to* their madness. One of these lunatics, who was *pretty well* recovered, was standing one day at the door of the house, and seeing a huntsman ride by with his hawks and hounds, he asked him what he was going to do. The huntsman answered, 'I am going *to hunt*.' '*At what price* do you value the animals which you catch in a year?' asked the lunatic. 'About two hundred pence,' replied the huntsman. 'And *what is the cost of* your horse, dogs, and hawks?' 'About two thousand pence,' answered the other. On hearing this, the lunatic besought the huntsman to go away *as quickly as possible* if he valued his liberty highly, and said that the physician would compel him to stand in the pond up to his chin if he found him there.

up to, *as far as*. in proportion to, *for (pro.)*. pretty well, *admodum*. to hunt, *supine in um*. at what price, *quanti*. what is the cost of, *at what price . . . stand to you*. as quickly as possible, *quam celerrime*.

Exercise 269.

Among the friends of Augustus was Mecenas, a Roman knight, whom he loved greatly, and who always so used the favour he had with the Emperor *as* to benefit all whom *he could*, and injure no one. His skill was very great in *softening* the temper of Augustus when he saw him incited by anger. Augustus was once pronouncing justice, and seemed *likely to condemn* many men *to death*. Mecenas, who was present, tried to approach the Emperor through the crowd; *being unable* to do this, he wrote on a tablet these words, 'Rise, *I pray*, butcher,' and threw the tablet to Augustus. When he had read it, Augustus at once stood up, *and no one* was condemned to death.

as, *ut*. he could, *subj., because no one in particular is meant; the ind. is the mood of fact, the subjunctive the mood of possibility*.
softening, *gerund*. likely to condemn, *fut. part*.
to death, *of the head*. being unable, *since he was not able*.
I pray, *tandem*. and no one, *neque quisquam*.

Exercise 270.

Lucilius was held by all so wise, that if any one had anything *to ask* he always consulted him, and often gave large sums of money that he might be admitted. Once there came a stranger, who said he was cleverer than any one *else*, and promised that if a large reward *were given* to the conqueror, he would engage with Lucilius in a contest of wisdom. Lucilius won easily in the following way. He told the stranger that a worm once climbed up a stalk ten feet high. It moved so slowly that each day it only ascended three feet, and slipped down two feet at night. The stranger said, 'Each day it is higher by one foot than the day before.' 'Certainly,' said Lucilius, 'but in how many days will it arrive at the top of the stalk?' 'In ten days,' said the stranger. Then Lucilius said, 'In seven days it has climbed seven feet, and since it ascends three feet daily, can you deny that it reaches the top of the stalk on the eighth day?' The stranger paid the money and departed.

to ask, *which he wished to ask.* else, *alius.*
were given, *should be given.*

LATIN-ENGLISH VOCABULARY.

ABBREVIATIONS USED.

abl., *ablative.*
acc., *accusative.*
adj., *adjective.*
adv., *adverb.*
c. abl., c. acc., *etc., with ablative, with accusative, etc.*
c., *common gender.*
conj., *conjunction.*
dat., *dative.*
def., *defective.*

dep., *deponent.*
distrib., *distributive.*
f. *feminine.*
gen., *genitive.*
impers., *impersonal.*
indcl., *indeclinable.*
intrans., *intransitive.*
m., *masculine.*
n., *neuter.*
num., *numeral.*

part., *participle.*
pass., *passive.*
pl., plur., *plural.*
prep., *preposition.*
pron., *pronoun.*
pronom., *pronominal.*
sing., *singular.*
subst., *substantive.*
trans., *transitive.*

The Conjugation of a Verb is denoted by a figure placed after it.

A, ab, abs, prep. *from, by* (c. abl.)
abdĭco, 1, *to resign, abdicate.*
abeo, ii, itum, 4, *to go away.*
absolvo, vi, ūtum, 3, *to acquit, finish.*
absum, fui, esse, *to be absent, at a distance.*
absūmo, sumpsi, sumptum, 3, *to take away, spend, destroy.*
accĭpio, cēpi, ceptum, 3, *to accept, receive, get* (capio).
accĭpĭter, tris, m. *a hawk.*
ācer, acris, acre, adj. *sharp, keen, active.*
Achaia, ae, f. *a province in the Peloponnesus.*
ācies, ei, f. *an edge, line of battle, battle.*
Actium, i, n. *Actium, a promontory in North Greece.*
ad, prep. *to, at, by, off, towards, against* (c. acc.)
adhaereo, haesi, haesum, 2, *to be attached to, adjoin.*
adhūc, adv. *hitherto, as yet.*
adĭmo, ēmi, emptum, 3, *to take away* (emo).
adĭpiscor, adeptus, 3, dep. *to obtain.*
admĭnistro, 1, *to manage.*

admitto, mīsi, missum, 3, *to commit.*
admŏneo, ui, ĭtum, 2, *to remind, warn.*
adŏlescens, ntis, m. *a youth.*
adsum, fui, esse, *to be present.*
advĕnio, vēni, ventum, 4, *to approach, arrive at.*
adversus, prep. *against, opposite to.*
aedes, is, f. *a temple;* in plur. *a house.*
aedĭfĭco, 1, *to build* (aedes-facio).
Aedui, ōrum, m. *the Aedui (a people of Italy).*
Aegyptius, a, um, adj. *Egyptian.*
Aegyptus, i, f. *Egypt.*
Aemĭlius, i, m. *Aemilius.*
Aequi, ōrum, m. *the Aequi (a people of Italy).*
aequus, a, um, adj. *calm, fair, equal.*
āër, ĕris, m. *the air.*
aestas, ātis, f. *summer.*
aestĭmo, 1, *to value.*
aetas, ātis, f. *age.*
affĕro, attŭli, allātum, afferre, *to bring to, cause, announce.*
Afrĭca, ae, f. *Africa.*
Afrĭcānus, a, um, *African (the title of honour bestowed on the Scipios).*
ăger, gri, m. *a field, territory.*

B. L. W.   L

Latin-English Vocabulary.

agrĭcŏla, ae, m. *a peasant.*
Agrippīna, ae, f. *Agrippina.*
Alba, ae, f. *Alba (a town in Latium).*
Alexander, dri, m. *Alexander.*
aliēnus, a, um, adj. *belonging to another;* aes alienum, *debt.*
ălĭquis, quă, quĭd, }
ălĭqui, quae, quŏd, } pron. *some one, any one* (alius—quis).
ălĭquot, indcl. *some, several* (aliusquot).
ălius, a, ud, pronom. adj. *other, another;* alius—alius, *one, another.*
alter, ĕra, ĕrum, pronom. adj. *the other;* alter—alter, *the one, the other.*
altus, a, um, adj. *high, deep.*
ămābĭlis, e, adj. *lovable* (amo).
ambo, ae, o, adj. *both.*
ambŭlo, 1, *to walk.*
ămīcĭtia, ae, f. *friendship* (amo).
ămīcus, i, m. *a friend.*
āmitto, mīsi, missum, 3, *to send away, lose.*
ămo, 1, *to love.*
amor, ōris, m. *love.*
amplector, plexus, 3, dep. *to embrace.*
an, conj. *or.*
ănas, ătis, f. *a duck.*
anceps, cĭpĭtis, adj. *doubtful.*
ango, xi, ctum, 3, *to grieve, torture.*
anguis, is, c. *a snake.*
ănĭmal, ālis, n. *an animal.*
ănĭmus, i, m. *spirit, disposition, courage.*
annŭlus, i, m. *a ring.*
annon, conj. *or not.*
annus, i, m. *a year.*
ante, adv. and prep. *before* (c. acc.)
antĕpōno, pŏsui, pŏsĭtum, 3, *to place before, prefer.*
antīquus, a, um, adj. *ancient.*
Antōnius, i, m. *Antonius.*
antrum, i, n. *a cave, den.*
ăper, pri, m. *a wild boar.*
ăpĕrio, rui, rtum, 4, *to open.*
appāreo, ui, 2, *to appear, come in sight, be manifest.*

ăpud, prep. *at, with, among, at the house of, before* (c. acc.)
ăqua, ae, f. *water.*
arbor, ŏris, f. *a tree.*
ardeo, si, sum, 2, *to burn, be on fire.*
ārea, ae, f. *a threshing-floor.*
argentum, i, n. *silver.*
arma, ōrum, n. *arms, armour.*
armĭger, ĕri, m. *an armour-bearer.*
ars, tis, f. *art, skill.*
artĭfex, fĭcis, c. *an artist, workman* (ars-facio).
arx, cis, f. *a citadel.*
as, sis, m. *a pound, an as* (a Roman coin).
Asia, ae, f. *Asia.*
aspecto, 1, *to look on, at.*
āter, tra, trum, adj. *jet black, deadly.*
Athēnae, ārum, f. *Athens.*
Attĭca, ae, f. *Attica.*
atrox, ōcis, adj. *fierce, warlike.*
audeo, sus sum, 2, dep. *to dare.*
audio, īvi *or* ii, ītum, 4, *to hear.*
aufĕro, abstŭli, ablātum, auferre, *to carry off.*
aureus, a, um, adj. *golden.*
aurum, i, n. *gold.*
aut, conj. *or;* aut—aut, *either—or.*
auxĭlium, i, n. *help.*
ăvĭdus, a, um, adj. *eager, greedy.*
ăvis, is, f. *a bird.*
ăvus, i, m. *a grandfather, ancestor.*

Babylon, ōnis, f. *Babylon.*
Balbus, i, m. *Balbus.*
barba, ae, f. *a beard.*
barbărus, a, um, . adj. *barbarous, foreign.*
Belga, ae, m. *a Belgian.*
bellum, i, n. *war.*
bēlua, ae, f. *a beast, monster.*
bestia, ae, f. *a beast.*
bĕnĕ, adv. *well.*
bĭbo, bĭbĭ, bĭbĭtum, 3, *to drink.*
bĭduum, i, n. *a space of two days* (bis-dies).
biennium, i, n. *a space of two years* (bis-annus).

Latin-English Vocabulary.

bīni, ae, a, distrib. num. *two each, two at a time.*
Boeōtia, ae, f. *Boeotia.*
bŏnus, a, um, adj. *good.*
bos, bŏvis, c. *an ox or cow.*
brĕvis, e, adj. *short.*
Brĭtanni, ōrum, m. *the Britons.*
Brĭtannia, ae, f. *Britain.*

Cado, cĕcĭdi, cāsum, 3, *to fall.*
caedes, is, f. *slaughter.*
caerŭleus, a, um, adj. *dark blue or green.*
Caesar, ăris, m. *Caesar.*
Caius, i, m. *Caius.*
Cămillus, i, m. *Camillus.*
cănis, is, c. *a dog.*
Cannensis, e, adj. *of Cannae (a town in South Italy).*
căno, cĕcĭni, cantum, 3, *to sing.*
canto, 1, *to sing.*
căpillus, i, m. *a hair.*
căpio, cēpi, captum, 3, *to catch, seize.*
Capĭtōlium, i, n. *the Capitol (one of the seven hills of Rome).*
captīvus, a, um, adj. *captive.*
Căpua, ae, f. *Capua.*
căput, ĭtis, n. *a head, capital;* capitis damnare or condemnare, *to condemn to death.*
carcer, ĕris, m. *a prison.*
carmen, ĭnis, n. *a song.*
căro, carnis, f. *flesh, meat.*
Carthāgo, ĭnis, f. *Carthage (a town in North Africa).*
cārus, a, um, adj. *dear.*
cāseus, i, m. *cheese.*
castra, ōrum, n. *a camp.*
cătella, ae, f. *a puppy.*
Catilīna, ae, m. *Catilina.*
caussa, ae, f. *a cause, suit.*
cēdo, cessi, cessum, 3, *to go away, yield, grant.*
cĕlĕrĭter, adv. *quickly.*
cēlo, 1, *to conceal.*
censeo, ui, 2, *to think.*
centum, indecl. num. *a hundred.*
centŭrio, ōnis, m. *a centurion, captain* (centum).

Ceres, ĕris, f. *Ceres.*
certo, 1. *to strive, contend.*
certus, a, um, adj. *sure, fixed, certain.*
cervus, i, m. *a stag.*
Chaldaei, ōrum, m. *the Chaldaeans.*
cĭbus, i, m. *food.*
Cicero, ōnis, m. *Cicero.*
Cincinnātus, i, m. *Cincinnatus.*
cĭnis, ĕris, m. *ashes, cinders.*
circa, circum, adv. and prep. *around, about* (c. acc.)
circumsto, stĕti, statum, 1, *to stand round.*
citra, prep. *on this side of* (c. acc.)
cīvis, is, c. *a citizen.*
cīvĭtas, ātis, f. *a state.*
clam, adv. *secretly;* prep. *without the knowledge of* (c. abl.)
clārus, a, um, adj. *bright, clear, renowned.*
classis, is, f. *a fleet.*
Claudia, ae, f. *Claudia.*
coepi, def., *to begin.*
cogĭto, 1, *to think, reflect.*
cognōmen, ĭnis, n. *a surname.*
cognosco, nōvi, nĭtum, 3, *to perceive, know, recognise.*
cōgo, coēgi, coactum, 3, *to compel, assemble* (cum-ago).
cŏhors, tis, f. *a cohort.*
cŏhortor, 1, dep. *to encourage.*
cŏlo, ui, cultum, 3, *to cultivate, worship.*
cŏmĕs, ĭtis, c. *a companion.*
committo, mīsi, missum, 3, *to commit, bring together;* aciem or pugnam committere, *to fight.*
commūnis, e, adj. *common.*
condemno, 1, *to condemn.*
condĭtio, ōnis, f. *a condition.*
confĕro, tŭli, collātum, ferre, 3, *to collect, compare, betake.*
confĭcio, fēci, fectum, *to finish, destroy* (facio).
confŏdio, fōdi, fossum, 3, *to pierce, stab.*
congruenter, adv. *agreeably to.*
conĭcio, iēci, iectum, 3, *to throw* (iacio).
coniūrātio, ōnis, f. *a conspiracy.*

Latin-English Vocabulary.

coniux, iŭgis, c. *a husband or wife.*
cōnor, 1, dep. *to try.*
conquiesco, ēvi, 3, *to rest.*
consĕquor, cūtus, 3, dep. *to follow after, reach, obtain.*
consīdo, sēdi, sessum, 3, *to sit down, encamp.*
constĭtuo, ui, ūtum, 3, *to determine, appoint.*
consto, stĭti, stātum, 1, *to halt, consist of;* impers. constat, *it is well known.*
consul, ŭlis, m. *a consul.*
consŭlo, ui, sultum, 3, *to consult.*
consumo, sumpsi, sumptum, 3, *to consume, destroy.*
contendo, di, tum, 3, *to hasten, strive.*
contentus, a, um, adj. *content (c. abl.)*
contra, adv. and prep. *against (c. acc.)*
contrăho, xi, ctum, 3, *to contract, assemble.*
convĕnio, vēni, ventum, 4, *to come together, agree.*
cōpia, ae, f. *plenty;* in plur. *forces.*
cor, dis, n. *the heart.*
cōram, adv. *publicly;* prep. *before (c. abl.)*
Cŏrinthus, i, f. *Corinth.*
cŏrōna, ae, f. *a crown.*
corpus, ŏris, n. *a body.*
corrumpo, rūpi, ruptum, 3, *to destroy, bribe.*
corvus, i, m. *a raven.*
Crassus, i, m. *Crassus.*
crēdo, dĭdi, dĭtum, 3, *to trust, believe.*
creo, 1, *to create.*
cresco, crēvi, crētum, 3, *to grow, increase.*
Croesus, i, m. *Croesus.*
crūdēlis, e, adj. *cruel.*
culpa, ae, f. *a fault.*
culpo, 1, *to blame.*
cŭpĭdus, a, um, adj. *desirous of, greedy.*

cŭpio, īvi *or* ii, ītum, 3, *to desire.*
cur, adv. *why?*
cūra, ae, f. *care.*
Cŭrio, ōnis, m. *Curio.*
Cŭrius, i, m. *Curius.*
curro, cŭcurri, cursum, 3, *to run.*

Damno, 1, *to condemn.*
damnum, i, n. *hurt, loss.*
Dărius, i, m. *Darius.*
dea, ae, f. *a goddess.*
dēbeo, ui, ĭtum, 2, *to owe.*
dĕcem, indcl. num. *ten.*
dĕcĭmus, a, um, adj. *tenth.*
dēcĭpio, cēpi, ceptum, 3, *to deceive (capio).*
dēdĕcus, ŏris, n. *disgrace, dishonour.*
dēdūco, xi, ctum, 3, *to lead down, escort.*
dēfendo, di, sum, 3, *to defend, ward off.*
deinde, adv. *then, next.*
dēlectus, ūs, m. *a levy* (lego).
dēleo, ēvi, ētum, 2, *to blot out, destroy.*
dēlībĕro, 1, *to take counsel.*
Dēmarātus, i, m. *Demaratus.*
dens, tis, m. *a tooth.*
despēro, 1, *to despair* (spes).
dēsum, fui, esse, *to be wanting, fail.*
detrăho, xi, ctum, 3, *to take off.*
dētrūdo, si, sum, 3, *to push off.*
deus, i, m. *a god.*
dēvinco, vīci, victum, 3, *to conquer utterly.*
dīco, xi, ctum, 3, *to say.*
dictātor, ōris, m. *a dictator.*
dictātūra, ae, f. *the dictatorship.*
dies, ēi, c. in sing., m. in plur., *a day;* in dies, *from day to day.*
diffĭcĭlis, e, adj. *difficult* (facilis).
dĭgĭtus, i, m. *a finger.*
dignus, a, um, adj. *worthy (c. abl.)*
dilĭgo, lexi, lectum, 3, *to love.*
Dionȳsius, i, m. *Dionysius.*
dīrĭpio, ui, reptum, 3, *to plunder* (rapio).
discedo, cessi, cessum, 3, *to depart.*

Latin-English Vocabulary. 165

discĭpŭlus, i, m. *a pupil* (disco).
disco, dĭdĭci, 3, *to learn.*
dissĕro, sĕrui, sertum, 3, *to argue.*
disto, 1, *to be distant.*
diu, adv. *long, for a long time.*
dīvĕs, ĭtis, adj. *rich.*
dīvĭdo, si, sum, 3, *to divide.*
dīvĭtiae, ārum, f. *riches.*
do, dĕdi, dătum, 1, *to give.*
dŏceo, ui, ctum, 2, *to teach.*
doctrīna, ae, f. *learning.*
doctus, a, um, adj. *learned.*
dŏlor, ōris, m. *pain.*
dŏmus, ūs, f. *a house, home.*
dōnum, i, n. *a gift.*
dormio, īvi *or* ii, ītum, 4, *to sleep.*
dūcēnī, ae, a, distrib. num. *two hundred each,* or, *at a time.*
dūcentī, ae, a, num. *two hundred.*
dūco, xi, ctum, 3, *to lead, marry.*
dulcis, e, adj. *sweet.*
duo, ae, o, num. *two.*
duodēvīginti, indcl. num. *eighteen.*
dux, dŭcis, m. *a leader.*

E *or* ex, prep. *out of, from.*
ĕdo, ēdi, ēsum, 3, *to eat.*
ēdo, ēdĭdi, ēdĭtum, 3, *to utter, produce.*
effŏdio, fōdi, fossum, 3, *to dig out.*
ĕgo, pron. *I.*
ĕlĕphantus, i, m. *an elephant.*
ēlŏquentia, ae, f. *eloquence.*
ĕmo, ēmi, emptum, 3, *to buy.*
ensis, is, m. *a sword.*
eō, adv. *thither.*
eo, īvi *or* ii, ītum, 4, *to go.*
epistŏla, ae, f. *a letter.*
ĕquĕs, ĭtis, m. *a horseman, knight.*
ĕquĭtātus, ūs, m. *cavalry.*
ĕquus, i, m. *horse.*
erro, 1, *to wander, err, stray.*
et, conj. *and, both;* et—et, *both—and.*
Etrūria, ae, f. *Etruria (a country in North Italy).*
exemplum, i, n. *an example.*
exercĭtus, ūs, m. *an army.*
exīgo, ēgi, actum, 3, *to drive out, require.*

exĭmius, a, um, adj. *remarkable.*
exĭtium, i, n. *destruction.*
expello, pŭli, pulsum, 3, *to expel, drive out.*
explōrātor, ōris, m. *a scout.*
expugno, 1, *to take by storm.*
exsisto, stĭti, stĭtum, 3, *to appear, exist.*
exsul, ŭlis, m. *an exile.*
extra, prep. *without, beyond* (c. acc.)

Facio, fēci, factum, 3, *to make, do.*
fācundus, a, um, adj. *eloquent.*
făveo, fāvi, fautum, 2, *to favour* (c. dat.)
fēcundus, a, um, adj. *fertile, fruitful.*
fel, lis, n. *gall.*
fēlix, īcis, adj. *happy.*
fĕra, ae, f. *a wild beast.*
fĕrē, adv. *nearly, almost, generally.*
fĕro, tŭli, lātum, ferre, *to bear, carry, say, pass (of a law).*
fertĭlis, e, adj. *fertile.*
ferrum, i, n. *iron.*
fīlia, ae, f. *a daughter.*
fīlius, i, m. *a son.*
fīnis, is, m. *an end;* in plur. *territory, boundaries.*
fīnĭtĭmus, a, um, adj. *neighbouring, bordering, akin to.*
fio, factus, fieri, 3, dep. *to become, be made.*
fluvus, a, um, adj. *yellow.*
flūmĕn, ĭnĭs, n. *a river.*
fluvius, i, m. *a river.*
fŏcus, i, m. *a hearth.*
foedus, ĕris, n. *a treaty.*
foedus, a, um, adj. *base.*
formīca, ae, f. *an ant.*
fortĕ, adv. *by chance.*
fortis, e, adj. *brave, strong.*
fortĭter, adv. *boldly, strongly.*
fortūna, ae, f. *fortune, luck.*
fŏrum, i, n. *the forum (the popular place of assembly at Rome).*
fossa, ae, f. *a ditch, trench.*
frango, frēgi, fractum, 3, *to break, wreck.*

Latin-English Vocabulary.

frāter, tris, m. *a brother.*
frāternus, a, um, adj. *of a brother, brotherly.*
fraus, dis, f. *deceit, fraud.*
frīgus, ŏris, n. *cold.*
frŭor, fructus *and* fruitus, 3, dep. *to enjoy* (*c. abl.*)
fŭga, ae, f. *flight.*
fŭgio, fŭgi, ĭtum, 3, *to fly, escape.*
fŭgo, 1, *to rout.*
fulmen, ĭnis, n. *a thunderbolt.*
fundo, fūdi, fūsum, 3, *to pour, disperse.*
fungor, functus, 3, dep. *to perform* (*c. abl.*)
furtum, i, n. *a theft.*

Gabii, ōrum, m. *Gabii (a town in Latium).*
Gallia, ae, f. *Gaul.*
gallīna, ae, f. *a hen.*
Gallus, i, m. *a Gaul.*
gaudium, i, n. *joy.*
gens, tis, f. *a race, family.*
gĕnu, ūs, n. *the knee.*
Germānus, a, um, adj. *German.*
gĕro, gessi, gestum, 3, *to do, wage, carry on.*
gĭgas, ntis, m. *a giant.*
gigno, gĕnui, genĭtum, 3, *to produce.*
glădius, i, m. *a sword.*
glōria, ae, f. *honour, glory.*
Graecia, ae, f. *Greece.*
Graecus, a, um, adj. *Greek, Grecian.*
grāmĕn, ĭnis, n. *grass.*
grăvis, e, adj. *heavy, important, unpleasant.*

Habeo, ui, ĭtum, 2, *to hold, have.*
hăbĭto, 1, *to inhabit.*
Hannĭbal, ălis, m. *Hannibal.*
hăruspex, ĭcis, m. *a soothsayer, augur.*
Hasdrŭbal, ălis, m. *Hasdrubal.*
hasta, ae, f. *a spear.*
Hector, ŏris, m. *Hector.*
Helvĕtii, ōrum, m. *the Helvetii (the Swiss).*

hīberna, ōrum, n. *winter-quarters* (castra, *understood*).
hīc, adv. *here.*
hīc, haec, hoc, pron. *this.*
hĭems, ĕmis, f. *winter.*
hinc, adv. *hence.*
Hispānia, ae, f. *Spain.*
hŏdiē, adv. *to-day* (hoc—die).
Hŏmērus, i, m. *Homer.*
hŏmo, ĭnis, c. *a human being.*
hōra, ae, f. *an hour.*
horreo, ui, 2, *to be rough.*
hortus, i, m. *a garden.*
hostis, is, c. *an enemy.*
hūc, adv. *hither.*
huiusmodi, *of this kind.*
hŭmus, i, f. *earth, ground;* humi, *on the ground.*

Iaceo, cui, cĭtum, 2, *to lie.*
iacio, iēci, iactum, 3, *to throw.*
iăcŭlum, i, n. *a javelin* (iacio).
iam, adv., *already, now.*
ibi, adv., *there* (*is*).
īco, īci, ictum, 3, *to strike.*
īdem, ĕădem, ĭdem, pronom. adj. *the same.*
ĭdōneus, a, um, adj. *useful, suitable.*
ignāvus, a, um, adj. *slothful, cowardly.*
ignis, is, m. *fire.*
ignosco, nōvi, nōtum, 3, *to forgive* (*c. dat.*)
ille, a, ud, pron. *he, she, it, that.*
imĭtor, 1, dep. *to imitate.*
immo, adv. *certainly, yes.*
immŏlo, 1, *to sacrifice.*
impĕrātor, ŏris, *a general, emperor.*
impĕrītus, a, um, adv. *unskilful, unskilled in* (*c. gen.*)
impĕro, 1, *to command* (*c. dat. of person*).
impĕtus, ūs, m. *a charge, attack.*
imprŏbus, a, um, adj. *importunate, wicked.*
in, prep. *in, into, on, to, against* (*c. acc. or abl.*)
incendium, i, n., *a fire.*

Latin-English Vocabulary.

incendo, di, sum, 3, *to burn, set on fire.*
incŏlŭmis, e, adj. *safe, unhurt.*
indĕ, adv. *thence.*
indīco, xi, ctum, 3, *to declare.*
indignus, a, um, adj. *unworthy* (c. abl.)
indo, dĭdi, dĭtum, 3, *to give to.*
ineo, ĭvi or ii, ĭtum, 4, *to enter, commence.*
infĕro, tŭli, illātum, ferre, *to advance, wage.*
ingens, tis, adj. *huge.*
ingĕnuus, a, um, adj. *high bred.*
ĭnĭmīcus, a, um, adj. *hostile;* as subst. *a private enemy.*
iniuria, ae, f. *injury, wrong.*
insĕro, sēvi, sĭtum, 3, *to implant.*
insons, tis, adj. *innocent.*
instruo, xi, ctum, 3, *to draw up.*
insŭla, ae, f. *an island.*
inter, prep. *among, between* (c. acc.)
interfĭcĭo, fēci, fectum, 3, *to kill* (facio).
intĕrĭmo, ēmi, emptum, 3, *to destroy* (emo).
ĭnūtĭlis, e, adj. *useless.*
invĕnio, vēni, ventum, 4, *to find.*
invĭdeo, vĭdi, visum, 2, *to envy, grudge* (c. dat.)
ipse, a, um, pron. *himself, herself, itself.*
Ira, ae, f. *anger.*
Irascor, 1, dep. *to be angry, angry with* (c. dat.)
is, ea, id, pron. *he, she, it, that.*
iste, a, ud, pron. *that* (near you).
Ister, tri, m. *the Danube.*
Itălia, ae, f. *Italy.*
Iter, ĭtĭnĕris, n. *a road, journey.*
Itĕrum, adv. *again.*
Iŭba, ae, m. *Juba.*
iūcundus, a, um, adj. *pleasant.*
iūdex, ĭcis, c. *a judge.*
iūdĭcĭum, i, n. *a judgment.*
iungo, xi, nctum, 3, *to join.*
Iuppĭter, Iŏvis, m. *Jupiter.*
iŭvĕnis, is. adj. *young;* as subst. *a young man.*
iŭventūs, ūtis, f. *youth.*

L *before proper name stands for Lucius.*
Lăbiēnus, i, m, *Labienus.*
lăbor, ōris, m. *labour.*
lac, tis, n. *milk.*
lăcesso, īvi, ītum, 3, *to provoke, annoy.*
lacrĭma, ae, f. *a tear.*
lăteo, ui, 2, *to lie hid.*
latro, ōnis, m. *a robber, pirate.*
lātus, a, um, adj. *broad.*
laudo, 1, *to praise.*
lēgātus, i, m. *an ambassador, lieutenant.*
lĕgio, ōnis, f. *legion.*
lĕgo, lēgi, lectum, 3, *to pluck, choose, read.*
leo, ōnis, m. *a lion.*
lĕpus, ŏris, m. *a hare.*
Lesbos, i, f. *Lesbos* (an island in the Aegean sea).
lĕvis, e, adj. *light.*
lex, lēgis, f. *a law.*
lĭber, bri, m. *a book.*
Lĭbĕr, ĕri, m. *Liber.*
Lĭbĕra, ae, f. *Libera.*
lībĕri, ōrum, m. *children.*
lībĕro, 1, *to free, liberate.*
lībertas, ātis, f. *liberty.*
lĭtĕra, ae, f. *a letter* (of the alphabet); in plur. *a letter.*
lŏcŭples, ētis, adj. *wealthy.*
lŏcus, i, m. *a place.*
longus, a, um, adj. *long.*
lŏquor, cūtus, 3, dep. *to speak.*
luctus, ūs, m. *grief.*
lūdo, si, sum, 3, *to play.*
lūmĕn, ĭnis, n. *light.*
lŭpa, ae, f. *a she-wolf.*
lŭpus, i, m, *a wolf.*
lux, lūcis, f. *light.*
Lўcurgus, i, m. *Lycurgus.*

Măgister, tri, m. *a master.*
măgistra, ae, f. *a mistress.*
magnĭtūdo, ĭnis, f. *size.*
magnus, a, um, adj. *great, large.*
māiōres, um, m. *ancestors.*
mălĕ, adv. *badly.*

mălĕdīco, xi, ctum, 3, *to abuse* (c. dat.)
mălum, i, n. *an evil.*
mălus, a, um, adj. *bad.*
mando, 1, *to command.*
măneo, si, sum, 2, *to remain.*
mănus, ūs, f. *a hand, band (of men).*
mărĕ, is, n. *the sea.*
Mars, tis, m. *Mars.*
māter, tris, f. *a mother.*
Mēcēnas, ātis, m. *Mecenas.*
mĕdĭcus, i, m. *a doctor.*
mĕdĭus, a, um, adj. *middle.*
mel, lis, n. *honey.*
mĕmĭni, def. *to remember.*
mĕmor, ŏris, adj. *mindful* (c. gen.)
mĕmŏria, ae, f. *memory.*
mĕmŏro, 1, *to call to memory, mention.*
mens, tis, f. *the mind.*
mentior, ītūs, 4, dep. *to lie.*
mercātor, ōris, m. *a merchant.*
Mercŭrius, i, m. *Mercurius.*
mergo, si, sum, 3, *to sink, drown.*
mīco, cui, 1, *to glitter, shine.*
mīlĕs, ĭtis, m. *a soldier.*
Mīlētus, i, f. *Miletus (a city in Asia Minor).*
mīlĭtia, ae, f. *warfare.*
mille, indcl. num. *a thousand.*
millia, ium, n. *thousands.*
mīna, ae, f. *a mina (about £4).*
mĭnĭmē, adv. *not at all.*
mīror, 1, dep. *to wonder at, admire.*
mīrus, a, um, adj. *strange, wonderful.*
mĭser, ĕra, ĕrum, adj. *wretched.*
mĭsĕret, uit, 2, impers. *it moves pity.*
mitis, e, adj. *gentle, mellow.*
mitto, mīsi, missum, 3, *to send.*
mŏdus, i, m. *a way, plan.*
moenia, ium, n. *town walls.*
mŏneo, ui, ĭtum, 2, *to warn.*
mons, tis, m. *a mountain.*
monstro, 1, *to show.*
mŏra, ae, f. *delay.*
mŏrior, mortuus, 3, dep. *to die.*
mŏror, 1, dep. *to delay.*

mors, tis, f. *death.*
mos, mōris, m. *a custom;* in plur. *manners.*
mox, adv. *soon.*
multĭtūdo, ĭnis, f. *a crowd, multitude.*
multo, 1, *to fine.*
multus, a, um, adj. *much.*
mūnio, īvi or ii, ītum, 4, *to fortify.*
mūnus, ĕris, n. *duty.*
mūrus, i, m. *a wall.*
mūto, 1, *to change.*

Nam, conj. *for.*
narro, 1, *to relate.*
nascor, nātus, 3, dep. *to be born.*
năto, 1, *to swim.*
nātūra, ae, f. *nature.*
nauta, ae, m. *a sailor.*
nāvĭgium, i, n. *a ship.*
nāvis, is, f. *a ship.*
nĕ, interrogative particle; *cannot be translated.*
nē, conj. *lest, that not, not.*
nĕfas, indcl. *wrong.*
nĕgōtium, i, n. *a business, thing.*
nēmo, nullius, *no one* (ne-homo).
nē quĭdem, *not even;* the word on which one wants to lay stress is put between *ne* and *quidem.*
Nĕro, ōnis, m. Nero.
neu, \
neve, / conj. *and not, neither, nor.*
nĭger, gra, grum, adj. *black.*
nĭhil, \
nīl, / indcl. *nothing.*
nix, nĭvis, f. *snow.*
nŏbĭlis, e, adj. *distinguished, noble.*
nŏceo, ui, ĭtum, 2, *to injure, hurt* (c. dat.)
nōlo, nōlui, nolle, *to be unwilling* (non-volo).
nōmen, ĭnis, n. *a name.*
nonnĕ, adv. *not; expecting answer, 'Yes?'*
nonnullus, a, um, adj. *some.*
noster, tra, trum, adj. *our.*
nox, noctis, f. *night.*
nūbo, psi, ptum, 3, *to take the veil for, marry* (c. dat.)

nullus, a, um, adj. *none.*
num, conj. *whether? expecting answer, 'No.'*
Nŭma, ae, m. *Numa.*
Nŭmantia, ae, f. *Numantia (a town in Spain).*
nŭmĕrus, i, m. *a number, quantity.*
numquis, numquid, pron. *any?*
nunquam, adv. *never.*
nuntius, i, m. *a messenger, news.*
nusquam, adv. *nowhere.*

Ob, prep. *on account of, for (c. acc.)*
obsĕs, ĭdis, c. *a hostage.*
occĭdo, cĭdi, cāsum, 3, *to fall, die* (ob-cado).
occīdo, cīdi, cīsum, 3, *to kill* (ob-caedo).
occŭpo, 1, *to seize, hold.*
occurro, curri, cursum, 3, *o meet* (ob-curro).
Ōcĕănus, i. m. *the Ocean.*
ōcĭus, adv. *more quickly.*
octāvus, a, um, adj. *eighth.*
ŏcŭlus, i, m. *an eye.*
ōdi, def. *to hate.*
ōlim, adv. *once upon a time, formerly.*
omnis, e, adj. *all.*
ŏnus, ĕris, n. *a burden.*
(ŏp,) ŏpem, ŏpis, ŏpe, f. *help;* in plur. *riches.*
ŏpĕra, ae, f. *work, care, assistance;* in plur. *workpeople.*
oppĭdum, i, n. *a town.*
opprĭmo, pressi, pressum, 3, *to overwhelm.*
ŏpus, ĕris, n. *work, need.*
ōrātio, ōnis, f. *a speech.*
ōrātor, ōris, m. *an orator.*
ordĭno, 1, *to set in order, draw up, dispose.*
ŏriundus, a, um, part. *descended from* (orior).
ōro, 1, *to pray, beseech.*
Orpheus, ei *or* ĕos, m. *Orpheus.*
ōtium, i, n. *rest.*
ōvum, i, n. *an egg.*

Paene, adv. *nearly, almost.*
pallium, i, n. *a cloak.*
pānis, is, m. *bread.*
pār, paris, adj. *equal.*
parco, pĕperci, parsum, 3, *to spare* (c. dat.)
pārens, tis, c. *a parent.*
pāreo, ui, 2, *to obey.*
păro, 1, *to prepare.*
părum, adv. *little.*
parvus, a, um, adj. *little, small.*
passim, adv. *everywhere.*
passus, ūs, m. *a step, pace;* mille passus, millia passuum, *a mile.*
pastor, ōris, m. *a shepherd.*
păter, tris, m. *a father.*
pătiens, tis, adj. *patient.*
pătior, passus, 3, dep. *to suffer, endure.*
patria, ae, f. *one's country, fatherland.*
pauper, ĕris, adj. *poor.*
pax, pācis, f. *peace.*
pĕcūnia, ae, f. *money.*
pĕcus, ŏris, n. *a herd.*
pĕcus, ŭdis, f. *a beast.*
Pĕlopŏnnēsus, i, f. *the Peloponnesus (now the Morea).*
Pĕlops, pis, m. *Pelops.*
pĕnes, prep. *in the power of (c. acc.)*
percŭtio, cussi, cussum, 3, *to strike* (per-quātio).
perdo, dĭdi, dĭtum, 3, *to lose, destroy.*
pĕreo, ii, ĭtum, 4, *to perish.*
perfĕro, tŭli, lātum, ferre, *to endure.*
Pĕricles, is, m. *Pericles.*
pĕrīcŭlum, i, n. *danger.*
pĕrītus, a, um, adj. *skilful, skilled in (c. gen.)*
Persa, ae, m. *a Persian.*
persuādeo, si, sum, 2, *to persuade* (c. dat.)
pervĕnio, vēni, ventum, 4, *to reach.*
pes, pĕdis, m. *the foot.*
pĕto, īvi *or* ii, ītum, 3, *to seek, make for.*
Philippus, i, m. *Philippus.*
phĭlŏsŏphia, ae, f. *philosophy.*

170 Latin-English Vocabulary.

phĭlŏsŏphus, i, m. *a philosopher.*
plăceo, ui, 2, *to please* (*c. dat.*)
Plăto, ōnis, m. *Plato.*
plausus, ūs, m. *applause.*
plebs, bis, f. *the common people.*
plēnus, a, um, adj. *full.*
pōcŭlum, i, n. *a cup.*
poenĭtet, uit, 2, impers. *it repents.*
Poenus, a, um, adj. *Carthaginian.*
poēta, ae, m. *a poet.*
Pompeius, i, m. *Pompeius.*
pōmum, i, n. *an apple, fruit.*
pondus, ĕris, n. *a weight.*
pōno, pŏsui, pŏsĭtum, 3, *to place, pitch.*
pons, tis, m. *a bridge.*
pŏpŭlus, i, m. *a people.*
porta, ae, f. *a door, gate.*
posco, pŏposci, 3, *to ask for, demand.*
possum, pŏtui, posse, *to be able.*
post, adv. and prep., *after, behind* (*c. acc.*)
postĕrus, a, um, adj. *next after.*
pŏtestas, ātis, f. *power.*
pŏtior, tītus, 4, dep. *to get possession of* (*c. abl. or gen.*)
praecĭpuē, adv. *especially.*
praeclārus, a, um, adj. *illustrious.*
praeda, ae, f. *booty.*
praefĭcio, fēci, fectum, 3, *to set over* (*c. dat.*)
praemitto, mīsi, missum, 3, *to send on* (*c. dat.*)
praemium, i, n. *a reward.*
praesĭdium, i, n. *a garrison, defence.*
praesto, stĭti, stĭtum, 1, *to stand out, pay, show, excel.*
praesum, fui, esse, *to be in command of.*
praeter, prep. *besides, except* (*c. acc.*)
praetĕreo, īvi *or* ii, ĭtum, 4, *to pass by.*
praetor, ōris, m. *a praetor* (*a Roman magistrate*).
prĕtiōsus, a, um, adj. *precious, valuable.*
prĕtium, i, n. *a price.*
primus, a, um, adj. *first.*
prŏcella, ae, f. *a storm.*
proelium, i, n. *a battle.*

profĭciscor, fectus, 3, dep. *to set out.*
prōgrĕdior, gressus, 3, dep. *to advance.*
prōmissus, a, um, adj. *long.*
prōmitto, mīsi, missum, 3, *to promise.*
prōmŏveo, mōvi, mōtum, 2, *to move forward.*
propter, prep. *on account of, near* (*c. acc.*)
prōsum, fui, esse, *to benefit* (*c. dat.*)
prōvincia, ae, f. *a province.*
proxĭmus, a, um, adj. *nearest.*
prūdens, tis, adj. *prudent* (pro— video).
pŭdet, uit, 2, *it shames.*
pudor, ōris, m. *modesty.*
puella, ae, f. *a girl.*
puer, ĕri, m. *a boy.*
pugna, ae, f. *a fight, battle.*
pugno, 1, *to fight.*
pulcher, chra, chrum, adj. *beautiful.*
pŭto, 1, *to think.*
Pȳrĕnaei, ōrum, m. *the Pyrenees.*

Quadraginta, indcl. num. *forty.*
quālis, e, adj. *of what kind, of such a kind.*
quando, conj. *when.*
quantus, a, um, adj. *how great, as great.*
quātuor, indcl. num. *four.*
quĕ, conj. *and, both.*
quīdam, quaedam, quiddam, *or* quoddam, pron. *a certain one.*
quĭdem, adv. *indeed.*
quiēs, ētis, f. *rest.*
Quinctius, i, m. *Quinctius.*
quinquāgintā, indcl. num. *fifty.*
quinquĕ, indcl. num. *five.*
quintus, a, um, adj. *fifth.*
Quĭrītēs, ium, m. *the Quirites* (*a name of the Roman people*).
quīs, quā, quĭd, *or* qui, quae, quod, pron. *any.*
quĭs, quid, *or* qui, quae, quod, pron. *who?*

Latin-English Vocabulary. 171

quisnam, quaenam, quidnam, or quodnam, pron. *who pray?*
quisquam, quaequam, quidquam, or quodquam, pron. *any, any one, anything.*
quisque, quaeque, quidque, or quodque, pron. *each.*
quivis, quaevis, quidvis *or* quodvis, pron. *any you will.*
quondam, adv. *once upon a time, formerly.*
quŏque, conj. *also.*
quŏt, indcl. *how many, as.*
quŏtidiē, adv. *daily.*
quŏtus, a, um, adj. *which (in order)?*

Rado, si, sum, 3, *to shave, scrape.*
rătio, ōnis, f. *a reason, plan.*
rătis, is, f. *a ship.*
rĕcĭpio, cēpi, ceptum, 3, *to retake, take back, betake* (capio).
rĕcĭto, 1, *to read aloud.*
rĕcordor, 1, dep. *to remember.*
reddo, dĭdi, dĭtum, 3, *to give back, restore.*
rĕdeo, ĭvi *or* ii, ĭtum, 4, *to return.*
rēgīna, ae, f. *a queen.*
rēgio, ōnis, f. *a region.*
rĕgo, xi, ctum, 3, *to rule.*
regrĕdior, gressus, 3, dep. *to return.*
Rēgŭlus, i, m. *Regulus.*
rĕlinquo, līqui, lictum, 3, *to leave, abandon.*
rellĭgio, ōnis, f. *religion, superstition.*
rĕmĕdium, i, n. *a remedy, cure.*
Rĕmus, i, m. *Remus.*
rĕpello, pŭli, pulsum, 3, *to repel.*
rĕpĕrio, rĕpĕri, rĕpertum, 4, *to find, discover.*
rĕquiesco, ēvi, 3, *to rest.*
res, rei, f. *a thing.*
rĕsisto, restĭti, restĭtum, 3, *to resist* (c. dat.).
respondeo, spondi, spousum, 2, *to answer* (c. dat.).

respublĭca, reipublĭcae, f. *a republic, state.*
rex, rēgis, m. *a king.*
Rhēnus, i, m. *the Rhine.*
rĭdeo, si, sum, 2, *to laugh.*
rŏgo, 1, *to ask.*
Rōma, ae, f. *Rome.*
Rōmānus, a, um, adj. *Roman.*
Rōmŭlus, i, m. *Romulus.*
Rŭbĭco, ōnis, m. *the Rubicon (a river in North Italy).*
rus, rūris, n. *the country.*

Sabini, orum, m. *the Sabines (a people of Central Italy).*
săcer, cra, crum, adj. *sacred.*
saepĕ, adv. *often.*
săgitta, ae, f. *an arrow.*
Săguntum, i, n. *Saguntum (a town in Spain).*
sălūs, ūtis, f. *safety, health.*
sălūto, 1, *to salute.*
Samnītes, ium, m. *the Samnites (a people of Central Italy).*
sanguis, ĭnis, m. *blood.*
săpiens, tis, adj. *wise.*
săpientia, ac, f. *wisdom.*
sătis, adv. *enough.*
sătisfăcio, fēci, factum, 3, *to satisfy* (c. dat.)
saxum, i, n. *a stone.*
scĕlus, ĕris, n. *a crime, wickedness.*
schŏla, ae, f. *a school.*
scio, scīvi *or* scii, scītum, 4, *to know.*
Scipio, ōnis, m. *Scipio.*
scŏpŭlus, i, m. *a rock.*
scrība, ae, m. *a clerk, secretary.*
Scȳtha, ae, m. *a Scythian (inhabitant of parts of North Europe and Asia).*
se, acc. no nom., pron. *self.*
sĕcūris, is, f. *an axe.*
sĕdeo, sēdi, sessum, 2, *to sit.*
sēdes, is, f. *a seat, home.*
semper, adv. *always.*
sĕnātus, ūs, m. *the senate.*
sĕnex, sĕnis, adj. *old;* as subst. *an old man.*

Latin-English Vocabulary.

sententia, ae, f. *an opinion.*
septemvir, i, m. *one of a commission of seven.*
Sĕquăni, ōrum, m. *the Sequani (a people of Gaul).*
sĕquor, cūtus, 3, dep. *to follow.*
servio, ii, ītum, 4, *to serve (c. dat.)*
servĭtūs, ūtis, f. *slavery.*
servus, i, m. *a slave.*
sex, indcl. num. *six.*
Sextus, i, m. *Sextus.*
Sĭcĭlia, ae, f. *Sicily.*
sīdus, ĕris, n. *a constellation, star.*
signum, i, n. *a sign, signal, standard.*
sĭmĭlis, e, adj. *like.*
sĭmĭlĭtūdo, ĭnis, f. *a likeness.*
sĭnĕ, prep. *without (c. abl.)*
Socrătes, is, m. *Socrates.*
sōl, sōlis, m. *the sun.*
solātium, i, n. *a solace, relief.*
sŏlĕo, ĭtus, 2, dep. *to be wont.*
sōlus, a, um, adj. *alone, lonely.*
solvo, vi, ūtum, 3, *to loose, pay.*
somnium, i, n. *a dream.*
sŏrŏr, ōris, f. *a sister.*
Sparta, ae, f. *Sparta (capital of Laconia in South Greece).*
spes, ei, f. *hope.*
sto, stĕti, stătum, 1, *to stand.*
stringo, nxi, ctum, 3, *to draw.*
stŭdeo, ui, 2, *to pay attention to, be fond of.*
stŭdiōsus, a, um, adj. *fond of.*
stultĭtia, ae, f. *folly.*
stultus, a, um, adj. *foolish.*
suāvis, e, adj. *sweet.*
sub, prep. *under (c. acc. and abl.)*
subsĭdium, i, n. *help.*
succēdo, cessi, cessum, 3, *to advance.*
Sulla, ae, m. *Sulla.*
sum, fui, esse, *to be.*
summus, a, um, adj. *top, highest* (superlative of *superus*).
sūmo, sumpsi, sumptum, 3, *to take, take up.*
sŭperbus, a, um, adj. *proud.*
sŭpĕrus, a, um, adj. *high.*
supplex, ĭcĭs, adj. *submissive, suppliant.*

supplĭcium, i, n. *punishment, torture.*
suppōno, pŏsui, pŏsĭtum, 3, *to place under.*
sustĭneo, ui, tentum, 2, *to support, endure.*
suus, a, um, adj. *his, her, its, their, own.*

T *before proper names stands for* Titus.
taedet, uit, 2, impers. *it wearies, it irks.*
talis, e, adj. *such, such as, as.*
tam, adv. *so.*
Tamĕsis, is, m. *the Thames.*
Tănais, is, m. *the Don (a river in South Russia).*
tango, tĕtĭgi, tactum, 3, *to touch.*
Tarquĭnius, i, m. *Tarquinius.*
tectum, i, n, *a roof, house.*
tēlum, i, n. *a dart.*
tĕmĕrĭtas, ātis, f. *rashness.*
templum, i, n. *a temple.*
tĕneo, ui, tentum, 2, *to hold.*
terra, ae, f. *the earth, land.*
terrŏr, ōris, m. *fear.*
tertius, a, um, adj. *third.*
Thēbae, ārum, f. *Thebes.*
Thĕmistocles, is, m. *Themistocles.*
tĭmeo, ui, 2, *to fear.*
tĭmŏr, ōris, m. *fear.*
tŏt, indcl. adv. *so many.*
tōtus, a, um, adj. *whole.*
trādo, dĭdi, dĭtum, 3, *to hand over, deliver up* (trans—do).
trăho, xi, ctum, 3, *to draw, drag.*
traiĭcio, iēci, iectum, 3, *to throw across, cross* (iacio).
trans, prep. *across (c. acc.)*
transdūco, xi, ctum, 3, *to lead across.*
transeo, ĭvi or ii, ĭtum, 4, *to cross.*
transfīgo, xi, xum, 3, *to pierce.*
transĭlio, ui, sultum, 4, *to leap across.*
transĭtus, ūs, m. *a crossing.*
transvĕho, xi, ctum, 3, *to bring across.*
trĕcentī, ae, a, num. *three hundred.*

Latin-English Vocabulary. 173

tremo, ui, ĭtum, 3, *to tremble.*
tres, tria, num. *three.*
trĭbūnus, i, m. *a tribune (a Roman magistrate or officer).*
trĭduum, i, n. *a space of three days* (tres—dies).
tristis, e, adj. *sad.*
Troia, ae, f. *Troy (a city on the North-west coast of Asia Minor.)*
tu, tui, pron. *thou.*
tum, adv. *then.*
turbo, 1, *to disturb, trouble.*
turpis, e, adj. *disgraceful, ugly.*
turris, is, f. *a tower.*
tŭus, a, um, adj. *thy, thine.*
tўrannus, i, m. *a despot.*

Ullus, a, um, adj. *any.*
ultĭmus, a, um, adj. *last.*
Ŭlysses, is, m. *Ulysses.*
undĭque, adv. *from all sides.*
ūnĭversus, a, um, adj. *whole, all, entire.*
unquam, adv. *ever.*
ūnus, a, um, num. *one.*
urbs, bis, f. *a city.*
ursus, i, m. *a bear.*
usus, ūs, m. *use, need.*
ŭter, tra, trum, pron. *which of the two?*
uterque, utraque, utrumque, pron. *both, either.*
ūtĭlis, e, adj. *useful.*
ūtŏr, ūsus, 3, dep. *to use (c. abl.)*
utrinque, adv. *on both sides.*
utrum, conj. *whether.*
uxŏr, ōris, f. *a wife.*

Vaco, 1, *to be at leisure for (c. dat.)*
vădum, i, n. *a shallow.*
văleo, ui, 2, *to be well, strong.*
vălĭdus, a, um, adj. *well, strong.*
vallis, is, f. *a valley.*
vallum, i, n. *a palisade.*
vasto, 1, *to lay waste, ravage.*
vĕ, conj. *or.*
vel, conj. *or.*

vēlox, ōcis, adj. *swift.*
vēnātŏr, ōris, m. *a hunter.*
vendo, dĭdi, dĭtum, 3, *to sell.*
vĕnēnum, i, n. *poison.*
vĕnĕror, 1, *to reverence.*
vĕnia, ae, f. *pardon.*
vĕnio, vēni, ventum, 4, *to come.*
ventus, i, m. *a wind.*
Vĕnus, ĕris, f. *Venus (the goddess of Love).*
vēr, vēris, n. *spring.*
verbum, i, n. *a word.*
vescor, 3, dep. *to eat, live on (c. abl.).*
Vesta, ae, f. *Vesta.*
vester, tra, trum, adj. *your.*
vestis, is, f. *a dress.*
via, ae, f. *a way.*
victŏr, ōris, m. *a conqueror.*
victōria, ae, f. *victory.*
vīcus, i, m. *a street, hamlet.*
vĭdeo, vīdi, vīsum, 2, *to see.*
vĭdeor, vīsus, 2, dep. *to seem.*
vīgintī, indcl. num. *twenty.*
vīlis, e, adj. *cheap.*
vincio, vinxi, vinctum, 4, *to bind.*
vinco, vīci, victum, 3, *to conquer.*
vīnum, i, n. *wine.*
vir, vĭri, m. *a man.*
virgo, ĭnis, f. *a virgin.*
vĭrĭdis, e, adj. *green.*
virtūs, ūtis, f. *virtue, courage.*
vīs, vim, vi, f. *force, violence;* in plur. vīres, ium, *strength.*
vīta, ae, f. *life.*
vīvo, xi, ctum, 3, *to live.*
vix, adv. *hardly, scarcely.*
vŏco, 1, *to call, summon.*
vŏlo, 1, *to fly.*
vŏlo, vŏlui, velle, *to wish, be willing.*
voltus, *see* vultus.
vŏluptas, ātis, f. *pleasure.*
vox, vōcis, f. *a voice.*
Vulcānus, i, m. *Vulcanus (the god of fire).*
vulnĕro, 1, *to wound.*
vulnus, ĕris, n. *a wound.*
vulpes, is, f. *a fox.*
vultus, ūs, m. *the face.*

ENGLISH-LATIN VOCABULARY.

Abhor, abhorreo, ui, 2.
abandon, rĕlinquo, līqui, lictum, 3; dēsĕro, rui, rtum, 3.
able, to be, possum, pŏtui, posse.
abode, sēdes, is, f.
abound, ăbundo, 1.
about, circum (c. acc. and adv.);. *nearly*, fĕre; *concerning*, de (c. abl.)
above, sŭper (c. acc. and abl.); *from above*, dēsŭper, adv.
abroad, fŏris.
absent, to be, absum, fui, esse.
abstain from, abstĭneo, ui, tentum, 2 (c. abl.)
abundantly, ăbundanter.
Acca, Acca, ae, f.
accept, accĭpio, cēpi, ceptum, 3.
acceptable, grātus, a, um.
access, ădĭtus, ūs, m.
accident, cāsus, ūs, m.; *by accident*, casu; forte (adv.)
accompany, cŏmĭtor, 1, dep.
accomplish, perfĭcio, fēci, fectum, 3.
according to, ex (c. abl.)
accordingly, ĭtăque, ĭgĭtur (adv.)
accusation, crimen, inis, n.
accuse, accūso, 1.
accused, the, reus, i, m.
accuser, accūsātor, oris, m.
accustomed, to be, sŏleo, sŏlĭtus, 2, dep.
Achilles, Achilles, is, m.
acknowledge, agnosco, nōvi, nĭtum, 3.
acquainted with, to be. See *to know*.

acquire, to, acquiro, sīvi, sītum, 3; ădĭpiscor, ădeptus, 3, dep.
acquit, absolvo, vi, ūtum, 3.
across, trans (c. acc.)
act, an, factum, i, n.
act, to, ago, ēgi, actum, 3.
Actium, Actium, i, n.
active, cĕler, is, e.
actor, an, mīmus, i, m.
adapted, aptus, a, um.
add, addo, dĭdi, dĭtum, 3.
address, allŏquor, cūtus, 3, dep.
admire, admīror, 1, dep.
admiration, admīrātio, onis, f.
admit, admitto, mīsi, missum, 3; (*confess*) confĭteor, fessus, 2, dep.
admonish, admŏneo, ui, ĭtum, 2.
admonition, admonĭtio, onis, f.
adopt, ădopto, 1.
adorn, orno, 1.
advance, to, progrĕdior, gressus, 3, dep.; prōcēdo, cessi, cessum, 3.
advantage, commŏdum, i, n.
adversary, adversārius, i, m.
adverse, inīquus, a, um.
advice, consĭlium, i, n.
advise, mŏneo, ui, ĭtum, 2.
aedile, aedīlis, is, m.
aedileship, aedīlĭtas, ātis, f.
Aegean, the, Aegeum mare.
Aemilius, Aemilius, i, m.
Aetna, Aetna, ae, f.
affability, făcĭlĭtas, ātis, f.
affair, res, rei, f.
affection, carĭtas, ātis, f.; *filial affection*, pĭĕtas, ātis, f.
affectionate, cārus, a, um; pius, a, um.

English-Latin Vocabulary. 175

affirm, assĕvēro, 1; affirmo, 1.
afflict, ango, xi, ctum, 3; vexo, 1.
afford, praebeo, ui, ĭtum, 2.
Africa, Afrĭca, ae, f.
after, post (*c. acc.*); ex (*c. abl.*)
afterwards, posteā.
again, rursus, ĭtĕrum.
against, adversus, contra, in (*all c. acc.*)
against one's will, invītus, a, um.
Agamemnon, Agămemnon, ŏnis, m.
age, aetas, ātis, f.; *old age*, sĕnectūs, ūtis, f.
age, an, saecŭlum, i. n.
agree, consentio, sensi, sensum, 4.
agreeably to, congruenter.
agreed, concors, cordis, adj.
agreement, conscnsus, ūs, m.
Agrippa, Agrippa, ae, m.
Agrippina, Agrippīna, ae, f.
aid, auxĭlium, i, n.
aid, to, auxĭlior.
air, aër, aëris, m.
alarm, an, tŭmultus, ūs, m.
alarm, to, excĭto, 1.
Alban, Albānus, a, um.
Alexander, Alexander, dri, m.
Alexandria, Alexandria, ae, f.
alliance, sociĕtas, ātis, f.
alien, ălĭēnus, a, um.
alike, părĭter.
alive, vīvus, a, um.
all, omnis, e; *from all sides*, undĭque; *in all*, omnīno; *on all sides*, passim.
allow, sino, sīvi, sĭtum, 3; *it is allowed*, lĭcet, uit, 2, impers.
ally, sŏcius, i, m.
almost, paene, fĕre.
alone, sōlus, a, um.
along, per (*c. acc.*)
Alps, Alpes, ium, f.
already, iam.
also, ĕt, ĕtiam.
altar, āra, ae, f.
altogether, omnīno.
always, semper.
ambassador, lēgātus, i, m.
ambush, insĭdiae, ārum, f.
America, Amerĭca, ae, f.

Ammon, Ammon, ōnis, m.
among, inter (*c. acc.*)
Amulius, Amūlius, i, m.
amuse, delecto, 1.
Anacharsis, Anacharsis, is, m.
ancestors, maiores, um, m.
ancestral, ăvītūs, a, um; patrius, a, um.
ancient, antīquus, a, um; priscus, a, um; vĕtus, ĕris.
Ancus, Ancus, i, m.
and, et; atquĕ; quĕ.
angry, to be, irascor, īrātus, 3, dep.
angry, īrātus, a, um.
animal, ănĭmal, alis, n.; *wild animal*, fĕra, ae, f.
announce, nuntio, 1.
annoy, to, vexo, 1.
annually, quŏtannis.
another, ălius, a, ud; *the other*, alter, ĕra, ĕrum.
answer, to, respondeo, di, nsum, 2.
answer, an, responsum, i, n.
ant, formīca, ae, f.
Antiochus, Antiŏchus, i, m.
antiquity, antīquĭtas, ātis, f.
Antisthenes, Antisthĕnes, is, m.
Antonius, Antōnĭus, i, m.
any, ullus, a, um; quisquam, quaequam, quicquam *or* quodquam (*only after negatives*); quis, qua, quid; *any you please*, quilĭbet, quaelĭbet, quidlĭbet *or* quodlĭbet.
anywhere, usquam.
Apollo, Apollo, ĭnis, m.
apparel, vestītus, ūs, m.; cultus, ūs, m.
appeal, prōvŏco, 1.
appear, vĭdeor, vīsus, 2, dep.; appāreo, ui, 2.
appearance, spĕcies, ei, f.
appease, plāco, 1.
Appian way, the, Appia via.
Appius, Appius, i, m.
applause, plausus, ūs, m.
apple, pōmum, i, n.
apply, appōno, pŏsui, pŏsĭtum, 3; adhĭbeo, ui, ĭtum, 2.

appoint, constĭtuo, ui, ūtum, 3.
approach, to, ădeo, ii, ĭtum; advĕnio, vĕni, ventum, 4.
approach, an, ădĭtus, ūs, m.
approve, prŏbo, 1.
apt, aptus, a, um.
Apulia, Apūlia, ae, f.
archer, săgittārius, i, m.
Archidamus, Archĭdāmus, i, m.
Archimedes, Archĭmēdes, is, m.
ardour, ardor, ōris, m.
Argolis, Argŏlis, ĭdis, f.
Argos, Argi, ōrum, m.
Arion, Arion, ŏnis, m.
Ariovistus, Ariovistus, i, m.
arise, ŏrior, ortus, 4, dep.; surgo, surrexi, surrectum, 3.
Aristippus, Aristippus, i, m.
arm, an, brachium, i, n.
arm, to, armo, 1.
armed, armātus, a, um.
armour-bearer, armĭger, ĕri, m.
arms, arma, ōrum, n.
army, exercĭtus, ūs, m.
around, circum (*prep. c. acc. and adv.*)
Arpinum, Arpīnum, i, n.
arrival, adventus, ūs, m.
arrive, advĕnio, vēni, ventum, 4.
arrow, săgitta, ae, f.
art, ars, tis, f.
artisan, artĭfex, ĭcis, c.
as, ut; *as if*, tanquam, quasi; *as long as*, dōnĕc; *as far as*, tĕnus (*c. abl.*)
ascend, ascendo, ndi, nsum, 3.
ashamed, to be, poenĭtet, uit, 2 (*impers.*)
Asia, Asia, ae, f.
ask, rŏgo, 1; *ask for*, pĕto, ĭvi or ii, ĭtum, 3, ōro, 1.
aspect, vultus, ūs, m; aspectus, ūs, m.
ass, ăsĭnus, i, m.
assault, to, oppugno, 1.
assault, an, impĕtus, us, m.
assemble, convĕnio, vēni, ventum, 4 (*intrans.*); convŏco, 1 (*trans.*)
assembly, concĭlium, i, n.
assign, dēfĕro, tŭli, lātum, ferre.

assist, auxĭlior, 1, dep.; subvĕnio, vēni, ventum, 4 (*c. dat.*)
assistance, auxĭlium, i, n.
astonished, attŏnĭtus, a, um.
astonishment, admīrātio, ōnis, f.
at, apud (*c. acc.*); ad (*c. acc.*)
at all, omnīno.
at any rate, saltem.
at length, tandem, aliquando.
at once, ūnā; simul, statim.
Athens, Athēnae, ārum, f.
Athenian, Athēniensis, e.
Atratinus, Atratīnus, i, m.
attach, allĭgo, 1.
attack, to, aggrĕdior, gressus, 3, dep.; oppugno, 1 (*to attack a town*).
attack, an, impĕtus, ūs, m.
Attalus, Attălus, i, m.
attempt, to, cōnor, 1, dep.
attempt, an, conātus, ūs, m.
attendant, 'sătcllĕs, ĭtis, c.
attention, to pay, ŏpĕram dăre.
attentively, intente.
Attica, Attĭca, ae, f.
attract, trăho, xi, ctum, 3.
Atys, Atys, Atyos, m.
audacity, audācia, ae, f.
augur, augur, ŭris, m.
augury, augurium, i, n.; ōmĕn, ĭnis, n.
Augustus, Augustus, i, m.
auspice, auspĭcium, i, n.
auspices, to take, auspĭcor, 1, dep.
author, auctor, ōris, m.
authority, auctorĭtas, ātis, f.
autumn, auctumnus, i, m.
auxiliary, auxĭliārius, a, um.
auxiliaries, auxĭlia, orum, n.
avail, văleo, ui, 2.
avarice, ăvārĭtia, ae, f.
avaricious, ăvārus, a, um.
avenge, ulciscor, ultus, 3, dep.
avoid, vīto, 1; fŭgio, fūgi, ĭtum, 3.
await, expecto, 1; mǎneo, nsi, nsum, 2.
awake, expergiscor, perrectus, 3, dep.

English-Latin Vocabulary. 177

aware of, gnārus, a, um (c. gen.)
awful, dīrus, a, um.
axe, secūris, is, f.

Bacchus, Bacchus, i, m.
back, tergum, i, n.
bad, mălus, a, um; badly, mălē.
baggage, impĕdimenta, ōrum, n.
bait, esca, ae, f.
banish, pello, pepŭli, pulsum, 3;
 expello, pŭli, pulsum, 3.
barbarian, barbărus, a, um.
barbarous, fĕrus, a, um.
barber, tonsor, ōris, m.
bare, nūdus, a, um.
bark, to, latro, 1.
barren, stĕrĭlis, e.
base, turpis, e.
baseness, turpĭtūdo, ĭnis, f.
basket, corbis, is, f.
bat, vespertīlio, ōnis, m.
bathe, lăvo, lāvi, lōtum, 1.
battle, proelium, i, n.; pugna, ae, f.
bay, laurus, i or ūs, f.
beak, rostrum, i, n.
bear, to, fĕro, tŭli, lātum, ferre.
bear, a, ursus, i, m.
beard, barba, ae, f.
beast, bestia, ae, f.; of burden, iūmentum, i, n.
beat, caedo, cĕcĭdi, caesum, 3.
beaten, to be, vāpŭlo, 1.
beautiful, pulcher, chra, chrum.
beauty, forma, ae, f.; pulchritūdo, ĭnis, f.
because, quia; quod.
become, fio, factus, fĭĕri; befit, dĕceo, ui, 2.
bed, lectus, i, m.
bed-chamber, cŭbĭcŭlum, i, n.
befall, contingo, tigi, tactum, 3 (c. dat.)
befit, see to become.
before (conj.), priusquam, antĕquam; (prep.) ante (c. acc.)
beforehand, ante.
beg, ōro, 1.
beggar, mendīcus, i, m.
 B.L.W.

begin, incĭpio, cēpi, ceptum, 3;
 coepi, def.; —a battle, committo, mīsi, missum, 3.
beginning, ĭnĭtium, i, n.
behind, post (c. acc.)
behold, aspĭcio, exi, ectum, 3;
 video, vīdi, visum, 3.
behoves, it, ŏportet, uit, 2; dĕcet, uit, 2.
believe, credo, dĭdi, dĭtum, 3 (c. dat. of person).
Belgae, Belgae, ārum, m.
bell, tintinnābŭlum, i, n.
Bellona, Bellōna, ae, f.
belly, venter, tris, m.
below, infrā (c. acc.)
benefactor, bĕnĕfactor, ōris, m.
benefit, to, bĕnĕfăcio, fēci, factum, 3; prōsum, fui, esse (c. dat.)
benefit, a, bĕnĕfactum, i, n.
benevolence, bĕnĕvŏlentia, ae, f.
beseech, ōro, 1.
beside, iuxtā (c. acc.)
besides (prep.) praeter (c. acc.);
 (adv.) praetĕreā.
besiege, obsĭdeo, sēdi, sessum, 2.
best, optĭmus, a, um.
betake, confĕro, tŭli, lātum, ferre;
 rĕcĭpio, cēpi, ceptum, 3.
betray, prōdo, dĭdi, dĭtum, 3.
betroth, spondeo, spŏpondi, sponsum, 3.
better, mĕlior, us.
between, inter (c. acc.)
bewail, plōro, 1.
beware, căveo, cāvi, cautum, 2.
beyond, ultra (c. acc.); practer (c. acc.)
big, see large.
bill, rostrum, i, n.
bind, vincio, vinxi, vinctum, 4;
 dēlīgo, 1.
bird, ăvis, is, f.
birth, partus, ūs, m; noble birth, nōbĭlĭtas, ātis, f.
bison, ūrus, i, m.
bite, a, morsus, ūs, m.
bite, to, mordeo, mŏmordi, morsum, 2.
bitter, ăcerbus, a, um.

M

black, nĭger, gra, grum; āter, tra, trum.
Black Sea, Pontus Euxīnus.
blame, culpa, ac, f.
blame, to, culpo.
blind, caecus, a, um.
blindness, caecĭtas, ātis, f.
blood, bloodshed, sanguis, ĭnis, m.; cruor, ōris, m.
bloodstained, cruentātus, a, um.
blot out, dēleo, ēvi, ētum, 2.
blow, ictus, ūs, m.
blue, caerŭleus, a, um.
blush, ērŭbesco, ui, 3.
boar, ăper, pri, m.
board, to, conscendo, di, sum, 3.
board, a, tăbŭla, ae, f.
boast, glōrior, 1, dep.; iacto, 1.
boat, cymba, ae, f.
body, corpus, ŏris, n.; *dead body*, cădāver, ĕris, n.
Boeotia, Boeōtia, ae, f.
bold, audax, ācis; fortis, e.
bone, os, ossis, n.
book, lĭber, bri, m.
boot, calceus, i, m.
booty, praeda, ae, f.
border, fīnis, is, m.
born, to be, nascor, nātus, 3 dep.
bosom, sĭnus, ūs, m.
both (adj.), ambo, ae, o; *(conj.)* et.
bottle, ūter, tris, m.
bottom, īmus, a, um, *adj.*
bound, boundary, fīnis, is, m.; termĭnus, i, m.
bow, arcus, ūs, m.
boy, puer, ĕri, m.
boyhood, puĕrĭtia, ae, f.
boxer, pŭgil, ĭlis, m.
bracelet, armilla, ae, f.
brag, iacto, 1.
branch, rāmus, i, m.
brandish, quătio, quassi, quassum, 3.
brave, fortis, e; *bravely*, fortĭter.
bravery, virtūs, ūtis, f.
bread, pānis, is, m.
break, frango, frēgi, fractum, 3; rumpo, rūpi, ruptum, 3.

break out, ērumpo, rūpi, ruptum, 3.
break down, dīruo, ui, ūtum, 3.
breast, pectus, ŏris, n.
breastplate, lōrīca, ae, f.
breath, ănĭma, ae, f.; halĭtus, us, m.
breed, ălo, ui, altum, 3.
bridge, pons, ntis, m.
bright, clārus, a, um; splendĭdus, a, um.
bring, affĕro, attŭli, allātum, afferre.
bring about, effĭcio, fēci, fectum, 3.
bring back, rĕdūco, duxi, ductum, 3.
bring down, dēdūco, duxi, ductum, 3.
bring in, infĕro, tŭli, illātum, ferre; introduco, xi, ctum, 3.
bring up, ēdūco, 1.
bring out, ēdūco, duxi, ductum, 3.
Britain, Britannia, ae, f.
brother, frāter, tris, m.
brow, frons, ntis, f.
Brutus, Brūtus, i, m.
build, aedĭfĭco, 1.
building, aedĭfĭcium, i, n.
bulk, magnĭtūdo, ĭnis, f.; mōles, is, f.
bull, taurus, i, m.
bundle, fascis, is, m.
burden, ŏnus, ĕris, n.
burn, uro, ussi, ustum, 3 (*trans.*); ardeo, arsi, arsum, 2 (*intrans.*)
burning, a, incendium, i, n.
bury, sĕpĕlio, ivi, sĕpultum, 4.
bush, dūmus, i, m.
bushel, mŏdius, i, m.
business, res, rei, f.; nĕgōtium, i, n.
but, sed; at; autem.
butcher, carnĭfex, ĭcis, m.
but that, quin (*only with negatives*).
buy, ĕmo, ēmi, emptum, 3.
buyer, emptor, ōris, m.

Cadiz, Gādes, ium, f.
Caesar, Caesar, ăris, m.
cage, căvea, ae, f.
Caius, Caius, i, m.
calamity, călămĭtas, ātis, f.; damnum, i, n.

English-Latin Vocabulary.

call, vŏco, 1.
call to witness, testor, 1, dep.
Callisthenes, Callisthĕnes, is, m.
calm, sĕrēnus, a, um; plăcĭdus, a, um.
Camillus, Cămillus, i, m.
camp, castra, ōrum, n.
Campania, Campānia, ae, f.
can, see *able*.
Caninius, Canīnius, i, m.
Cannae, Cannae, ārum, f.
canton, pāgus, i, m.
cap, pĭleus, i, m.
capital, căput, ĭtis, n.
Capitol, Căpĭtolium, i, n.
captive, captīvus, a, um.
capture, to, căpio, cēpi, captum, 3.
Capua, Căpua, ae, f.
car, currus, ūs, m.
carcass, cădāver, ĕris, n.
care, cūra, ae, f.
care, to, cūro, 1.
care, to take, ŏpĕram dăre.
carefully, dīlĭgenter.
careless, neglĭgens, ntis.
carelessness, incūria, ae, f.; neglĭgentia, ae, f.
carry, porto, 1; vĕho, vexi, vectum, 3.
carry down, dēfĕro, tŭli, lātum, ferre.
carry off, aufĕro, abstŭli, ablātum, auferre; răpio, ui, ptum, 3.
carry off (a victory), rĕporto, 1.
cart, plaustrum, i, n.
Carthage, Carthāgo, ĭnis, f.
Carthaginian, Poenus, a, um.
Casilinum, Casĭlīnum, i, n.
cast, iăcio, iēci, iactum, 3; mitto, mīsi, missum, 3.
cast down, dēmitto, mīsi, missum, 3.
cat, fēles, is, f.
catapult, cătăpulta, ae, f.
catch, căpio, cēpi, captum, 3.
Catiline, Catilīna, ae, m.
cattle, pĕcus, ŏris, n.
Caudine Forks, Furcŭlae Caudīnae, f.
cause, caussa, ae, f.

cause, to, efficio, fēci, fectum, 3.
cautiously, caute.
cavalry, ĕquĭtes, um, m; ĕquĭtātus, ūs, m.
cease, dēsĭno, sīvi *or* sii, situm, 3.
celebrate, cĕlebro, 1.
celebrated, cĕlĕber, bris, bre; insignis, e; praeclārus, a, um.
centaur, centaurus, i, m.
centurion, centūrio, ōnis, m.
century, centūria, ae, f.
Ceres, Cĕres, ĕris, f.
ceremony, rītus, ūs, m.
certain, certus, a, um; *a certain person*, quidam.
certainly, immo.
chain, cătēna, ae, f.; vincŭlum, i, n.
challenge, to, provŏco, 1.
chamber, cŭbĭcŭlum, i, n.
champion, vindex, ĭcis, c.
chance, sors, tis, f.; cāsus, ūs, m.
chance (adj.), fortuītus, a, um.
change, mūtātio, ōnis, f.; vĭces, ium, f.
change (money), nummus, i, m.
change, to, mūto, 1.
character, mōres, um, m; indŏles, is, f.
charge, a, impĕtus, ūs, m.
charge, to, impĕtum făcere.
charm, dēlecto, 1.
chariot, currus, ūs, m.; essĕdum, i, n.
charioteer, aurīga, ae, m.
cheap, vīlis, e.
check, reprĭmo, pressi, pressum, 3; impĕdio, ivi *or* ii, ītum, 4.
cheese, cāseus, i, m.
cherish, fŏveo, fōvi, fōtum, 2.
chew, mando, di, sum, 3.
chicken, pullus, i, m.
chief, dux, cis, m.
chief men, prīmōres, um, m.
chiefly, maxĭme; imprīmis.
child, infans, ntis, c.
children, lĭbĕri, orum, m.
chin, mentum, i, n.
Chinese, Sēres, ae, m.
choice, ēlectio, ōnis, f.
choose, ēlĭgo, lēgi, lectum, 3.

English-Latin Vocabulary.

Christian, Christiānus, a, um.
Cicero, Cicĕro, ōnis, m.
Cincinnatus, Cincinnatus, i, m.
circuit, ambĭtus, ūs, m.
circus, circus, i, m.
circumstance, res, rei, f.
citadel, arx, cis, f.
citizen, cīvis, is, c.
city, urbs, bis, f.
civil, cīvīlis, e.
claim, posco, pŏposci, 3; vindĭco, 1.
clamour for, postŭlo, 1.
claw, unguis, is, m.
Claudia, Claudia, ae, f.
Claudius, Claudius, i, m.
clean, purgo, 1.
clear, clārus, a, um.
clear, it is, constat, 1, impers.
clemency, clēmentia, ae, f.
Cleopatra, Cleopatra, ae, f.
clerk, scrība, ae, m.
clever, pĕrītus, a, um; hăbĭlis, e.
climb, scando, di, sum, 3.
cling-to, amplector, plexus, 3, dep.
cloak, păludāmentum, i, n.
Clodius, Clodius, i, m.
Cloelia, Cloelia, ae, f.
close, claudo, si, sum, 3.
closely, arcte.
close to, prŏpe (c. acc.)
close quarters, at, comĭnus.
cloth, pannus, i, m.
clothe, vestio, īvi *or* ii, ītum, 4.
clothing, vestītūs, ūs, m.
cloud, nūbes, is, f.
club, clāva, ae, f.
Clypea, Clypea, ae, f.
Clytemnestra, Clytemnestra, ae, f.
coast, lītus, ŏris, n.; ōra, ae, f.
coat, vestis, is, f.
cobbler, sūtor, ōris, m.
cock, gallus, i, m.
Cocles, Coclĕs, Ĭtis, m.
coin, nummus, i, m.
cold, frīgus, ŏris, n.
cold, frīgĭdus, a, um.
collar, torquis, is, c.
colleague, collēga, ae, m.

collect, collĭgo, lēgi, lectum, 3; cōgo, coēgi, coactum, 3.
colony, cŏlōnia, ae, f.
colour, cŏlor, ōris, m.
column, cŏlumna, ae, f.; *of men*, agmen, ĭnis, n.
combat, pugna, ae, f.
come, vĕnio, vēni, ventum, 4.
command, mandātum, i, n.; iussum, i, n.; *power*, impĕrium, i, n.
command, to, impĕro, 1; praesum, fui, esse (*both c. dat. of person*); iŭbeo, iussi, iussum, 2.
command of, to be in, see *to command*.
commander, imperātor, ōris, m.; dux, dŭcis, m.
commence, incĭpio, cēpi, ceptum, 3.
commit, committo, mīsi, missum, 3.
common, commūnis, e.
common-people, plebs, plēbis, f.; vulgus, i, n.
commonwealth, respublĭca, reipublicae, f.
commotion, mōtus, ūs, m; tŭmultus, ūs, m.
companion, cŏmes, ĭtis, c.
compare, compăro, 1; confĕro, tŭli, collātum, ferre.
compassion, mĭsĕrĭcordia, ae, f.
compel, cōgo, coēgi, coactum, 3.
complain, quĕror, questus, 3, dep.
complaint, quĕrēla, ae, f.
complete, to, confĭcio, fēci, fectum, 3.
conceal, cēlo, 1.
concede, concēdo, cessi, cessum, 3.
conceive, concĭpio, cēpi, ceptum, 3.
concern, attĭnet, 2 impers. (*c. ad with acc.*)
concerning, de (*c. abl.*)
conciliate, concĭlio, 1.
concord, concordia, ae, f.
concourse, concursus, ūs, m.
condemn, damno, 1; condemno, 1.
condition, condĭtio, ōnis, f.
confer, confĕro, tŭli, collātum, ferre.
conference, collŏquium, i, n.
confess, confĭteor, fessus, 2, dep.

English-Latin Vocabulary. 181

confession, confessio, ōnis. f.
confidence, fĭdes, ei, f.
confine, contĭneo, ui, tentum, 2.
confirm, confirmo, 1.
confiscate, publĭco, 1.
Conon, Conon, ōnis, m.
congratulate, grātŭlor, 1, dep. (*c. dat.*)
conquer, vinco, vīci, victum, 3; supĕro, 1.
conqueror, victor, ōris, m.
conquest, victōria, ae, f.
conscious, conscius, a, um (*c. gen.*)
consciousness, conscientia, ae, f.
consecrate, consecro, 1.
consecutive, contĭnuus, a, um.
consent, to, consentio, sensi, sensum, 4.
consent, consensus, ūs, m.
consider, pŭto, 1.
consist, consto, stĭti, statum, 1.
consolation, sōlātium, i, n.
console, sōlor, 1, dep.
conspiracy, coniūrātio, ōnis, f.
conspire, coniuro, 1.
conspirator, coniūrātŏr, ōris, m.
constancy, constantia, ae, f.
constrain, cōgo, coēgi, coactum, 3.
consul, consul, ŭlis, m.
consulate, consŭlātus, ūs, m.
consult, consŭlo, ui, sultum, 3.
consult, to deliberate, dēlībĕro, 1.
consume, consūmo, sumpsi, sumptum, 3.
contempt, contemptus, ūs, m.
contend, contendo, di, tum, 3.
content, contentus, a, um (*c. abl.*)
contest, certāmen, ĭnis, n.
continual, contĭnuus, a, um.
continue, măneo, mansi, mansum, 2; *to go on*, pergo, perrexi, rectum, 3.
contract, contrăho, traxi, tractum, 3.
contradict, contradīco, dixi, dictum, 3 (*c. dat.*)
contrary, contrarius, a, um.
contrary, on the, contra.
contrary-to, contra (*c. acc.*)
convenient, commŏdus, a, um.
conversation, sermo, ōnis, m.; collŏquium, i, n.

convey, vĕho, vexi, vectum, 3.
cook, cŏquus, i, m.
cook, to, cŏquo, coxi, coctum, 3.
coop, căvea, ae, f.
copper, aes, acris, n.
Corinth, Cŏrinthus, i, m.
Corinthian, Cŏrinthius, a, um.
cormorant, phălăcrŏcŏrax, acis, m.
corn, frūmentum, i, n.
Cornelia, Cornēlia, ae, f.
corpse, cădāver, eris, n.
correct, corrĭgo, rexi, rectum, 3; ēmendo, 1.
corrupt, corrumpo, rūpi, ruptum, 3.
Corvus, Corvus, i, m.
cost, prĕtium, i, n.; *expense*, sumptus, ūs, m.
cost, to, sto, stĕti, statum, 1 (*c. dat. of person*).
costume, vestītus, ūs, m.
cottage, căsa, ae, f.
cover, tĕgo, texi, tectum, 3.
covet, cŭpio, īvi, ītum, 3.
covetous, cŭpĭdus, a, um.
couch, lectus, i, m., cubīle, is, n.
council, concilium, i, n.
counsel, consilium, i, n.
counsellor, suāsor, ōris, m.; consĭliārius, i, m.
count, nŭmĕro, 1.
countenance, vultus, ūs, m.
country, terra, ae, f.; *the country*, rus, rūris, n.; *one's own country*, patria, ae, f.
courage, virtūs, ūtis, f.
course, cursus, ūs, m.
cover, tĕgo, xi, ctum, 3; conspergo, si, sum, 3.
coward, cowardly, ignāvus, a, um.
cowardice, ignāvia, ae, f.
craft, callĭdĭtas, ātis, f.
crafty, callĭdus, a, um.
crane, grus, gruis, c.
crash, frăgor, ōris, m.
Crassus, Crassus, i, m.
create, creo, 1.
creature, ănĭmal, ālis, n.
credible, crēdĭbĭlis, e.
credit, fĭdes, ei, f.
Cremera, Cremĕra, ae, m.

crescent, lūnŭla, ae, f.
crest, signum, i, n.
Crete, Crēta, ae, f.
crime, scĕlus, ĕris, n.
crocodile, crŏcodīlus, i, m.
Croesus, Croesus, i, m.
crop, sĕges, ĕtis, f.
cross, crux, crŭcis, f.
cross, to, traiĭcio, iēci, iectum, 3 ; transeo, īvi *or* ii, ĭtum, 4.
crow, corvus, i, m.
crow of a cock, cantus, ūs, m.
crowd, turba, ae, f.
crown, cŏrōna, ae, f.
crown, to, cŏrōno, 1 ; cingo, cinxi, cinctum, 3.
cruel, crūdēlis, e.
cruelty, crūdēlitas, ātis, f.
crumb, frustum, i, n.
crush, opprĭmo, pressi, pressum, 3.
cry, vŏco, 1 ; clāmo, 1 ; *like a child*, vāgio, īvi *or* ii, ītum, 4.
cry out, exclāmo, 1.
cry, a, clāmor, ōris, m.
cub, cătŭlus, i, m.
cultivate, cŏlo, cŏlui, cultum, 3.
cultivation, cultūra, ae, f.
cunning, callĭdus, a, um.
cup, pōcŭlum, i, n.
cure, rĕmĕdium, i, n.
cure, to, sāno, 1.
curiae, cūriae, ārum, f.
Curiatii, the, Curiātii, ōrum, m.
Curius, Cŭrius, i, m.
curtain, vēlum, i, n.
custom, mos, mōris, m.
cut, caedo, cĕcīdi, caesum, 3 ; scindo, scĭdi, scissum, 3.
cut down, concīdo, di, sum, 3.
cut off, abscindo, scīdi, scissum, 3.
cut to pieces, concīdo, di, sum, 3.
Cyprus, Cyprus, i, f.

Dagger, pūgio, ōnis, m.
daily, quŏtīdiānus, a, um ; *adv*. quŏtīdie.
damage, damnum, i, n. ; dētrīmentūm, i, n.
damage, to, nŏceo, ui, ĭtum, 2 (*c. dat.*)
dance, salto, 1.
danger, pĕrīcŭlum, i, n.
dangerous, pĕrīcŭlōsus, a, um.
Danube, Ister, tri, m.
dare, audeo, ausus sum, 2, dep.
Darius, Darius, i, m.
dark, obscūrus, a, um ; pullus, a, um.
darken, obscūro, 1.
darkness, cālīgo, ĭnis, f. ; tĕnebrae, ārum, f.
dart, tēlum, i, n. ; iacŭlum, i, n.
daughter, fīlia, ae, f.
dawn, prima lux ; māne, indcl.
dawn, to, illūcesco, illuxi, 3.
day, dies, ei, c. in sing. m. in plural ; *daybreak*, prima lux.
dead, mortuus, a, um.
dead body, cădāver, ĕris, n.
deadly, fătālis, e.
deaf, surdus, a, um.
dear, cārus, a, um.
death, mors, mortis, f.
debt, aes ălienum.
deceive, dēcĭpio, cēpi, ceptum, 3.
deceit, dŏlus, i, m.
decide, constĭtuo, ui, ūtum, 3 ; dēcerno, crēvi, crētum, 3.
Decius, Decius, i, m.
declare, declaro, 1 ; *to declare war*, bellum indīcĕre.
decree, to, dēcerno, crēvi, crētum, 3.
decree, a, decrētum, i, n. ; ēdictum, i, n.
deed, factum, i, n. ; făcĭnus, ŏris, n.
deem worthy, dignor, 1, dep.
deep, altus, a, um.
deer, dāma, ae, c.
defeat, a, clādes, is, f.
defeat, to, vinco, vīci, victum, 3.
defect, vĭtium, i, n.
defence, praesĭdium, i, n.
defend, dēfendo, di, sum, 3.
defendant, reus, i, m.
defile, polluo, ui, ūtum, 3.
Deianira, Dēiănīra, ae, f.
deity, nūmen, ĭnis, n.
delay, mŏra, ae, f.

English-Latin Vocabulary. 183

delay, to, mŏror, 1, dep. ; cunctor, 1, dep.
deliberate, delībĕro, 1.
delight, gaudium, i, n.
delight, to, dēlecto, 1 ; iūvo, 1.
deliver, lībĕro, 1.
Delos, Delos, i, f.
Demades, Dĕmădes, is, m.
demand, posco, pŏposci, 3; postŭlo, 1.
Demosthenes, Dēmosthĕnes, is, m.
deny, nĕgo, 1.
depart, excēdo, cessi, cessum, 3 ; discēdo, cessi, cessum, 3.
departure, discessus, ūs, m.
deplore, plōro, 1.
deprive, spŏlio, 1 ; prīvo, 1.
descend, descendo, di, sum, 3.
descended from, ŏriundus, a, um.
describe, descrībo, scripsi, scriptum, 3.
desert, dēsĕro, rui, rtum, 3 ; linquo, līqui, lictum, 3.
deserter, transfŭga, ae, m.
deserve, mĕreor, mĕrĭtus, 2, dep.
design, consĭlium, i, n.
desire, cŭpīdo, ĭnis, f.
desire, to, cŭpio, īvi, ĭtum, 3 ; opto, 1.
desirous, cŭpĭdus, a, um.
desist from, dēsisto, destiti, destĭtum, 3.
desolate, sōlus, a, um ; dēsertus, a, um.
despair, to, despēro, 1.
despair, despērātio, ōnis, f.
despatch, conficio, fēci, fectum, 3.
despise, contemno, tempsi, temptum, 3.
destiny, fātum, i, n.; sors, sortis, f.
destroy, perdo, dĭdi, dĭtum, 3.
destructive, exĭtiōsus, a, um.
detain, dĕtĭneo, ui, tentum, 2.
detect, ănĭmadverto, verti, versum, 3.
determine, stătuo, ui, ūtum, 3.
detract, dētrăho, traxi, tractum, 3.
devastate, vasto, 1.
devote, dĕvŏveo, vōvi, vōtum, 2.
devour, cŏmĕdo, edi, ēsum, 3 ; dēvŏro, 1.

diadem, diădēma, ătis, n.
Diana, Diāna, ae, f.
dictator, dictātor, ōris, m.
dictatorship, dictatūra, ae, f.
die, mŏrior, mortuus, 3, dep.
differ, differo, distŭli, dīlātum, differre.
difference, discrīmen, ĭnis, n.
difficult, difficilis, e.
difficulty, difficultas, ătis, f. ; *with difficulty,* vix.
dig, fŏdio, fōdi, fossum, 3.
dig up, effŏdio, fōdi, fossum, 3.
digest, concŏquo, coxi, coctum, 3.
dignity, dignĭtas, ătis, f.
diligent, strēnuus, a, um ; stŭdiōsus, a, um.
diminish, mĭnuo, ui, ūtum, 3.
dine, prandeo, di, sum, 2 ; coeno, 1.
Diocles, Diocles, is, m.
Diogenes, Diogĕnes, is, m.
Dionysius, Diōnỹsius, i, m.
dip, tinguo, tinxi, tinctum, 3.
dire, dīrus, a, um.
disappear, ēvānesco, ui, 3.
disaster, damnum, i, n.; clādes, is, f.
discern, cerno, crēvi, crētum, 3.
discharge, fungor, functus, 3, dep ; (*darts*), conĭcio, iēci, iectum, 3.
disciple, discĭpŭlus, i, m.
discipline, disciplīna, ae, f.
discord, discordia, ae, f.
discover, invĕnio, vēni, ventum, 4 ; rĕperio, reperi, repertum, 4.
disease, morbus, i, m.
disembark, egrĕdior, egressus, 3, dep.
disgrace, dēdĕcus, ōris, n.
disgrace, to, foedo, 1.
disgraceful, turpis, e.
disguise, dissĭmŭlo, 1.
disgust, taedium, i, n.
disgusts, it, taedet, uit, 2, impers.
dish, pătella, ae, f.
dishevelled, passus, a, um.
dishonour, see *disgrace.*
dismiss, dīmitto, mīsi, missum, 3.
dismount, descendo, di, sum, 3.
dispense, distrĭbuo, ui, ūtum, 3 ; (— *justice*), dīco, xi, ctum 3.

display, ostendo, di, sum, 3; ostento, 1.
displease, displĭceo, ui, ĭtum, 2.
dispose, dispōno, pŏsui, posĭtum, 3.
disposition, indŏles, is, f.; ingĕnium, i, n.
dispute, a, rixa, ae, f.; contentio, ōnis, f.
dispute, to, dispŭto, 1.
dissemble, dissĭmŭlo, 1.
dissembler, dissĭmŭlātor, ōris, m.
dissension, dissensio, ōnis, f.
distance, distantia, ae, f.; *space between*, intervallum, i, n.
distant, to be, absum, fui, esse.
distinguish, dēcerno, crēvi, crētum, 3.
distinguished, insignis, e; clārus, a, um.
distribute, distrĭbuo, ui, ūtum, 3.
disturb, turbo, 1.
disturbance, mōtus, ūs, m.
ditch, fossa, ae, f.
dive, mergor (*pass. of mergo*).
diver, ūrīnātor, ōris, m.
divide, dīvĭdo, si, sum, 3.
divine, dīvīnus, a, um.
division, a, pars, rtis, f.
do, făcio, fēci, factum, 3.
docility, dŏcĭlĭtas, ātis, f.; mansuetŭdo, inis, f.
doctor, mĕdĭcus, i, m.
doe, cerva, ae, f.
dog, cănis, is, c.
dolphin, delphīn, īnis, m.
domestic, dŏmestĭcus, a, um.
door, iānua, ae, f.; fŏres, um.
Don, Tănais, is *or* ĭdis, m.
doubt, to, dŭbĭto, 1.
doubtful, incertus, a, um; dŭbius, a, um; *without doubt*, sine dubio.
dove, cŏlumba, ae, f.
downcast, dēmissus, a, um.
down from, dē (*c. abl.*)
drachma, drachma, ae, f.
Draco, Draco, ōnis, m.
drag, trăho, traxi, tractum, 3.
draw (a sword), stringo, nxi, ictum, 3.
draw along, dūco, xi, ctum, 3.

draw back, reduco, xi, ctum, 3.
draw off, abdūco, xi, ctum, 3.
draw up (an army), instruo, struxi, structum, 3.
draw by lot, sortior, tītus, 4, dep.
draw water, ăquor, 1, dep.
dreadful, dīrus, a, um.
dream, a, somnium, i, n.
dream, to, somnio, 1.
dress, vestītus, ūs, m; vestis, is, f.
dress, to, vestio, īvi *or* ii, ītum, 4.
drink, bibo, bĭbi, bibĭtum, 3; poto, 1.
drive, ago, ēgi, actum, 3; pello, pepŭli, pulsum, 3.
drive away, out, expello, pŭli, pulsum, 3.
drop, a, gutta, ae, f.
drown, mergo, mersi, mersum, 3.
drunk, ebrius, a, um.
dry, siccus, a, um; ārĭdus, a, um.
duck, ănas, atis, f.
Duilius, Duilius, i, m.
duly, rītē.
dutiful conduct, pĭĕtas, ātis, f.
duty, offĭcium, i, n.
dwelling, dŏmus, ūs, f.
dye, tinguo, tinxi, tinctum, 3; imbuo, ui, ūtum, 3.

Each, quisque, quaeque, quidque, *or* quodque.
eager, cŭpĭdus, a, um.
eagle, ăquĭla, ae, f.
ear, auris, is, f.
early, matūre.
earnest, strēnuus, a, um; stŭdiōsus, a, um.
earth, terra, ae, f.; tellūs, ūris, f.
ease, ōtium, i, n.
easily, făcĭle.
east, the, ŏriens, entis, m.
easy, făcĭlis, e.
eat, ĕdo, ĕdi, ēsum, 3; vescor, 3, dep. (*c. abl.*)
ebony, ĕbĕnus, i, f.
eclipse, dēfectus, ūs, m.
educate, ēdŭco, 1.
Edward, Edvardus, i, m.

English-Latin Vocabulary. 185

effect, to, efficio, fēci, fectum, 3.
effeminate, mollis, e.
effort, cōnātus, ūs, m.; impĕtus, ūs, m.
egg, ōvum, i, n.
Egypt, Aegyptus, i, f.
Egyptian, Aegyptius, a, um.
eight, octo, indcl.
eighth, octāvus, a, um.
eighty, octoginta, indcl.
either, ūter, tra, trum; (*conj.*) aut; vel; sive; seu.
eject, ēǐcio, ēiēci, ēiectum, 3.
elated, ēlātus, a, um.
elder, sĕnior.
elect, ēlīgo, lēgi, lectum, 3.
elegance, grātia, ae, f.
elephant, ĕlĕphantus, i, m.; ĕlĕphas, antis, m.
elk, alces, is, f.
eloquence, fācundia, ae, f.
eloquent, fācundus, a, um.
else, ălius, a, ud.
elsewhere, ălibi.
elude, ēlūdo, lūsi, lūsum, 3.
embark, to, ascendo, di, sum, 3.
embassy, lēgātio, ōnis, f.
embrace, to, amplector, plexus, 3, dep.
embrace, amplexus, ūs, m.
eminent, clārus, a, um.
emperor, impĕrātor, ōris, m.
empire, impĕrium, i, n.
empty, văcuus, a, um.
encourage, hortor, 1, dep.; cŏhortor, 1, dep; stĭmŭlo, 1.
end, fīnis, is, m.
endeavour, cōnor, 1, dep.
endued with, praedĭtus, a, um (*c. abl.*)
endurance, pătientia, ae, f.
endure, pătior, passus, 3, dep.
enemy, hostis, is, m.; *a private enemy,* inĭmīcus, a, um.
energetic, strĕnuus, a, um.
enervate, mollio, ivi *or* ii, ītum, 4.
engagement, certāmen, ĭnis, n.; pugna, ae, f.
England, Anglia, ae, f.
enjoy, fruor, fruitus, 3, dep. (*c. abl.*)

enjoyment, vŏluptas, ātis, f.
Ennius, Ennius, i, m.
enormous, ingens, ntis.
enough, sătis.
enraged, īrātus, a, um.
enrol, conscribo, scripsi, scriptum, 3.
enter, intro, 1; ineo, īvi *or* ii, ĭtum, 4.
enterprise, cōnātus, ūs, m.
entirely, omnīno.
entrails, viscĕra, um, n.
entrenchment, vallum, i, n.; agger, ĕris, n.
entrust, crēdo, dĭdi, dĭtum, 3.
entry, introĭtus, ūs, m.; ădĭtus, ūs, m.
envious, invĭdus, a, um.
envoy, lēgātus, i, m.
envy, invĭdia, ae, f.
envy, to, invĭdeo, vīdi, vīsum, 2 (*c. dat.*)
Epaminondas, Epaminondas, ae, m.
Ephesus, Ephĕsus, i, f.
Epirus, Epīrus, i, f.
equal, aequus, a, um; aequālis, e, par, is.
equal, to, adaequo, 1.
equally, părĭter.
equipped, instructus, a, um, part. (*instruo*).
erect, erĭgo, rexi, rectum, 3.
err, erro, 1.
escape, fŭga, ae, f.
escape, to, effŭgio, fŭgi, fŭgĭtum, 3.
escape the notice of, fallo, fĕfelli, falsum, 3.
escort, dēdūco, duxi, ductum, 3.
especially, praesertim; praecĭpue; imprīmis.
establish, constĭtuo, ui, ūtum, 3.
estimate, aestĭmo, 1.
Etruria, Etruria, ae, f.
Etrurian, Tuscus, a, um.
Europe, Eurōpa, ae, f.
Eurydice, Eurydĭce, ēs, f.
Eurystheus, Eurystheus, ei, m.
even, ĕtiam; vel; *not even,* nē— quidem.
event, ēventus, ūs, m.

ever, unquam ; *always*, semper.
everlasting, aeternus, a, um.
every, omnis, e ; quisque, quaeque, quodque.
every day, quŏtīdie.
everywhere, passim.
evil, mălus, a, um ; *subst.* mălum, i, n.
examine, investīgo, 1.
example, exemplum, i, n.
excel, antĕcello, ui, 3 (*c. dat.*) ; sŭpĕro, 1.
excellent, egrĕgius, a, um ; praeclārus, a, um.
except, praeter (*c. acc.*)
excessive, nĭmius, a, um.
exchange, mūto, 1.
excite, excīto, 1 ; mŏveo, mōvi, mōtum, 2.
excitement, mōtus, ūs, m.
exclaim, exclāmo, 1.
excuse, excūso, 1.
exercise, exercĭtātio, ōnis, f.
exercise, to, exerceo, ui, ĭtum, 2.
exhort, cŏhortor, atus, 1, dep.
exile, exĭlium, i, n.
exile, an, exsul, ŭlis, m.
exist, exsisto, stĭti, stĭtum, 3.
expect, expecto, 1.
expectation, expectātio, ōnis, f. ; spes, spei, f.
expediency, ūtĭlĭtas, ātis, f.
expedient, ūtĭlis, e.
expedition, expĕdītio, ōnis, f.
expel, expello, pŭli, pulsum, 3.
expense, sumptus, ūs, m.
experience, expĕrientia, ae, f. ; ūsus, ūs, m.
experience, to, expĕrior, pertus, 4, dep.
expiate, expio, 1.
expire, exeo, ivi *or* ii, ĭtum, 4.
explain, explĭco, 1.
exploit, factum, i, n. ; făcĭnus, ŏris, n.
export, exporto, 1.
expose, expōno, pŏsui, positum, 3.
exposure, expŏsĭtio, ōnis, f.
extend, păteo, ui, 2 (*intrans.*) ; pando, di, sum, 3 (*trans.*)

extent, spătium, i, n. ; distantia, ae, f.
extinguish, exstinguo, nxi, nctum, 3.
extol, laudo, 1.
extract, extrăho, traxi, tractum, 3.
extraordinary, mīrus, a, um.
extreme, extrēmus, a, um.
extremely, valde.
extremity, extrēmum, i, n.
eye, ŏcŭlus, i, m.

Fabian, Făbius, a, um.
Fabius, Făbius, i, m.
fable, făbŭla, ae, f.
Fabricius, Fabrĭcius, i, m.
fabulous, făbŭlōsus, a, um.
face, făcies, ei, f. ; os, ōris, n. ; vultus, ūs, m.
factions, partes, ium, f.
fade, marcesco, 3.
fail, dēfĭcio, fēci, fectum, 3.
fair, pulcher, chra, chrum ; *just*, aequus, a, um.
faith, fĭdes, ei, f.
faithful, fĭdēlis, e ; fīdus, a, um.
fall, a, cāsus, ūs, m.
fall, to, cădo, cecĭdi, casum, 3 ; lābor, lapsus, 3, dep.
fall asleep, to, obdormio, ii *or* ivi, ĭtum, 4.
false, falsus, a, um.
fame, fāma, ae, f.
family, fămĭlia, ae, f. ; dŏmus, ūs, f.
famine, fămes, is, f.
far, prŏcul ; longe.
farm, praedium, i, n.
farming, agrĭcultūra, ae, f.
fat, pinguis, e.
fate, fātum, i, n.
father, păter, tris, m.
fatherland, patria, ae, f.
fatigue, lassĭtūdo, inis, f.
fatten, săgīno, 1.
fault, culpa, ae, f.
favour, grātia, ae, f.
favour, to, făveo, fāvi, fautum, 2 (*c. dat.*)

English-Latin Vocabulary.

Faustulus, Faustŭlus, i, m.
fear, tĭmor, oris, m.; mĕtus, ūs, m.
fear, to, tĭmeo, ui, 2; mĕtuo, ui, 3.
fearful, terrĭbĭlis, e.
fearless, impăvĭdus, a, um.
feast, ĕpŭlae, ārum, f.
feast, to, ĕpŭlor, ātus, 1, dep.
feather, penna, ae, f.; plūma, ae, f.
features, ōra, ōrum, n.; see *countenance*.
feeble, infirmus, a, um.
feed, pasco, pāvi, pastum, 3 (*trans.*); pascor, *passive* (*intrans.*)
feed on, vescor, 3, dep. (*c. abl.*).
feel, sentio, sensi, sensum, 4.
feign, sĭmŭlo, 1; fingo, finxi, fictum, 3.
fellow, hŏmo, ĭnis, c.
female, fēmĭna, ae, f.; (*adj.*) fēmĭneus, a, um.
ferocity, saevĭtia, ae, f.
fertile, fertĭlis, e.
fetch, see *bring*.
fetter, compes, ĕdis, f.
few, paucus, a, um.
field, ăger, gri, m.
fierce, fĕrox, ōcis.
fifty, quinquāginta, indcl.
fig, fig-tree, fīcus, i *and* ūs, f.
fight, pugna, ae, f.
fight, to, pugno, 1.
figure, fĭgūra, ae, f.
filial affection, pĭĕtas, ātis, f.
fill, repleo, plēvi, plētum, 2.
finally, dēnique.
find, invĕnio, vēni, ventum, 4.
fine, multa, ae, f.
fine, to, multo, 1.
finger, dĭgĭtus, i, m.
finish, confĭcio, fēci, fectum, 3; pĕrăgo, ēgi, actum, 3.
fire, ignis, is, m.
firm, firmus, a, um.
first, prīmus, a, um.
fish, piscis, is, m.
fisherman, piscātor, ōris, m.
fit, aptus, a, um; ĭdōneus, a, um.
five, quinque, indcl.
fix, fīgo, xi, xum, 3.

fixed, certus, a, um.
flame, flamma, ae, f.
flapping, plausus, ūs, m.
flatter, ădūlor, 1, dep.
flee, fŭgio, fūgi, fŭgĭtum, 3.
fleet, classis, is, f.
flesh, căro, carnis, f.
flight, fŭga, ae, f.; *of a bird*, vŏlatus, ūs, m.
floor, tăbŭlātum, i, n.
flourish, floreo, ui, 2.
flow, fluo, xi, ctum, 3.
flower, flos, ōris, m.
flute-player, fĭdīcen, ĭnis, m.
fly, a, musca, ae, f.
fly, to, see *flee; of a bird*, vŏlo, 1.
fly away, aufŭgio, fūgi, 3.
foam, spūma, ae, f.
foe, hostis, is, m.
follow, sĕquor, sĕcūtus, 3, dep.
follower, cŏmĕs, ĭtis, c.
folly, stultĭtia, ae, f.
food, cĭbus, i, m.
fond of, stŭdiōsus, a, um.
fool, foolish, stultus, a, um.
foolishly, stultē.
foot, pes, pĕdis, m.
for (*conj.*), nam, ĕnim; (*prep.*) pro (*c. abl.*).
foray, incursio, ōnis, f.
forbid, vĕto, ui, ĭtum, 1; prŏhĭbeo, ui, ĭtum, 2.
force, vis, acc. vim, *abl.* vi, f.
force, to, see *compel*.
forced marches, magna itĭnĕra.
forces, cōpĭae, ārum, f.
forehead, frons, ntis, m.
foreign, externus, a, um; pĕregrīnus, a, um.
foresee, prōvĭdeo, vīdi, visum, 2.
forest, silva, ae, f.
foretell, praedīco, dixi, dictum, 3.
forget, oblīviscor, oblītus, 3, dep. (*c. gen.*).
forgetful, immĕmor, ŏris (*c. gen.*).
form, forma, ae, f.
former, prior, prius.
formerly, ōlim, quondam.
formidable, formīdŏlōsus, a, um.
fort, castrum, i, n,; castellum, i, n.

fortify, mūnio, īvi *or* ii, ītum, 4.
fortunate, fēlix, īcis.
fortune, fortūna, ae, f.
forty, quadrāginta, indcl.
forum, fŏrum, i, n.
found, condo, dĭdi, dĭtum, 3.
founder, condĭtor, ōris, m.
four, quātuor, indcl.
fourteen, quātuordecim, indcl.
four horse chariot, quadrīgae, arum, f.
fourth, quartus, a, um.
four times, quăter.
fowl, vŏlucris, is, f.; *domestic fowl*, gallīna, ae, f.
fowler, auceps, cŭpis, m.
France, Gallia, ae, f.
free, līber, era, erum.
free, to, lībĕro, 1.
freedman, lībertus, i, m.
freedom, lībertas, ātis, f.
French, Gallĭcus, a, um.
frequent, crēber, bra, brum.
frequently, saepe.
fresh, rĕcens, ntis; nŏvus, a, um.
friend, friendly, ămīcus, a, um.
friendship, ămīcĭtia, ae, f.
frighten, terreo, ui, 2.
frog, rāna, ae, f.
from, ā, ē, *or* ex, dē (*all c. abl.*)
from a distance, ēmĭnus.
front, in, adversus, a, um.
frost, gĕlu, indcl.
frugal, parcus, a, um.
frugality, parsĭmōnia, ae, f.
fruit, fructus, ūs, m.
fruitful, fertĭlis, e.
Fuffetius, Fuffĕtius, i, m.
fugitive, fŭgĭtīvus, a, um.
fulfil, perfĭcio, fēci, fectum, 3; expleo, plēvi, plētum, 2.
full, plēnus, a, um.
funeral, fūnus, ĕris, n.; *funeral rites*, infĕriae, arum, f.
funny, iŏcōsus, a, um.
furrow, sulcus, i, m.
fury, fŭror, ōris, m., impĕtus, ūs, m.
future, fŭtūrus, a, um.

Gabii, Găbii, ōrum, m.
gain, quaestus, ūs, m.; lucrum, i, n.
gain, to, acquīro, quisīvi, quisītum, 3; păro, 1.
gain possession of, pŏtior, ītus, 4, dep. (*c. abl.*)
Gallic, Gallĭcus, a, um.
gallows, crux, crŭcis, f.
game, lūdus, i, m.
garden, hortus, i, m.
gaoler. See *jailer*.
garland, sertum, i, n.
garment, vestis, is, f.
garrison, praesĭdium, i, n.
gate, iānua, ae, f.; porta, ae, f.
gather, lĕgo, lēgi, lectum, 3; collĕgo, lēgi, lectum, 3.
Gaul, Gallia, ae, f.
Gaul, a, Gallus, i, m.
gem, gemma, ae, f.
general, dux, dŭcis, m.; impĕrātor, ōris, m.
generally, fĕre.
generosity, lībĕrālĭtas, ātis, f.
Geneva, Gĕnēva, ae, f.
genius, ingĕnium, i, n.
gentleness, comĭtas, ātis, f.
gently, lēnĭter.
German, Germānus, a, um.
Germany, Germānia, ae, f.
get possession of, pŏtĭor, ītus, 4, dep. (*c. abl.*).
giant, gĭgas, antis, m.
gift, dōnum, i, n.
gild, ĭnauro, 1.
gird, cingo, nxi, nctum, 3.
girl, puella, ae, f.
give, do, dĕdi, dătum, 1.
give back, reddo, dĭdi, dĭtum, 3.
give birth to, părio, pepĕri, partum, 3.
give up, trādo, dĭdi, dĭtum, 3.
glad, laetus, a, um.
glass, vitrum, i, n.
Glaucus, Glaucus, i, m.
glitter, mĭco, ui, 1.
gloomy, tristis, e.
glorious, praeclārus, a, um.
glory, glōria, ae, f.

English-Latin Vocabulary.

glow, to, ardeo, rsi, rsum, 2.
go, eo, ivi *or* ii, itum, 4.
go away, abeo, ii, itum, 4.
go by, praetereo, ivi *or* ii, itum, 4.
go forth, or out, exeo, ivi *or* ii, itum, 4.
go on, procedo, cessi, cessum, 3.
go under, subeo, ii, itum, 4.
goal, meta, ae, f.
goat, caper, pri, m.; *she-goat*, capella, ae, f.
goat-footed, capripes, pedis.
god, deus, i, m.
goddess, dea, ae, f.
gods below, the, Inferi, orum, m.
gold, aurum, i, n.
golden, aureus, a, um.
good, bonus, a, um.
good-nature, facilitas, atis, f.
goodwill, benevolentia, ae, f.
goose, anser, eris, m.
Gorgon, Gorgon, onis, f.
govern, rego, rexi, rectum, 3.
government, imperium, i, n.
grace, gratia, ae, f.
Graces, the, Gratiae, arum, f.
graciousness, facilitas, atis, f.; comitas, atis, f.
grandfather, avus, i, m.
grandson, nepos, otis, m.
grant, see *give*.
grape, uva, ae, f.
grapnel, uncus, i, m.
grapple with, prehendo, di, sum, 3.
grass, herba, ae, f.
grateful, gratus, a, um.
gratitude, gratia, ae, f.
gray, canus, a, um.
great, magnus, a, um.
greatly, magnopere, valde.
greatness, magnitudo, inis, f.
Grecian, Greek, Graecus, a, um.
Greece, Graecia, ae, f.
greedy, avidus, a, um.
green, viridis, e.
green, to grow, viresco, 3.
greeting, salus, utis, f.
grief, dolor, oris, m.; luctus, us, m.

grieve, doleo, ui, 2 (*intrans.*); ango, xi, ctum, 3 (*trans.*)
groan, gemitus, us, m.
groan, to, gemo, ui, itum, 3.
ground, humus, i, f.; *on the ground*, humi.
grove, lucus, i, m.
grow, cresco, crevi, cretum, 3.
guard, custos, odis, c.
guard, to, custodio, ivi *or* ii, itum, 4.
guest, hospes, itis, c.
guide, dux, ducis, m.
guide, to, duco, duxi, ductum, 3.
guilt, culpa, ae, f; scelus, eris, n.

Habit, mos, moris, m.
hail, grando, inis, f.
hail, salve, def.
hair, crinis, is, m; *of an animal*, pilus, i, m.
half, dimidium, i, n.
hall, aula, ae, f.
halt, consisto, stiti, stitum, 3.
hand, manus, us, f; *right hand*, dextra; *left hand*, sinistra.
hand down, trado, didi, ditum, 3.
handsome, pulcher, chra, chrum.
hang, pendeo, pependi, pensum, 2 (*intrans.*); pendo, pependi, pensum, 3 (*trans.*)
hanging, suspendium, i, n.
Hannibal, Hannibal, alis, m.
Hanno, Hanno, onis, m.
happen, accido, cidi, 3; contingo, tigi, 3.
happy, felix, icis.
harass, vexo, 1.
harbour, portus, us, m.
hard, durus, a, um.
harden, duro, 1.
hardy, robustus, a, um.
hare, lepus, oris, m.
harm, detrimentum, i, n.
harmful, noxius, a, um.
harmless, innoxius, a, um.
harp, cithara, ae, f.
harper, citharista, ae, m.
harvest, messis, is, f.

Hasdrubal, Hsadrŭbal, ălis, m.
hasten, festīno, 1; prŏpĕro, 1; mātūro, 1.
hastily, tĕmĕre.
hatch, exclūdo, si, sum, 3.
hate, ōdium, i, n.
hate, to, ōdi, def.
hated, invīsus, a, um.
hatred, see hate.
have, hăbeo, ui, ĭtum, 2.
haughty, fĕrox, ōcis.
haunt, frĕquento, 1.
hawk, accĭpĭter, tris, m.
hazard, ālĕa, ae, f.
he, ille, a, ud; is, ea, id.
head, căput, ĭtis, n.
headlong, praeceps, cĭpĭtis.
health, sălūs, ūtis, f.
healthy, sānus, a, um; *healthful*, sălūber, bris, bre.
heap, ăcervus, i, m.
hear, audio, īvi *or* ii, ĭtum, 4.
hearer, audītor, ōris, m.
heart, cor, dis, n.
hearth, fŏcus, i, m.
heat, călor, ōris, m.
heaven, caelum, i, n.
heavy, grăvis, e.
hedgehog, ĕchīnus, i, m.
heel, calx, cis, f.
he-goat, căper, pri, m.
heir, hēres, ēdis, c.
Helena, Hĕlĕna, ae, f.
helmet, gălea, ae, f.
help, auxĭlium, i, n.
help, to, iŭvo, iūvi, iūtum, 1; subvĕnio, vēni, ventum, 4 (*c. dat.*)
Helvetii, the, Helvetii, ōrum, m.
hemlock, cĭcūta, ae, f.
hen, gallīna, ae, f.
hence, hinc.
herald, praeco, ōnis, m.
herb, *herbage*, herba, ae, f.; grāmen, ĭnis, n.
Hercules, Hercŭles, is, m.
herd, pĕcus, ŏris, n.
here, hic.
hero, hēros, ōis, m.
hesitate, dŭbĭto, 1.
hesitation, cunctātio, ōnis, f.

hide, cŏrium, i, n.
hide, to, condo, dĭdi, dĭtum, 3; abdo, dĭdi, dĭtum, 3.
hiding place, lătebra, ae, f.
high, altus, a, um.
highbred, ingĕnuus, a, um.
highest, summus, a, um.
highly, magni.
hill. collis, is, m.
himself, se (acc.)
hind, cerva, ae, f.
hinder, impĕdio, īvi *or* ii, ītum, 4.
hire, condūco, duxi, ductum, 3.
historian, auctor, ōris, m.
hither, hūc.
hitherto, adhūc.
hold, tĕnco, ui, 2; hăbeo, ui, itum, 2.
hold out, porrĭgo, rexi, rectum, 3.
hole, căvum, i, n.
holiday, fēriae, ārum, f.
hollow, căvus, a, um.
holy, săcer, cra, crum.
home, dŏmus, ūs, f.; *at home*, domi.
honest, prŏbus, a, um.
honesty, prŏbĭtas, ātis, f.
honey, mel, lis, n.
honour, hŏnor, ōris, m.
honour, to, hŏnōro, 1.
honourable, hŏnestus, a, um.
hoof, ungŭla, ae, f.
hook, hāmus, i, m.
hope, spes, spei, f.
Horatius, Horatius, i, m.
Horatii, the, Horatii, ōrum, m.
horn, cornu, ūs, n.
horrible, dīrus, a, um.
horrid, horrĭdus, a, um.
horse, ĕquus, i, m.
horseman, ĕques, ĭtis, m.
hospitality, hospĭtium, i, n.
host, hospĕs, ĭtis, m.
hostage, obsĕs, ĭdis, c.
hostile, infestus, a, um.
Hostilius, Hostilius, i, m.
hound, cănis, is, c.
hour, hōra, ae, f.
house, dŏmus, ūs, f.
household, fămĭlia, ae, f.

English-Latin Vocabulary. 191

how, quam, quomŏdo; *how great*, quantus, a, um; *how many*, quot; *how often*, quŏties; *how long*, quamdiu.
howdah, turris, is, f.
however, tămen.
huge, ingens, tis.
human, hūmānus, a, um.
human being, hŏmo, ĭnis, c.
humanity, see *clemency*.
humble, hŭmĭlis, e.
hundred, centum, indcl.
hunger, fămes, is, f.
hungry, to be, ēsŭrio, ītum, 4.
hunt, vēnor, atus, 1 dep.
hunter, huntsman, vēnātor, ōris, m.
hunting, vēnātio, ōnis, f.
hurdle, crātes, is, f.
hurl, iăcio, iēci, iactum, 3.
hurl down, dēĭcio, iēci, iectum, 3.
hurry, see *hasten*.
hurtful, noxius, a, um.
husband, mărītus, i, m.
husbandman, agrĭcŏla, ae, m.
Hydra, Hydra, ae, f.

I, ĕgo, mei.
Ibis, ĭbis, ĭdis, f.
ichneumon, ichneumon, ŏnis, m.
idea, nōtio, onis, f.
idle, ignāvus, a, um.
idleness, ignāvia, ae, f.
if, si.
ignorant, ignārus, a, um.
ignorant, to be, ignōro, 1; nescio, ii, 4.
ill, mălus, a, um; *sick*, aeger, gra, grum; (*subst.*) mălum, i, n.
ill (*adv.*), aegre.
illness, morbus, i, m.
ill-timed, ĭnopportūnus, a, um.
ill-tongued, mălĕdĭcus, a, um.
illustrious, clārus, a, um; illustris, e.
image, ĭmāgo, ĭnis, f.
imagine, pŭto, 1.
imitate, ĭmĭtor, 1, dep.
immediately, stătim.
immense, ingens, ntis.

immortal, immortālis, e.
immortality, immortalĭtas, ātis, f.
impatient, impătiens, tis.
impede, impĕdio, ĭvi *or* ii, ītum, 4.
impel, impello, pŭli, pulsum, 3.
imperial, impĕrātōrius, a, um.
impertinence, insŏlentia, ae, f.
impious, impius, a, um.
implore, ōro, 1.
important, magnus, a, um.
importune, fatīgo, 1.
impose, impōno, pŏsui, pŏsĭtum, 3.
impudent, impŭdens, tis.
impudently, impŭdenter.
impulse, mōtus, ūs, m.
impunity, with, impūne.
impute, attrĭbuo, ui, ūtum, 3.
in, in (*c. abl.*)
in the power of, pĕnes (*c. acc.*)
in the presence of, cōram (*c. abl.*)
incite, stĭmŭlo, 1; mŏveo, mōvi, mōtum, 2.
increase, augeo, auxi, auctum, 2 (*trans.*); cresco, crēvi, crētum (*intrans.*)
incredible, incrēdĭbĭlis, e.
incur, contraho, traxi, tractum, 3.
incursion, incursio, ōnis, f.
indecency, impŭdentia, ae, f.
indeed, quĭdem.
India, India, ae, f.
Indian, Indĭcus, a, um.
indolence, ignāvia, ae, f.
industry, industria, ae, f.
infantry, pĕdĭtātus, ūs, m.
infect, infĭcio, fēci, fectum, 3.
infirm, infirmus, a, um.
infirmity, infirmĭtas, ātis, f.
infernal regions, see *gods below*.
inflame, incendo, di, sum, 3.
inflict, infĕro, tuli, illātum, ferre.
influence, mŏveo, mōvi, mōtum, 2.
inform, certiorem făcĕre.
informer, dēlātor, oris, m.; index, ĭcis, c.
in front, adversus, a, um.
ingenuity, sollertia, ae, f.
inglorious, inglōrius, a, um.
inhabit, incŏlo, colui, cultum, 3; hăbĭto, 1.

inhabitant, incŏla, ae, c.
injure, laedo, si, sum, 3 ; nŏceo, ui, ĭtum, 2 (*c. dat.*)
injury, iniūria, ae, f.
inn, dīversorium, i, n.
innkeeper, caupo, ōnis, m.
innocence, innŏcentia, ae, f.
innocent, innŏcens, tis.
innumerable, innŭmĕrābĭlis, e.
inquire, quaero, quaesīvi, quaesītum, 3 ; rŏgo, 1.
inquiry, quaestio, ōnis, f.
insatiable, inexplēbĭlis, e.
inscribe, inscrībo, scripsi, scriptum, 3.
insert, insĕro, ui, tum, 3.
insolence, insŏlentia, ae, f.
insolent, insŏlens, tis.
inspect, inspĭcio, spexi, spectum, 3.
inspire, stĭmŭlo, 1.
instance, exemplum, i, n.
instead of, pro (*c. abl.*)
instinct, instinctus, ūs, m.
instruct, dŏceo, ui, ctum, 2.
instrument, instrumentum, i, n.
insufficient, impar, is.
insult, contŭmēlia, ae, f.
insult, to, illūdo, si, sum, 3 (*c. dat.*)
integrity, prŏbĭtas, ātis, f.
intellect, ingĕnium, i, n.
intend, stătuo, ui, ūtum, 3.
intent, intentus, a, um.
intention, consĭlium, i, n.
inter, sĕpĕlio, īvi *or* ii, pultum, 4.
intercept, interclūdo, si, sum, 3.
intercourse, consuētūdo, inis, f.
interfere with, intercēdo, cessi, cessum, 3 (*c. dat.*)
interpret, interprĕtor, 1.
interrupt, interrumpo, rūpi, ruptum, 3.
into, in (*c. acc.*)
introduce, indūco, duxi, ductum, 3.
invade, invādo, si, sum, 3.
in turn, invĭcem.
in vain, frustra.
invaluable, prĕtiōsissĭmus, a, um.
inventor, inventor, ōris, m.
invincible, invictus, a, um.
invite, invīto, 1.

invoke, invŏco, 1.
involved, obstrictus, a, um.
Iphigenia, Iphigĕnīa, ae, f.
Ireland, Hibernia, ae, f.
Irishman, Hibernus, a, um.
iron (*subst.*), ferrum ; (*adj.*), ferreus, a, um.
irritate, irrīto, 1.
island, insŭla, ae, f.
it, see *he.*
Italy, Itălia, ae, f.
ivory (*subst.*), ĕbur, ŏris, n ; (*adj.*) ĕburnus, a, um.
ivy, hĕdĕra, ae, f.

Jailer, iānĭtor, ōris, m.
Janiculum, Ianĭcŭlum, i, n.
jar, vas, vāsis, n.
javelin, iacŭlum, i, n.
jaw, māla, ae, f.
jest, iŏcus, i, m ; *pl.* i *and* a.
join, iungo, nxi, nctum, 3.
joint, artĭcŭlus, i, m.
journey, Iter, itĭnĕris, n.
joy, gaudium, i, n.
joyful, laetus, a, um.
joyfully, laete.
judge, iūdex, ĭcis, m.
judge, to, iūdīco, 1.
judgment, iūdĭcium, i, n.
juice, ius, iūris, n.
Julia, Iūlia, ae, f.
jump, saltus, ūs, m.
jump, to, salto, 1.
jumper, saltātor, oris, m.
Juno, Iūno, ōnis, f.
Jupiter, Iuppĭter, Iŏvis, m.
just, iustus, a, um.
just (*adv.*), tantum non.
justice, iustĭtia, ae, f.; ius, iuris. m.

Keep, tĕneo, ui, 2 ; servo, 1.
keep off, arceo, ui, 2.
keeper, custos, ōdis, c.
key, clāvis, is, f.
kill, interfĭcio, fēci, fectum, 3.
kind, gĕnus, ĕris, n.
kindle, incendo, di, sum, 3.
kindly, bĕnigne.

English-Latin Vocabulary.

kindliness, kindness, bŏnĭtas, ātis,
  f. ; a kindness, bĕnĕfĭcium, i, n.
kindred, prŏpinqui, ōrum, m.
king, rex, rēgis, m.
kingdom, regnum, i, n.
kiss, oscŭlor, 1 dep.
knave, nĕbŭlo, ōnis, m.
knee, gĕnu, ūs, n.
knife, culter, tri, m.
knight, ĕques, ĭtis, m.
knightly, ĕquester, tris, tre.
knot, nŏdus, i, m.
know, scio, īvi or ii, ītum, 4.
knowledge, scientia, ae, f
known, nōtus, a, um.

Labienus. Lăbiēnus, i, m.
laborious, arduus, a, um.
labour, lăbor, ōris, m.
labour, to, lăbōro, 1.
Lacedaemonian, Lăcĕdaemŏnius, a,
  um : Lacedaemonian woman,
  = Lăcaena, ae, f.
lack, ĕgeo, ui, 2 ; căreo, ui, 2.
Laconia, Lăcōnia, ae, f.
laden, ŏnustus, a, um.
Laevinus, Laevīnus, i, m.
lady, mŭlier, ĕris, f.
lake, lăcus, ūs, m.
lamb, agnus, i, m.
lame, claudus, a, um.
lament, lūgeo, xi, ctum, 2 (trans.) ;
  dōleo, ui, itum, 2 (intrans.)
lamentation, maeror, ōris, m., see
  grief.
lance, hasta, ae, f.
land, terra, ae, f.; ăger, gri, m.
land (adj.), terrestris, e.
landlord, caupo, ōnis, m.
large, magnus, a, um.
last, ultĭmus, a, um.
last, at, tandem.
lasting, pĕrennis, e.
late, tardus, a, um   crus, a, um.
lately, nūper.
Latin, Latīnus, a, um.
latter, the former . . . the latter,
  ille . . . hic.
Latōna, Latōna, ae, f.
  B. L. W.

laugh, rīdeo, si, sum, 2.
laugh at, irrīdeo, si, sum, 2 (c. dat.)
laughing-stock, lūdibrium, i, n.
Laurentia, Laurentia, ae, f.
lavish, prŏdĭgus, a, um.
law, lex, lēgis, f.
lawful, lĕgĭtĭmus, a, um.
lawful, it is, lĭcet, uit, 2, impers.
lay, lay aside, see place.
lay down, depōno, pŏsui, posĭtum, 3.
lay (eggs), părio, pĕperi, partum, 3.
lay waste, vasto, 1.
laziness, inertia, ae, f.
lazy, segnis, e ; ĭners, tis.
lead, plumbum, i, n.
lead, dūco, xi, ctum, 3.
lead out, ēdūco, xi, ctum, 3.
leaden, plumbeus, a, um.
leader, dux, dŭcis, m.
leaf, frons, dis, f.
leap, saltus, ūs, m.
leap, to, sălio, ii or ŭi, saltum, 4.
leap across, transĭlio, ui, sultum, 4.
leap down, desĭlio, sĭlui, sultum, 4.
leap forth, exsĭlio, sĭlui, sultum, 4.
leaper, saltātor, ōris, m.
learn, disco, didĭci, 3.
learned, doctus, a, um.
learning, doctrīna, ae, f.
least, minĭmus, a, um.
leave, to, linquo, līqui, lictum, 3 ;
  rĕlinquo, līqui, lictum, 3.
leave, pŏtestas, ātis, f.
left, relĭquus, a, um.
left (hand), sĭnister, tra, trum.
leg, crus, crūris, n.
legate, lēgātus, i, m.
legion, lĕgio, ōnis, f.
legionary, lĕgiōnārius, a, um.
leisure, ōtium, i, n.
leisure, to have, văco, 1.
Lemnos, Lemnos, i, f.
lend, crēdo, dĭdi, ditum, 3.
length, longitūdo, ĭnis, f.
length, at, tandem.
Lentulus, Lentŭlus, i, m.
Leonidas, Leonĭdas, ae, m.
less, minor, us.
less, for, minōris.

N

lessen, dēmĭnuo, ui, ūtum, 3.
lest, nē.
let go, dīmitto, mīsi, missum, 3.
letter, lĭtĕrae, arum, f.; *letter of the alphabet*, lītĕra, ae, f.
level, aequus, a, um.
level, to, aequo, 1.
levy, a, dēlectus, ūs, m.
levy, to, conscrībo, psi, ptum, 3.
liar, mendax, ācis.
liberality, mūnĭfĭcentia, ae, f.
liberate, lībĕro, 1.
liberty, lībertas, ātis, f.
lick, lingo, nxi, nctum, 3.
lictor, lictor, ōris, m.
lie (to tell lies), mentior, ĭtŭs, 4 dep.
lie, lie down, iăcco, ui, ĭtum, 2.
lie hid, lăteo, ui, 2.
lie in ambush, in wait for, insĭdior, 1 dep. (c. dat.)
life, vīta, ae, f.
light, lux, lūcis, f.; lūmen, ĭnis, n.
light, lĕvis, e.
lighted, accensus, a, um.
lighten, lĕvo, 1.
lightning, fulgŭr, ŭris, n.
like, sĭmĭlis, e.
like, to, see *to love.*
likeness, sĭmĭlĭtūdo, inis, f.
limb, membrum, i, n.
limit, fīnis, is, m; līmes, ĭtis, m.
line—of battle, ăcies, ei, f.
line—of march, agmen, ĭnis, n.
linger, cunctor, 1 dep.
lion, leo, ōnis, m.
lip, labrum, i, m.
listen to, audio, īvi *or* ii, ītum, 4.
literature, lĭtĕrae, ārum, f.
litter, lectīca, ae, f.
little, parvus, a, um.
live, to, vīvo, vixi, victum, 3.
live on, vescor, 3 dep. (c. abl.)
load, ŏnus, ĕris, n.
load, to, ŏnĕro, 1.
lofty, altus, a, um.
log, lignum, i, n.
long, longus, a, um.
long-haired, cŏmātus, a, um.
look, look at, aspĭcio, spexi, spectum, 3.

look back, respĭcio, spexi, spectum, 3.
look for, quaero, quaesīvi, quaesītum, 3.
look on, aspecto, 1.
look, a, vultus, ūs, m.
lord, dŏmĭnus, i, m.
lose, perdo, dĭdi, dĭtum, 3 ; āmitto, mīsi, missum, 3.
loss, damnum, i, n.
lot, sors, tis, f.
loud, altus, a, um ; magnus, a, um.
lovable, ămābĭlis, e.
love, ămor, ōris, m.
love, to, ămo, 1 ; dīlĭgo, lexi, lectum, 3.
lover, ămātor, ōris, m.
loving, ămans, tis.
low, lowly, hŭmĭlis, e.
lower, infĕrior, us.
lower, to, dēmitto, mīsi, missum, 3.
Lucilius, Lūcīlius, i, m.
Lucius, Lūcius, i, m.
luck, fortūna, ae, f.
lucky, fēlix, īcis ; faustus, a, um.
Lucullus, Lŭcullus, i, m.
lunatic, insānus, a, um ; āmens, tis.
luxury, luxŭria, ae, f.
Lydia, Lydia, ae, f.
lyre, lyra, ae, f.
Lysimachus, Lȳsĭmăchus, i, m.

Macedon, Macedonia, Măcĕdŏnia, ae, f.
Macedonian, Măcĕdonĭcus, a, um.
Macedonians, the, Măcĕdŏnes, ŏnum, m.
machine, machīna, ae, f.
mad, insānus, a, um ; āmens, tis.
mad, to be, insānio, īvi *or* ii, 4.
madness, insānia, ac, f.; āmentia, ae, f.
magistrate, măgistrātus, ūs, m.
magnanimity, magnănĭmĭtas, ātis, f.
magpie, pīca, ae, f.
Maharbal, Măharbal, ălis, m.
Maia, Maia, ae, f.
maid, ancilla, ae, f.

English-Latin Vocabulary. 195

maintain, conservo, 1, sustĭneo, ui, tentum, 2.
make, făcio, fēci, factum, 3.
make haste, festīno, 1 ; prŏpĕro, 1 ; mātūro, 1.
make way, cēdo, cessi, cessum, 3.
male, mas, māris.
malignant, mălĕfĭcus, a, um.
mallet, malleus, i, m.
man, vir, i, m ; hŏmo, inis, c.
manage, admĭnistro, 1.
manager (*of a theatre*), lŭdīmăgister, tri, m.
manifest, mănĭfestus, a, um.
Manius, Manius, i, m.
Manlius, Manlius, i, m.
manly, vĭrīlis, e ; *brave*, fortis, e.
manner, mos, mōris, m ; mŏdus, i, m.
manure, stercus, ŏris, n.
many, multus, a, um.
marble, marmor, ŏris, n ; (*adj.*) marmŏreus, a, um.
march, to, prŏfĭciscor, fectus, 3 dep.; contendo, di, tum, 3.
march, ĭter, itinĕris, n.
Marcus, Marcus, i, m.
mark, signum, i, n ; nŏta, ae, f.
marry, *as a man*, dūco duxi, ductum, 3 ; *as a woman*, nūbo, nupsi, nuptum, 3 (*c. dat.*)
Mars, Mars, tis, m.
marsh, pălūs, ūdis, f.
martial, martius, a, um.
mass, mōles, is, f.
master, dŏmĭnus, i, m ; *of a school*, măgister, tri, m.
matter, res, rei, f.
matters, *it*, rēfert, *impers.*
mayor, praefectus, i, m.
meadow, prătum, i, n.
meanness, ăvārĭtia, ae, f.
means, ŏpes, um, f.; cōpia, ae, f.
meanwhile, intĕreā, intĕrim.
measure, mŏdus, i, m.
measure, to, mētior, mensus, 4, dep.
meat, căro, carnis, f.
Mecenas, Mecēnas, ātis, m.
meditate, cōgĭto, 1.
Medusa, Medūsa, ae, f.

meet, aptus, a, um.
meet, to, occurro, curri, cursum, 3 (*c. dat.*) ; (*adv.*), obviam (*c. dat.*)
memorable, insignis, e.
Menelaus, Menĕlāus, i, m.
Menenius, Menēnius, i, m.
mention, mentio, ōnis, f.
merchant, mercātor, ōris, m.
merchantman, ŏnĕrāria nāvis.
mercy, clēmentia, ae, f.
merited, mĕrĭtus, a, um.
message, nuntius, i, m.
messenger, nuntius, i, m.
metal, mĕtallum, i, n.
Metellus, Mĕtellus, i, m.
middle, mĕdius, a, um ; *in the midst*, in medio ; *midnight*, media nox.
might, vis, *acc.* vim, *abl.* vi, f.
mighty, pŏtens, tis ; ingens, tis.
mildness, lēnĭtas, ātis, f.
mile, say *a thousand paces*.
milestone, termĭnus, i, m.
Miletus, Mīlētus, i, f.
military, mīlĭtāris, e.
milk, lac, tis, n.
Milo, Milo, ōnis, m.
mina, mīna, ae, f.
mind, mens, tis, f.; ănĭmus, i. m.
mindful, mĕmor, ŏris (*c. gen.*)
mine, meus, a, um.
mingle, misceo, ui, xtum, 2.
miracle, mīrăcŭlum, i, n.
miraculous, mīrus, a, um.
mirth, laetĭtia, ıe, f.
miserable, mĭsĕrābĭlis, e ; mĭser, era, erum.
miserably, mĭsĕre.
misery, dŏlor, ōris, m.
misfortune, mălum, i, n ; călămĭtas, ātis, f.
mistake, error, ōris, m.
mistress, hĕra, ae, f.; dŏmĭna, ae, f.
mix, see *mingle*.
mob, turba, ae, f.
mock, lūdo, si, sum, 3.
mockery, lūdibrium, i, n.
moderation, mŏdĕrātio, ōnis, f.
modest, mŏdestus, a, um.
modesty, mŏdestia, ae, f.
moist, hūmĭdus, a, um.

English-Latin Vocabulary.

moisture, hŭmor, ōris, m.
mole, talpa, ae, c.
money, *sum of money*, pĕcūnia, ae, f.
monster, monstrum, i, n.
month, mensis, is, m.
monument, mŏnŭmentum, i, n.
moon, lūna, ae, f.
more, plus, pluris ; (*adv*.), măgis.
moreover, praetĕreā.
morning, māne, indcl.
mortal, mortālis, e.
mother, māter, tris, f.
motion, mōtus, ūs, m.
mound, tŭmŭlus, i, m.
mount, ascendo, di, sum, 3 ; conscendo, di, sum, 3.
mountain, mons, tis, m.
mourn, lūgeo, xi, ctum, 2.
mournful, maestus, a, um.
mourning, luctus, ūs, m.
mouse, mus, mūris, c.
mouth, os, ōris, n.
move, mŏveo, vi, tum, 2.
much, multus, a, um ; (*adv*.), multum.
Mucius, Mŭcius, i, m.
mud, līmus, i, m.
multitude, multĭtūdo, ĭnis, f.
Mummius, Mummius, i, m.
munificence, mŭnĭfĭcentia, ae, f.
murder, caedes, is, f.
murder, *to*, interfĭcio, fēci, fectum, 3 ; trucīdo, 1.
murderer, interfector, ōris, m.
murmur, murmur, ŭris, n.
murmur, *to*, murmŭro, 1.
mutilate, mŭtĭlo, 1.
Mutina, Mŭtĭna, ae, f.
my, meus, a, um.
myrrh, myrrha, ae, f.
myrtle, myrtus, i, f.

Naked, nūdus, a, um.
name, nōmen, ĭnis, n.
name, *to*, nōmĭno, 1 ; vŏco, 1.
narrate, narro, 1 ; refĕro, tŭli, lātum, ferre.
narrow, angustus, a, um.
nation, gens, tis, f.; popŭlus, i, m.

national, patrius, a, um.
native, a, incŏla, ae, c.
nature, nātūra, ae, f.
naval, nāvālis, e.
navigation, nāvĭgatio, ōnis, f.
near, prŏpinquus, a, um ; (*prep*.), prŏpe, ad (*c. acc.*)
nearly, fĕre, paene.
near side of, *on the*, cis, citra (*c. acc.*)
necessary, nĕcessārius, a, um.
necessity, nĕcessĭtas, ātis, f.
neck, collum, i, n.
need, ŏpus, n. (*c. abl.*)
needle, ăcus, ūs, f.
neglect, neglĭgo, lexi, lectum, 3.
negligence, incūria, ae, f.
neigh, hinnītus, ūs, m.
neigh, *to*, hinnio, īvi *or* ii, 4.
neigh at, adhinnio, īvi *or* ii, ītum, 4.
neighbour, *neighbouring*, vīcīnus, a, um ; fīnĭtĭmus, a, um.
neither, neuter, tra, trum ; (*conj*.), nec, nĕque.
nephew, nĕpos, ōtis, m.
Neptune, Neptūnus, i, m.
Nessus, Nessus, i, m.
Nero, Nero, ōnis, m.
nest, nīdus, i, m.
net, rēte, is, n.
never, nunquam.
nevertheless, tămen.
new, nŏvus, a, um.
news, nuntius, i, m.
next, proxĭmus, a, um.
night, nox, noctis, f.; *by night*, noctu.
nightingale, phĭlŏmēla, ae, f.
Nile, Nīlus, i, m.
nine, nŏvem, indcl.
nobility, nōbĭlĭtas, ātis, f.
noble, nōbĭlis, e.
noble, *nobleman*, princeps, cĭpis, m.
noise, sŏnus, i, m ; clāmor, ōris, m.
nominate, nomĭno, 1.
none, nullus, a, um ; *no one*, *nobody*, nēmo, *acc*. nemĭnem.
nose, nāsus, i, m.
not, non ; *not even*, nē . . . quĭdem.
noted, nōtus, a, um.

English-Latin Vocabulary.

nothing, nĭhil *or* nil, indcl.
notice, ănĭmadverto, ti, sum, 3.
notwithstanding, tămen.
nourish, alo, alui, altum *or* alĭtum, 3.
novelty, nŏvĭtas, ātis, f.
now, nunc; iam.
nowhere, nusquam.
Numa, Nŭma, ae, m.
number, nŭmĕrus, i, m.
numerous, multus, a, um.
Numitor, Numĭtor, ōris, m.
nurse, nutrix, īcis, f.
nurse, to, fŏvco, fōvi, fotum, 2.
nut, nux, nŭcis, f.
nymph, nympha, ac,

Oak, quercus, ûs, f.
oar, rēmus, i, m.
oath, iusiūrandum, iurisiurandi; *military oath*, sacrāmentum, i, n.
obedience, obsĕquium, i, n.
obedient, ŏbēdiens, tis (*c. dat.*)
obey, pārco, ui, ĭtum, 2 (*c. dat.*)
object, obiĭcio, iēci, iectum, 3.
oblige, cōgo, coēgi, coactum, 3.
obscure, to, obscūro, 1.
observe, observo, 1.
obstinacy, pertĭnacia, ae, f.
obstinate, pertĭnax, ācis.
obstruct, impĕdio, īvi *or* ii, ītum, 4.
obtain, potior, ītus, 4 (*c. abl.*)
obtain by entreaty, impetro, 1.
obtain by lot, sortior, ītus, 4 dep.
occasion, tempus, ŏris, n.
occupy, possĭdeo, sēdi, sessum, 2.
ocean, ōcĕănus, i, m.
Octavianus, Octāviānus, i, m.
odour, ŏdor, ōris, m.
off, ad (*c. acc.*)
offend, offendo, di, sum, 3.
offer, offĕro, obtŭli, oblātum, offerre.
offering, dōnum, i, n.
office, offĭcium, i, n.; mūnus, ĕris, n.
officer, lēgātus, i, m.
offspring, prōles, is, f.
often, saepe.
oil, ŏlĕum, i, n.

old, antīquus, a, um; vĕtus, ĕris.
old age, sĕnectûs, ûtis, f.
old man, sĕnex, is.
old woman, ănus, ûs, f.
Olympic, Olympĭcus, a, um.
omen, ōmen, ĭnis, n.
omit, ŏmitto, mīsi, missum, 3.
on, in (*c. abl.*)
on account of, ob, propter (*c. acc.*)
once, sĕmel; *once upon a time*, ōlim, quondam.
one, ūnus, a, um; *one by one*, singuli, ae, a.
one—another, ălius—ălius; *the one —the other*, alter—alter.
only, mŏdo; (*adj.*) sōlus, a, um.
onset, impĕtus, ûs, m.
open, ăpertus, a, um.
open, to, ăpĕrio, ui, rtum, 4.
opinion, sententia, ae, f.
opponent, adversārius, i, m.
opportunity, occāsio, ōnis, f.
oppose, oppōno, pŏsui, pŏsitum; obsisto, stĭti, stĭtum, 3.
oppress, opprĭmo, pressi, pressum, 3.
or, aut, vel; vĕ (*enclitic*); sīve, seu.
orator, ōrātor, ōris, m.
oratory, făcundia, ae, f.
orb, orbis, is, m.
order, ordo, ĭnis, m; *command*, mandātum, i, n.
order, to, iŭbeo, iussi, iussum, 2; impĕro, 1 (*c. dat.*)
orderly, an, tăbellārius, i, m.
Orgetorix, Orgĕtŏrix, ĭgis, m.
ornament, ornātus, ûs, m.
Orpheus, Orpheûs, ĕos, m.
ostentation, ostentātio, ōnis, f.
ostrich, strūthiŏcămēlus, i, m.
other, ălius, a, ud.
otherwise, ălioquin, ălias.
ought, dĕbeo, ui, ĭtum, 2.
our, noster, tra, trum.
out of, e, ex (*c. abl.*)
outline, descriptio, ōnis, f.
outrage, iniūria, ae, f.
outside, extra (*c. acc.*)
outstrip, praevĕnio, vēni, ventum, 4.

English-Latin Vocabulary.

outwork, prōpugnācŭlum, i, n.
over, sŭper (*c. acc. and abl.*), *across*. trans (*c. acc.*)
overcome, vinco, vīci, victum, 3.
overflow, ĭnundo, 1.
overlook, prospĭcio, spexi, spectum, 3.
overthrow, see *overcome*.
overturn, subverto, verti, versum, 3.
overwhelm, opprĭmo, pressi, pressum, 3.
owe, dēbeo, ui, itum, 2.
owner, dŏmĭnus, i, m.
ox, bos, bŏvis, c.

Pace, passus, ūs, m
pacify, pāco, 1.
pain, dŏlor, ōris, m.
paint, pingo, nxi, ctum, 3.
painter, pictor, ōris, m.
painting, pictūra, ae, f.
palace, pălātium, i, n.
palm, palma, ae, f.
panic, păvor, ōris, m.
pant, ănhēlo, 1.
pantry, cella, ae, f.
paper, charta, ae, f.
parched, ārĭdus, a, um ; tostus, a, um.
pardon, vĕnia, ae, f.
pardon, to, ignosco, nōvi, nōtum, 3.
parent, parens, tis, c.
Parrhasius, Parrhăsius, i, m.
parricide, parrĭcīda, ae, m.
parrot, psittăcus, i, m.
part, pars, tis, f. ; (*of an actor*), partes, pl.
partner, sŏcius, i, m.
party, pars, tis, f. (*generally in pl.*)
pass, pass by, pass on, praetĕreo, ĭvi or ii, ĭtum, 4.
pass on (trans.), trādo, dĭdi, dĭtum, 3.
path, callis, is, m.
patrician, patrĭcius, a, um.
patron, patrōnus, i, m.
Paullus, Paullus, i, m.
pay, stīpendium, i, n.
pay, to, solvo, vi, ūtum, 3.
pay attention, operam dare.

pea, cĭcer, ĕris, n.
peace, pax, pācis, f.
peacock, pāvo, ōnis, m.
peasant, rustĭcus, i, m.
pelican, pĕlĭcānus, i, m.
penalty, poena, ae, f.
penetrate, penetro, 1.
penitence, poenĭtentia, ae, f.
penny, dēnārius, i, m ; as, sis, m.
people, pŏpŭlus, i, m.
perceive, animadverto, ti, sum, 3.
perch, to, insīdo, sēdi, sessum, 3.
perfectly, plāne.
perform, fungor, functus, 3 (*c. abl.*)
perfume, ŏdor, ōris, m.
perhaps, forsĭtan, fortasse.
Periander, Periander, dri, m.
peril, pĕrīcŭlum, i, n.
perish, pĕreo, ivi *or* ii, 4.
permission, pŏtestas, ātis, f.
permit, pătior, passus, 3, dep.
Perse, Perse, ēs, f.
perseverance, persĕvērantia, ae, f.
Perseus, Perseus, eos, m.
persevere, persĕvĕro, 1.
Persian, Persa, ae, m.
persistently, assĭdue.
person, hŏmo, ĭnis, c.
persuade, persuādeo, si, sum (*c. dat. of person*).
pestilential, pestĭlens, tis.
Philip, Phĭlippus, i, m.
Philoctetes, Philoctētes, is, m.
philosopher, phĭlŏsŏphus, i, m.
philosophy, phĭlŏsŏphia, ae, f.
Phocion, Phocion, ōnis, m.
Phocus, Phocus, i, m.
physician, mĕdĭcus, i, m.
pickle, condio, ĭvi *or* ii, ītum, 4.
picture, tăbŭla, ae, f.
pierce, transfīgo, xi, xum, 3.
pig, porcus, i, m ; porcellus, i, m.
pigeon, cŏlumba, ae, f.
pillow, culcĭta, ae, f.
pilot, gŭbernātor, ōris, m.
pious, pius, a, um.
pirate, praedo, ōnis, m.
Piso, Pīso, ōnis, m.
pitch (*a camp*), pōno, pŏsui, pŏsĭtum, 3.

English-Latin Vocabulary.

piteously, mĭsĕre.
pitfall, fŏvĕa. ae, f.
pitiful, mĭserĭcors, cordis.
pity, mĭserĭcordia, ae, f.
pity, to, mĭsĕreor, sĕrĭtus *or* sertus, 2 dep. (*c. gen.*)
placable, plăcābĭlis, e.
place, lŏcus, ĭ, m ; *plural*, lŏca.
place, to, pōno, pŏsui, pŏsĭtum, 3.
place before, antĕpono, pŏsui, pŏsĭtum, 3.
plain, campus, i, m.
plan, consĭlium, i, n.
plant, planta, ae, f.
plant, to, see *place*.
plaster, oblĭno, lēvi, lĭtum, 3.
Plataea, Plataea, ae, f.
plate, vas, vāsis, n.
platform, trĭbūnal, ālis, n.
Plato, Plato, ōnis, m.
play, lūdus, i, m.
play, to, lūdo, si, sum, 3.
plead (*a cause*), dīco, xi, ctum, 3.
pleasant, grātus, a, um : jūcundus, a, um.
please, plăceo, ui, ĭtum (*c. dat.*) delecto.
pleasure, vŏluptas, ātis, f.
plot, consĭlium, i, n.
plough, ărătrum, i, n.
plough, to, ăro, 1.
ploughshare, vŏmer, ĕris, m.
pluck, carpo, psi, ptum, 3.
plucking, vellicatio, ōnis, f.
plunder, praeda, ae, f.
plunder, to, dīrĭpio, rĭpui, reptum, 3.
plunderer, praedātor, ōris, m.
Pluto, Pluto, ōnis, m.
poet, poēta, ae, m.
point out, ostendo, di, sum, 3.
poison, vĕnēnum, i, n.
poisonous, vĕnēnātus, a, um.
Polycarp, Polycarpus, i, m.
Polyxena, Polyxĕna, ae, f.
pomp, pompa, ae, f.
Pompeius, Pompeius, i, m.
Pomponius, Pompōnius, i, m.
pond, pool, stagnum, i, n.
poor, pauper, ĕris.
poppy, păpăver, ĕris, n.

populace, vulgus, i, n. *or* m.
populous, frĕquens, tis.
porch, portĭcus, ūs, f.
Porcia, Porcia, ae, f.
Porsena, Porsĕna, ae, m.
port, portus, ūs, m.
portent, prodĭgium, i, n.
portion, pars, tis, f.
portrait, effĭgies, ēi, f.
Porus, Porus, i, m.
Poseidon, Poseidon, ōnis, m.
position, see *place*.
possess, hăbeo, ui, ĭtum, 2.
possession, possessio, ōnis, f.
possession of, to take, occŭpo, 1.
posterity, postĕri, ōrum, m.
pour, fundo, fūdi, fūsum, 3.
poverty, paupertas, ātis, f.
power, pŏtestas, ātis, f. ; *in the power of*, penes (*c. acc.*)
powerful, pŏtens, tis.
practice, usus, ūs, m.
practise, exerceo, ui, ĭtum, 2.
praetor, praetor, ōris, m.
praise, laus, dis, f.
praise, to, laudo, 1.
pray, ōro, 1 ; prĕcor, 1 dep.
prayers, prĕces, um, f.
precept, praeceptum, i, n.
precious, prĕtiōsus, a, um.
prefer, mălo, ui, malle ; antĕpono, pŏsui, pŏsĭtum, 3.
prepare, păro, 1.
presence of, in, cōram (*c. abl.*)
present, a, dōnum, i, n ; mūnus, ĕris, n.
present, to, dōno, 1.
present, to be, adsum, fui, esse.
preserve, servo, 1.
press, prĕmo, pressi, pressum, 3.
pretence, spĕcies, ei, f. ; sĭmŭlātio, ōnis, f.
pretend, sĭmŭlo, 1.
pretender, sĭmŭlātor, ōris, m.
pretty, pulcher, chra, chrum.
prevail, văleo, ui, 2.
prevent, prŏhĭbeo, ui, itum, 2 ; impĕdio, ivi *or* ii, ĭtum, 4.
previously, ante, antea.
prey, praeda, ae, f.

Priam, Priămus, i, m.
price, prĕtium, i, n.
pride, sŭperbia, ae, f.
priest, priestess, săcerdos, ōtis, c.
prince, princeps, cĭpis, m.
prison, carcer, ĕris, m.
prisoner, captīvus, i, m.
private, prīvātus, a, um.
prize, praemium, i, n.
proceed, prōgredior, gressus, 3 dep.
proclaim, prōnuntio, 1 ; ēdīco, dixi, dictum, 3.
proconsul, prōconsul, ŭlis, m.
proconsular, prōconsulāris, e.
Proculus, Prŏcŭlus, i, m.
procure, păro, 1.
Procus, Procus, i, m.
prodigal, prōdĭgus, a, um.
produce, părio, pĕpĕri, partum, 3 ; prodūco, duxi, ductum, 3.
profane, prŏfānus, a, um.
proficiency, pĕrītia, ae, f.
profit, quaestus, ūs, m.
profuse, see *prodigal*.
project, ēmĭneo, ui, 2.
prolong, prōdūco, duxi, ductum, 3.
promise, pollĭceor, cĭtus, 2 dep.; promitto, mīsi, missum, 3.
prompt, promptus, a, um.
promptitude, cĕlĕrĭtas, ātis, f.
prone, prōnus, a, um.
pronounce, prōnuntio, 1.
property, res, rei, f.; bŏna, ōrum, n.
prophet, vātes, is, c.
propitious, prŏpĭtius, a, um.
propose, prōpōno, pŏsui, pŏsĭtum, 3 ; *to propose a law*, rŏgo, 1.
proscribe, proscrībo, psi, ptum, 3.
prosperity, res secundae.
prosperous, sĕcundus, a, um.
protect, tueor, tuĭtus, 2 dep.; tutor, 1 dep.
protection, praesĭdium, i, n.
protract, trăho, xi, ctum, 3, see *prolong*.
proud, sŭperbus, a, um.
prove, dēmonstro, 1.
provide, prōvĭdeo, vīdi, vīsum, 2.
provided, instructus, a, um.

provided that, dum, modo (*both c. subj.*)
province, prōvincia, ae, f.
provisions, commeātus, ūs, m.
provoke, lăcesso, īvi, ītum, 3.
prudence, consĭlium, i, n.
prudent, prūdens, tis.
public, publĭcus, a, um.
Publius, Publius, i, m.
pull, trăho, xi, ctum, 3.
pull out, extrăho, xi, ctum, 3.
punish, pūnio, īvi or ii, ītum, 4.
punishment, poena, ae, f.
puppy, cătellus,|i, m.; cătella, ae, f.
pure, pūrus, a, um.
purple, purpŭreus, a, um.
purpose, on, de industria.
purse, lŏcŭli, ōrum, m.
pursue, sĕquor, cūtus, 3 dep.
push down, dētrūdo, si, sum, 3.
put, pōno, pŏsui, pŏsĭtum, 3.
put over, praefĭcio, fēci, fectum, 3 (*c. dat.*)
put back, rĕpōno, pŏsui, pŏsĭtum, 3.
put under, suppōno, pŏsui, pŏsĭtum, 3.
pyre, rŏgus, i, m.
Pyrenees, Pȳrēnaei montes.
Pyrrhus, Pyrrhus, i, m.

Quadruped, quadrŭpes, pĕdis.
quaestor, quaestor, ōris, m.
quail, cŏturnix, ĭcis, f.
quantity, cōpia, ae, f.; vis, vim, vi, f.
quarrel, rixa, ae, f.
quarrel, to, contendo, di, tum; rixor, 1 dep.
quarters, winter, hīberna, ōrum, n.
queen, rēgīna, ae, f.
question, percontātio, ōnis, f.
question, to, interrŏgo, 1 ; rŏgo, 1 ; percontor, 1 dep.
quickly, cĕlĕrĭter.
quickness, cĕlĕrĭtas, ātis, f.
quiet, tranquillus, a, um ; quietus, a, um.
quietly, quiēte.
Quintus, Quintus, i, m.
Quirinus, Quĭrīnus, i, m.

English-Latin Vocabulary. 201

Race, gĕnus, ĕris, n.
race, a, cursus, ūs, m.
raft, rătis, is, f.
rage, Ira, ae, f.; fŭror, ōris, m.
rage, to, saevio, ii, Itum, 4.
raid, incursio, ōnis, f.
rain, imber, bris, m; plŭvia, ae, f.
raise, tollo, sustŭli, sublātum, 3.
rally, collĭgo, legi, lectum, 3.
rampart, vallum, i, n.
rank, ordo, Inis, m.
ransom, rēdemptio, ōnis, f.
rapacious, răpax, ācis.
rapid, răpĭdus, a, um; cĕler, is, e.
rapidity, cĕlĕrĭtas, ātis, f.
rapine, răpīna, ae, f.
rare, rārus, a, um.
rascal, scĕlestus, a, um.
rash, praeceps, cĭpĭtis.
rashly, tĕmĕre.
rashness, tĕmĕrĭtas, ātis, f.
rat, mus, mūris, c.
rather, pŏtĭus.
ravage, vasto, 1.
ravager, vastātor, ōris, m.
rave, fŭro, ui, 3.
raven, corvus, i, m.
raw, crūdus, a, um.
ray, rădius, i, m.
reach, attingo, tĭgi, tactum, 3; pervĕnio, vēni, ventum, 4.
rebuke, incrĕpo, ui, Itum, 1.
read, lĕgo, lēgi, lectum, 3.
readily, lŭbenter.
ready, promptus, a, um; părātus, a, um.
real, vērus, a, um.
reality, vērĭtas, ātis, f.
really, vēre.
reap, mĕto, messui, messum, 3.
rear, ălo, ălui, altum or alĭtum, 3.
reason, reasoning, rătio, ōnis, f.; cause, caussa, ae, f.; by reason of, ob, propter (both c. acc.)
rebuke, incrĕpo, ui, Itum, 1.
recall, rĕvŏco, 1.
receive, accĭpio, cēpi, ceptum, 3.
recent, rĕcens, tis; nŏvus, a, um.
recently, nūper.
receptacle, rĕceptācŭlum, i. n.

recite, narro, 1; rĕcĭto, 1.
reckon, nŭmĕro, 1.
recline, discumbo, cŭbui, cŭbitum, 3; reclīno, 1.
recognise, agnosco, nōvi, nĭtum, 3.
recognition, cognĭtio, ōnis, f.
recollection, mĕmŏria, ae, f.
recommence, rĕdintĕgro, 1; rĕnŏvo, 1.
recover, rĕcŭpĕro, 1; recĭpio, cēpi, ceptum, 3.
recount, narro, 1.
refrain from, abstĭneo, ui, tentum, 2.
refresh, rĕcreo, 1.
refuge, ăsўlum, i, n.
refuse, rĕcūso, 1.
refute, arguo, ui, ūtum, 3.
regard, aspĭcio, spexi, spectum, 3; estimate, aestĭmo, 1.
region, rĕgio, ōnis, f.
regret, dēsīdĕrium, i, n.
regret, to, dēsīdĕro, 1.
Regulus, Rĕgŭlus, i, m.
reign, regnum, i, n.
reign, to, regno, 1; reign over. impĕro (c. dat.)
rein, hăbēna, ae, f.
reinforcement, subsĭdium, i, n.
reject, rēĭcio, rūiēci, rūiectum, 3.
rejoice, gaudeo, gāvĭsus, 2 dep.
relate, narro, 1.
relation, prŏpinquus, i, m.
reliance, fĭdūciă, ae, f.
relieve, lĕvo, 1.
religion, rĕlĭgio, ōnis, f.
relying, frētus, a, um (c. abl.)
remain, măneo, mansi, nsum, 2.
remain over, sŭpersum, fui, esse.
remaining, rĕlĭquus, a, um.
remark, inquam, def.
remarkable, insignis, e.
remedy, rĕmĕdium, i, n.
remember, mĕmĭni, def.; rĕcordor, atus, 1 dep.
remembrance, mĕmŏria, ae, f.
remind, admŏneo, ui, Itum, 2.
remove, āmŏveo, mōvi, mōtum, 2.
remorse, dŏlor, ōris, m.; poenĭtentia, ae, f.

Remus, Rĕmus, i, m.
render, reddo, dĭdi, dĭtum, 3.
renew, rĕnŏvo, 1.
renown, fāma, ae, f.
renowned, clārus, a, um.
repair, rĕfĭcio, fēci, fectum, 3.
repeat, ĭtĕro, 1.
repel, repello, pŭli, pulsum, 3.
repent, poenĭtet, uit, 2 impers.
repentance, poenĭtentia, ae, f.
replace, rĕpōno, pŏsui, pŏsĭtum, 3.
reply, responsum, i, n.
reply, in, contrā.
reply, to, respondeo, di, sum, 2.
report, fāma, ae, f.; rūmor, ōris, m.
report, to, nuntio, 1.
repose, quies, ētis, f.
represent, effingo, finxi, fictum, 3.
repress, rĕprĭmo, pressi, pressum, 3.
republic, respublĭca, reipublĭcae, f.
repulse, pello, pĕpŭli, pulsum, 3.
reputation, fāma, ae, f.
resign, abdĭco, 1.
resist, rĕsisto, stĭti, stĭtum, 3 (c. dat.)
resolve, constituo, ui, ūtum, 3.
resound, rĕsŏno, 1.
resources, ŏpes, um, f.
respect, observantia, ae, f.
response, responsum, i, n.
rest, quies, ētis, f.
rest, the, rĕlĭquus, a, um.
rest, to, quiesco, ēvi, ētum, 3.
restore, reddo, dĭdi, dĭtum, 3 ; restĭtuo, ui, ūtum, 3.
restrain, cŏhĭbeo, ui, ĭtum, 2.
result, ēventus, ūs, m.
retain, rĕtĭneo, ui, tentum, 2.
retake, rĕcĭpio, cēpi, ceptum, 3.
retinue, comĭtātus, ūs, m.
retire, see *retreat*.
retirement, ōtium, i, n.
retreat, rĕceptus, ūs, m.
retreat, to, cēdo, cessi, cessum, 3.
return, rĕdĭtus, ūs, m.
return, to, rĕdeo, ĭvi or ii, ĭtum, 4 ; rĕgrĕdior, gressus, 3 dep.
reveal, pătĕfăcio, fēci, factum, 3.
revel, commissātio, ōnis, f.
revenge, ultio, ōnis, f.

revenge, to, ulciscor, ultus, 3 dep.
revenue, vectīgal, ālis, n.
reverence, rĕvĕrentia, ae, f.
revere, reverence, vĕnĕror, atus, 1 dep. ; vĕreor, ĭtus, 2 dep.
review, lustro, 1.
revolt, sēdĭtio, ōnis, f.
revolt, to, dēfĭcio, fēci, fectum, 3.
reward, praemium, i, n ; merces, ēdis, f.
reward, to, rĕmūnĕror, 1 dep.
Rhea, Rhĕa, ae, f.
Rhodes, Rhŏdus, i, f.
rich, dīves, ĭtis.
riches, ŏpes, um, f.; dīvitiae, arum, f.
ride, ĕquĭto, 1 ; vĕhor, vectus, 3.
rider, ĕques, ĭtis, m.
ridiculous, rĭdĭcŭlus, a, um.
right, prŏbus, a, um.
right, ius, iūris, n.; fas, indcl.
right-hand, dexter, tra, trum ; (*subst.*), dextra *or* dextĕra, ae, f.
rightly, rīte ; iure.
ring, annŭlus, i, m.
ripe, mātūrus, a, um.
ripen, mātūresco, rui, 3.
rise, surgo, surrexi, rectum, 3 ; ŏrĭor, ortus, 4 dep.
risk, pĕrīcŭlum, i, n.
rite, rītūs, ūs, m.
rivalry, aemŭlātio, ōnis, f.
river, flūmen, ĭnis, n.; amnis, is, m.; flŭvius, i, m.
road, via, ae, f.; ĭter, itĭnĕris, n.
roam, văgor, ātus, 1 dep.
roast, torreo, torrui, tostum, 2.
rob, răpio, ui, ptum, 3 ; spŏlio, 1.
robber, latro, ōnis, m.
rock, scŏpŭlus, i, m ; rūpes, is, f.
roedeer, caprea, ae, f.
roll, volvo, vi, volūtum, 3 (*trans.*); volvor (*intrans.*)
Rome, Rōma, ae, f.
Roman, Rōmānus, a, um.
Romulus, Rōmŭlus, i, m.
roof, tectum, i, n.
room, conclāve, is, n.
root, rādix, ĭcis, f.
rope, fūnis, is, m.

English-Latin Vocabulary. 203

rose, rŏsa, ae, f.
rough, asper, ĕra, ĕrum.
round, rŏtundus, a, um ; tĕres, ĕtis.
round (*prep.*), circum (*c. acc.*)
rouse, excito, 1.
rout, fŭgo, 1 ; fundo, fūdi, fusum, 3.
royal, rēgālis, e ; rēgius, a, um.
rude, rŭdis, e ; incultus, a, um.
Rufus, Rufus, i, m.
ruin, ruīna, ae, f ; exĭtium, i, n.
ruin, to, dīruo, ui, ūtum, 3 ; confĭcio, fēci, fectum, 3.
rule, to, rĕgo, xi, ctum ; impĕro, 1 (*c. dat.*)
rule, impĕrium, i, n.
rumour, fāma, ae, f ; rūmor, ōris, m.
run, curro, cŭcurri, cursum, 3.
run up, accurro, curri, cursum, 3.
run away, aufŭgio, fūgi, fugĭtum, 3.
running, cursus, ūs, m.
rush, impĕtus, ūs, m.
rush (*bulrush*), iuncus, i, m.
rush, to, rŭo, ui, rŭtum, 3.
rush forth, ērumpo, rūpi, ruptum, 3.
rush forward, procurro, curri, cursum, 3.
Russian, Scȳthĭcus, a, um.
rustic, rustĭcus, a, um.
Rutilius, Rŭtĭlius, i, m.

Sabine, Săbīnus, a, um.
sacred, săcer, cra, crum.
sacrifice, săcrĭfĭcium, i, n.
sacrifice, to, sacrĭfĭco, 1.
sad, tristis, e.
saddle, ĕphippium, i, n.
safe, tūtŭs, a, um ; incŏlŭmis, e.
safely, tūte.
safety, sălŭs, ūtis, f.
Saguntum, Săguntum, i, n.
sail, a, vēlum, i, n.
sail, to, nāvĭgo, 1.
sailor, nauta, ae, m.
sake, for the, caussa.
Salinator, Sălĭnātor, ōris, m.
salt, sāl, is, m.
salutation, sălūtātio, ōnis, f.
salute, sălūto, 1.

saluter, sălūtātor, ōris, m.
same, Idem, ĕădem, Idem.
Samos, Sămos, i, f.
Samnites, Samnītes, ium, m.
sanction, sancio, sanxi, sanctum, 4.
sanctity, sanctĭtas, ātis, f.
sand, ărēna, ae, f.
sate, satiate, sătio, 1 ; explĕo, plēvi, plētum, 2.
satisfy, sătisfăcio, fēci, factum, 3 (*c. dat.*)
Saturn, Sāturnus, i, m.
satyr, sătȳrus, i, m.
sauce, condīmentum, i, n.
savage, saevus, a, um.
save, servo, 1.
say, dīco, xi, ctum, 3.
saying, dictum, i, n.
Scaevola, Scaevola, ae, m.
scanty, exĭguus, a, um.
scar, cĭcătrix, īcis, f.
scarcely, vix.
scarcity, ĭnŏpia, ae, f.
scatter, spargo, rsi, rsum, 3 ; fundo, fūdi, fusum, 3.
Scaurus, Scaurus, i, m.
scent, odor, ōris, m.
school, schŏla, ae, f.
science, scientia, ac, f.
Scipio, Scīpio, ōnis, m.
scorch, adūro, ussi, ustum 3 ; torreo, ui, tostum, 2.
scorn, contemno, tempsi, temptum, 3.
Scotchman, Scŏtus, i, m.
scout, explōrātor, ōris, m.
scream, clāmor, ōris, m.
sculptor, sculptor, ōris, m.
sculpture, sculptūra, ac, f.
Scyros, Scȳros, i, f.
Scythian, Scȳtha, ae, m.
sea, măre, is, n.; (*adj.*) mărīnus, a, um ; nāvālis, e.
seagull, mergus, i, m.
search, explōro, 1 ; quaero, sīvi, sītum, 3.
season, tempus, ŏris, n.; tempestas, ātis, f.
season, to, condio, īvi *or* ii, ītum, 4.
seasonable, opportūnus, a, um.

seat, sēdes, is, f.
second, sĕcundus, a, um ; alter, ĕra, ĕrum.
secret, secrētus, a, um.
secretary, scrība, ae, m.
secretly, clam.
secure, sēcūrus, a, um ; see *safe*.
security, see *safety*.
sedition, sēdĭtio, ōnis, f.
see, vĭdeo, vīdi, visum 2.
seed, sēmen, ĭnis, n.
seek, quaero, sīvi, sītum, 3 ; peto, īvi *or* ii, ĭtum, 3.
seem, vĭdeor, vīsus, 2 dep.
seize, occŭpo, 1 ; răpio, ui, ptum, 3; corrĭpio, ui, reptum, 3.
seldom, rāro.
select, lĕgo, lēgi, lectum, 3.
self, ipse, a, um.
sell, vendo, dĭdi, dĭtum, 3.
seller, vendĭtor, ōris, m.
senate, sĕnātus, ūs, m.
senate-house, cūria, ae, f.
senator, sĕnātor, ōris, m.
senatorial, sĕnātōrius, a, um.
send, mitto, mīsi, missum, 3.
send away, dīmitto, mīsi, missum 3.
send for, arcesso, īvi, ītum, 3.
send on, praemitto, mīsi, missum, 3.
sentinel, vĭgil, ĭlis, m.
separate, sēpăro, 1.
serious, grăvis, e.
serpent, serpens, tis, c.
Sertorius, Sertōrius, i, m.
servant, servus, i, m.; fămŭlus, i, m.; *maid-servant*, ancilla, ae, f.
serve, servio, ivi *or* ii, ītum, 4 (*c. dat.*)
serve up, appōno, pŏsui, posĭtum, 3.
service, servĭtium, i, n. ; (*benefit*), bĕnĕficium, i, n.
servile, servīlis, e.
servitude, see *service*.
set, occīdo, cīdi, cāsum, 3.
set out, proficiscor, fectus, 3 dep.
set up, constĭtuo, ui, ūtum, 3.
setting, occāsus, ūs, m.
seven, septem, indcl.
seventy, septuāginta, indcl.

several, plūres, a.
severe, grăvis, e.
severely, grăvĭter.
severity, sĕvērĭtas, ātis, f.
Sextius, Sextius, i, m.
shade, *shadow*, umbra, ae, f.
shady, umbrōsus, a, um.
shake, quătio, quassi, quassum, 3 ; concŭtio, cussi, cussum, 3.
shame, pŭdor, oris, m.
shameful, turpis, e.
shameless, impŭdens, tis.
shamelessness, impŭdentia, ae, f.
shape, forma, ae, f.
share, pars, tis, f.
share, *to*, dīvĭdo, si, sum, 3.
sharp, ăcūtus, a, um ; ācer, acris, acre.
sharpen, ăcuo, ui, ūtum, 3.
shatter, see *break*.
shave, rādo, si, sum, 3.
she, see *he*.
shear, tondeo, tŏtondi, tonsum, 2.
shears, forfex, ĭcis, f.
shed, fundo, fūdi, fūsum, 3.
sheep, ŏvis, is, c.
shepherd, pastor, ōris, m.
shield, scūtum, i, n.; clĭpĕus, i, m.
shine, lūceo, xi, 2 ; nĭteo, ui, 2.
ship, nāvis, is, f.
shipwreck, naufrăgium, i, n.
shirt, tŭnĭca, ae, f.
shock, impĕtus, ūs, m.
shoe, calceus, i, m.
shop, tăberna, ae, f.
shore, lītus, ŏris, n.; ōra, ae, f.
short, brĕvis, e.
shoulder, hŭmĕrus, i, m.
shout, clāmor, ōris, m.
shout, *to*, clāmo, 1.
show, *to*, ostendo, di, sum, 3 ; ostento, 1 ; monstro, 1 ; praebeo, ui, ĭtum, 2.
shower, imber, bris, m.
shriek, ŭlŭlātus, ūs, m.
shriek, *to*, ŭlŭlo, 1.
shrine, ădўtum, i, n.; dēlūbrum, i, n.
shrub, arbustum, i, n.
shun, fŭgio, fūgi, fugĭtum, 3 ; vīto, 1.

English-Latin Vocabulary. 205

shut, claudo, si, sum, 3.
sick, sickly, aeger, gra, grum; infirmus, a, um.
side, on this, citra, cis (*c. acc.*)
side, lătus, ĕris, n.
sides, on all, passim.
sides, from all, undĭque.
sight, vīsus, ūs, m; conspectus, ūs, m.
sign, signal, signum, i, n.
silence, sĭlentium, i, n.
silent, sĭlens, tis; tăcĭtus, a, um.
silently, tăcĭte.
silent, to be, tăceo, ui, ĭtum, 2; sĭlco, ui, 2.
Silenus, Sĭlēnus, i, m.
silver, argentum, i, n.; (*adj.*) argenteus, a, um.
Simonides, Simōnĭdes, is, m.
simple, simplex, ĭcis.
sin, peccātum, i, n.; scĕlus, ĕris, n.
sin, to, pecco, 1.
since, quum, quŏniam.
sincere, sincērus, a, um.
sing, căno, cecĭni, cantum, 3; canto, 1.
single, ūnus, a, um.
singular, singulāris, e.
sink, mergo, rsi, rsum, 3 (*trans.*); mergor (*intrans.*)
sister, sŏror, ōris, f.
sit, sĕdeo, di, ssum, 2.
sit down, consīdo, sēdi, sessum, 3.
situated, sĭtus, a, um.
six, sex, indcl.
size, magnitūdo, ĭnis, f.
skilful, skilled, pĕrītus, a, um.
skill, pĕrītia, ae, f.
skin, cŭtis, is, f.; pellis, is, f.
skirmish, lĕve praelium.
sky, caelum, i, n.
slander, mălĕdīco, xi, ctum, 3 (*c. dat.*)
slaughter, caedes, is, f.
slave, servus, i, m.
slavery, servĭtūs, ūtis, f.
slay, interfĭcio, fēci, fectum, 3; occīdo, cīdi, cīsum, 3.
sleep, somnus, i, m.
sleep, to, dormio, ivi *or* ii, ītum, 4.

slender, tĕnuis, e.
slip, lābor, lapsus, 3 dep.
slip down, delābor, lapsus, 3 dep.
sloth, ignāvia, ae, f.
slow, tardus, a, um.
slowly, tardē.
sluggishness, see *sloth*.
slumber, somnus, i, m.
small, parvus, a, um.
smear, oblĭno, lēvi, lĭtum, 3.
smell, ŏdor, ōris, m.
smile, rīdeo, si, sum, 2.
smith, făber, bri, m.
Smyrna, Smyrna, ae, f.
snake, anguis, is, c.
snare, insĭdiae, ārum, f.
snatch, răpio, ui, ptum, 3.
snatch away, abrĭpio, ui, reptum, 3.
snow, nix, nĭvis, f.
snipe, scŏlōpax, ācis, f.
so, ita, sic, tam.
so great, tantus, a, um.
so many, tŏt, indcl.
Socrates, Socrătes, is, m.
soft, mollis, e.
soften, mollio, īvi *or* ii, ītum, 4.
soil, sŏlum, i, n.; hŭmus, i, f.
soldier, mĭles, ĭtis, m.
sole, ūnus, a, um; ūnĭcus, a, um.
solemn, sollennis, e.
some, quidam, quaedam, quoddam nonnullus, a, um; aliquot.
sometimes, interdum, alĭquando.
son, fīlius, i, m.
son-in-law, gĕner, ĕri, m.
song, carmen, ĭnis, n.; cantus, ūs, m.
soon, mox.
soothsayer, hăruspex, ĭcis, m.
sorrow, dŏlor, ōris, m.
sort, gĕnus, ĕris, n.
soul, ănĭma, ae, f.
sound, a, sŏnus, i, m; sŏnĭtus, ūs, m.
sound, to, sŏno, ui, ĭtum, 1.
sound, altus, a, um.
soundly, altē, bĕnē.
soup, ius, iūris, n.
sour, acerbus, a, um.
sow, sĕro, sēvi, sătum, 3.

space, spătium, i, n.
spacious, magnus, a, um.
spade, lĭgo, ōnis, m.
Spain, Hispānia, ae, f.
spare, parco, pĕperci, parsum, 3 (*c. dat.*)
Sparta, Sparta, ae, f.
Spartan, Spartānus, a, um.
speak, lŏquor, cūtus, 3 dep; dīco, xi, ctum, 3.
spear, hasta, ae, f.
spectacle, spectācŭlum, i, n.
spectre, spectrum, i, n.
speech, ōrātio, ōnis, f.
spend, consūmo, sumpsi, sumptum, 3.
spider, ărānea, ae, f.
spirit, spīrĭtus, ūs, m.; ănĭmus, i, m.
spit, vĕru, ūs, n.
spit, to, conspuo, ui, ūtum, 3.
splendid, splendĭdus, a, um.
splendour, splendor, ōris, m.
spoil, spŏlio, 1.
spoils, spŏlia, ōrum, n.
sport, lūdus, i, m.
spot, lŏcus, i, m.; plur. lŏca.
spread out, extendo, di, sum *and* tum, 3.
spring, ver, veris, n.
spring forward, prōsĭlio, ui, sultum, 4.
spy, explōrātor, ōris, m.
squander, dissĭpo, 1.
stab, confŏdio, fōdi, fossum, 3.
stag, cervus, i, m.
stain, infĭcio, fēci, fectum, 3.
stake, pālus, i, m.
stalk, culmus, i, m.
stand, sto, stĕti, statum, 1.
stand by, asto, stĭti, 1.
stand up, consurgo, surrexi, 3.
standard, signum, i, n.
star, stella, ae, f.; sīdus, ĕris, n.
start, contendo, di, tum, 3.
starting-post, carcĕres, um, m.
state, cīvĭtas, ātis, f., respublĭca, reipublĭcae, f.
station, a, stătio, ōnis, f.
station, to, lŏco, l.

statue, stătua, ae, f.
stature, stătūra, ae, f.
stay, mǎneo, nsi, nsum, 2; mŏror, ātus, 1 dep.
steadily, constanter.
steal, fūror, ātus, 1 dep.
stern, sĕvĕrus, a, um.
sternness, sĕvērĭtas, ātis, f.
stick, băcŭlus, i, m.
stick, to, adhaereo, si, sum, 2.
stick out, exsĕro, sĕrui, sertum, 3.
still, tranquillus, a, um.
still (i.e. *yet*), adhūc.
stir, mŏveo, mōvi, mōtum, 2.
stone, lăpis, ĭdis, m; saxum, i, n.
stop, consisto, stĭti, stĭtum, 3.
stop (*trans.*), mŏror, 1 dep.
store, thēsaurus, i, m.
storm, prŏcella, ae, f.; tempestas, ātis, f.
storm, to, expugno, 1.
story, fābŭla, ae, f.
straggler, pālans, tis.
straight, rectus, a, um.
strange, mīrus, a, um.
stranger, hospĕs, ĭtis, m.; advĕna, ae, c.
stratagem, dŏlus, i, m.
strategy, consĭlium, i, n.
stream, flūmen, ĭnis, n.
street, vīcus, i, m.
strength, vīres, ium, f.; stabilitas, ātis, f.
strengthen, firmo, 1.
stretch out, extendo, di, sum, 3.
strew, sterno, strāvi, strātum, 3.
strike, strike down, caedo, cĕcīdi, caesum, 3.
strive, nītor, nīsus *or* nixus, 3 dep; certo, 1.
strong, vălĭdus, a, um; fortis, e.
struggle, certāmen, ĭnis, n.
struggle, to, luctor, 1 dep.
study, stŭdium, i, n.
study, to, stŭdeo, ui, 2.
stupid, stultus, a, um.
subdue, *subjugate*, sŭbĭgo, ēgi, actum, 3.
subject, to be, pāreo, ui, 2 (*c. dat.*)
subside, decresco, crēvi, crētum, 3.

substitute, vĭcārius, i, m.
subtle, callĭdus, a, um; subdŏlus, a, um.
succeed, succēdo, ssi, ssum, 3 (*c. dat.*)
success, victōria, ae, f.; successus, ūs, m.
successful, *to be*, succēdo, cessi, cessum, 3.
succour, auxĭlium, i, n.; subsĭdium, i, n.
succour, to, subvĕnio, vēni, ventum, 4 (*c. dat.*)
such, tālis, e.
sudden, sŭbĭtus, a, um.
suddenly, rĕpente, sŭbĭto, stătim.
Suevi, Suēvī, ōrum, m.
suffer, pătior, passus, 3 dep.
sufficient, sătis, indcl.; ĭdōneus, a, um.
sufficiently, sătis.
suited for, *suitable*, aptus, a, um; ĭdōneus, a, um.
Sulla, Sulla, ae, m.
sum of money, pĕcūnia, ae, f.
summer, aestas, ātis, f.
summit, culmen, ĭnis, n.
summon, vŏco, 1; convŏco, 1.
sun, sol, sōlis, m.
sundial, sōlārium, i, n.
sunrise, lux, lūcis, f.; solis ortus.
sunset, solis occāsus.
sup, coeno, 1.
superstition, superstĭtio, ōnis, f.
supper, coena, ae, f.
suppliant, supplex, ĭcis.
supplies, commeātus, ūs, m.
support, sustĭneo, ui, tentum, 2; sustento, 1.
suppose, pŭto, 1.
supreme, suprēmus, a, um; summus, a, um.
sure, certus, a, um.
surgeon, mĕdĭcus, i, m.
surname, cognōmen, ĭnis, n.
surpass, sŭpĕro, 1.
surrender, dedĭtio, ōnis, f.
surrender, dēdo, dĭdi, dĭtum, 3.
surround, circumdo, dĕdi, dătum, 1; cingo, nxi, nctum, 3.

survive, sŭpersum, fui, esse.
suspicion, suspĭcio, ōnis, f.
swallow, hĭrundo, ĭnis, f.
swallow, to, dĕvŏro, 1.
swamp, pălūs, ūdis, f.
swan, cycnus, i, m.
swear, iūro, 1.
sweat, sūdor, ōris, m.
sweet, dulcis, e; suāvis, e.
swift, cĕler, is, e.
swiftly, celĕrĭter.
swiftness, celĕrĭtas, ātis, f.
swim, no, 1; năto, 1.
swim across, trano, 1.
sword, glădius, i, m.
Sylvia, Sylvia, ae, f.
Syracuse, Syracūsae, ārum, f.
Syracusan, Syracusānus, a, um.
Syria, Sўria, ae, f.
system, rătio, ōnis, f.

Table, mensa, ae, f.
tablet, tessĕra, ae, f.
tail, cauda, ae, f.
tailor, sartor, ōris, m.
taint, infĭcio, fēci, fectum, 3.
take, căpio, cēpi, captum, 3.
take away, adĭmo, ēmi, emptum, 3; aufĕro, abstŭli, ablātum, aufcrre.
take by storm, expugno, 1.
take care of, cūro, 1.
take in hand, suscĭpio, cēpi, ceptum, 3.
take out, exĭmo, ēmi, emptum, 3.
take up, sūmo, sumpsi, sumptum, 3.
take place, see *happen*.
talent, ingĕnium, i, n.
talk, lŏquor, lŏcūtus, 3 dep.
talkative, lŏquax, ācis.
tall, prŏcērus, a, um.
tame, mansuētus, a, um.
tame, to, dŏmo, ui, ĭtum, 1.
tardy, sērus, a, um; tardus, a, um.
Tarentum, Tărentum, i, n.
Tarentine, Tărentīnus, a, um.
Tarpeia, Tarpeia, ae, f.
Tarquin, Tarquĭnius, i, m.
tarry, mŏror, cunctor, 1 dep.
taste, gusto, 1.

English-Latin Vocabulary.

Tatius, Tatius, i, m.
tax, trĭbūtum, i, n.; vectīgal, ālis, n.
teach, dŏceo, ui, ctum, 2.
teacher, măgister, tri, m.
tear, lăcrĭma, ae, f.
tear, to, scindo, scĭdi, scissum, 3; (*snatch*), rapio, ui, ptum, 3.
tear asunder, in pieces, dīlănio, 1.
tear out, ēvello, velli, vulsum, 3.
tell, dīco, xi, ctum, 3; nuntio, 1.
temerity, tĕmĕrĭtas, ātis, f.
temper, ănĭmus, i, m.
temperate, mŏdĭcus, a, um.
tempest, tempestas, ātis, f.; prŏcella, ae, f.
temple, templum, i, n.; aedes, is, f.
ten, dĕcem, indcl.
tent, tentōrium, i, n.
terrible, dīrus, a, um.
terrify, terreo, ui, ĭtum, 2; terrĭto, 1.
territory, fīnes, ium, m.
terror, terror, ōris, m.
test, tento, pertento, 1; expĕrior, pertus, 4 dep.
Thames, Tămĕsis, is, m.
than, quam.
thanks, grātiae, ārum, f.
that, ille, a, ud; is, ea, id; iste, a, ud.
that (*conj.*), ut, quo.
theatre, theatrum, i, n.
Theban, Thēbānus, i, m.
Thebes, Thēbae, ārum, f.
theft, furtum, i, n.
their, eōrum, eārum, eōrum; (*own*), suus, a, um.
Themistocles, Thĕmistocles, is, m.
then, tum; tunc; deinde.
thence, inde.
there, ĭbi, illic.
therefore, ĭgĭtur, ĭtăque.
Thermopylae, Thermŏpўlae, ārum, f.
Thetis, Thĕtis, ĭdis, f.
thick, crassus, a, um; densus, a, um.
thicket, dūmētŭm, i, n.
thief, fur, is, c.

thin, măcer, cra, crum; tĕnuis, e.
thing, res, rei, f.
think, pŭto, 1; censeo, ui, 2; existĭmo, 1; cogĭto, 1.
third, tertius, a, um.
thirst, sĭtis, is, f.
thirteen, trĕdĕcim, indcl.
thirty, trīginta, indcl.
this, hic, haec, hoc.
thither, eo, illūc.
thou, tu, tui.
though, quamvis (*c. subj.*); quanquam (*c. ind.*).
thousand, mille, *indcl. adj.;* millia, ium, *subst.*
threaten, mĭnor, 1 dep. (*c. dat. of person.*)
three, tres, tria.
three hundred, trĕcenti, ae, a.
three times, thrice, ter.
threshing-floor, ārea, ae, f.
thrift, parsĭmōnia, ae, f.
thrifty, parcus, a, um.
throat, fauces, ium, f.; guttur, ŭris, n.
throne, sŏlium, i, n.
through, per (*c. acc.*).
throw, coniicio, iēci, iectum, 3.
thrush, turdus, i, m.
thrust, inĭĭcio, iēci, iectum, 3.
thumb, pollex, ĭcis, m.
thunder, thunderbolt, tŏnĭtrus, ūs, m.
thunder, to, tŏno, ui, ĭtum, 1.
thunderbolt, fulmen, ĭnis, n.
thus, sīc, ĭtă.
thy, tuus, a, um.
thyrsus, thyrsus, i, m.
Tiber, Tībĕris, is, m.
ticket, tessĕra, ae, f.
tide, aestus, ūs, m.
tie, allĭgo, 1.
tiger, tigris, is, c.
tight, contentus, a, um.
tile, tēgŭla, ae, f.
till, dōnec, dum, quoad.
till, to, cŏlo, ui, cultum, 3.
time, tempus, ŏris, n.
timely, opportūnus, a, um.
timid, tĭmĭdus, a, um.

English-Latin Vocabulary.

Timon, Timon, ōnis, m.
Tiryns, Tīryns, ynthis, f.
Titus, Tītus, i, m.
to, in, ad. (*c. acc.*)
to-day, hŏdie.
together, sĭmul, ūna.
toil, lăbor, ōris, m.
token, indĭcium, i, n.; *pledge*, pignus, ŏris, n.
tolerably, sătis, admŏdum.
tolerate, pătior, passus, 3 dep.; tŏlĕro, 1.
tomb, sĕpulcrum, i, n.; tŭmŭlus, i, m.
to-morrow, cras.
tongue, lingua, ae, f.
too, *too much*, nĭmis, nĭmium; (*adj.*) nĭmius, a, um.
tooth, dens, tis, m.
top, summus, a, um.
torch, taeda, ae, f.; fax, făcis, f.
torment, crŭciātus, ūs, m.
torn, lacer, ĕra, ĕrum.
Torquatus, Torquātus, i, m.
touch, tango, tetĭgi, tactum, 3.
touch at, appello, pŭli, pulsum, 3.
towards, versus, ergā, ad (*all c. acc.*)
tower, turris, is, f.
town, oppĭdum, i, n.
townsman, oppĭdānus, i, m.
trace, vestīgium, i, n.
tract, tractus, ūs, m.
train, exerceo, ui, ĭtum, 2.
traitor, prodĭtor, ōris, m.
tranquil, tranquillus, a, um.
tranquillity, tranquillĭtas, ātis, f.
transact, ago, ēgi, actum, 3.
transcribe, transcrībo, scripsi, scriptum, 3.
transfer, *transport*, transfĕro, tŭli, lātum, ferre.
travel, ĭter facĕre.
traveller, viātor, ōris, m.
treacherous, perfĭdus, a, um.
treachery, perfĭdia, ae, f.
tread on, conculco, 1.
treason, prōdĭtio, ōnis, f.
treasure, thēsaurus, i, m.
treasury, aerārium, i, n.
treat, tracto, 1.
treaty, foedus, ĕris, n.

tree, arbor, ŏris, f.
tremble, trĕmo, ui, 3.
tribe, trĭbus, ūs, f.
tribunal, trĭbūnal, ālis, n.
tribune, trĭbūnus, i, m.
tribuneship, trĭbūnātus, ūs, m.
tribute, trĭbūtum, i, n.
triumph, triumphus, i, m.
triumph, to, triumpho, 1.
Trojan, Troiānus, i, m.
troop, turma, ae, f.
troops, cōpiae, ārum, f.
trophy, trŏpaeum, i, n.
trouble, ŏpĕra, ae, f.
trouble, to, turbo, 1.
troublesome, mŏlestus, a, um.
Troy, Troia, ae, f.
truce, indūtiae, ārum, f.
true, vērus, a, um ; *truly*, vēre.
trumpet, tŭba, ae, f.; lĭtuus, i, m.
trumpeter, tŭbĭcen, ĭnis, m.
trunk, truncus, i, m.; (*of an elephant*), prōboscis, ĭdis, f.
trust, to, crēdo, dĭdi, dĭtum, 3; confīdo, fīsus sum, 3.
trust, fĭdes, ei, f.
trusty, fĭdēlis, e; fīdus, a, um.
truth, vērĭtas, ātis, f.; vērum, i, n.
try, cōnor, 1, dep.
tuft, floccus, i, m.
Tullius, Tullius, i, m.
Tullus, Tullus, i, m.
tumult, tŭmultus, ūs, m.
turn, verto, ti, sum, 3.
turn, out, ēvĕnio, vēni, ventum, 4.
turn, in, invĭcem.
turnip, răpum, i, n.
twelve, duodĕcim, indcl.
twentieth, vicesĭmus, a, um.
twenty, vĭginti, indcl.
twice, bis.
twig, virga, ae, f.
twist, torqueo, si, tum, 2.
two, duo, ae, o.
two hundred, dŭcenti, ae, a.
Tyler, Tȳlĕrius, i, m.
tyrant, tȳrannus, i, n.

Ugliness, dēformĭtas, ātis, f.
ugly, turpis, e.

Ulysses, Ulysses, is, m.
unaccustomed, insŏlītus, a, um.
unarmed, ĭnermis, e.
unavenged, ĭnultus, a, um.
uncertain, incertus, a, um.
uncle, patrŭus, i, m.
uncultivated, incultus, a, um.
undaunted, impăvĭdus, a, um.
under, sub (*c. abl. or acc.*).
undergo, sŭbeo, ĭvi *or* ii, 4.
undermine, subruo, ui, ŭtum, 3.
understand, intellĭgo, lexi, lectum, 3.
undertake, suscĭpio, cēpi, ceptum, 3.
undertaking, inceptum, i, n.
undisciplined, rŭdis, e.
undutiful, impius, a, um.
unequal, impar, paris.
unexpected, inspērātus, a, um; něcŏpīnātus, a, um.
unfair, inīquus, a, um.
unfortunate, infēlix, ĭcis.
unfriendly, ĭnĭmīcus, a, um.
ungrateful, ingrātus, a, um.
unhappy, infēlix, ĭcis.
unharmed, *unhurt*, intĕger, gra, grum.
unity, concordia, ae, f.
universal, ūnĭversus, a, um.
unjust, iniustus, a, um.
unknown, ignōtus, a, um.
unless, nĭsi.
unlike, dissĭmĭlis, e.
unlucky, infēlix, ĭcis; infaustus, a, um.
unmindful, immĕmor, ŏris (*c. gen.*)
unpleasant, ingrātus, a, um.
unpunished, ĭnultus, a, um.
unseasonable, ĭnopportūnus, a, um.
unsuspecting, imprūdens, tis.
until, dum; dōnec; quoad.
untouched, intactus, a, um.
unwarlike, imbellis, e.
unwilling, invītus, a, um.
unwilling, to be, nolo, nolui, nolle.
unworthy, indignus, a, um (*c. abl.*)
upbraid, exprobro, 1.
uphold, sustĭneo, ui, tentum, 2.
upon, sŭper (*c. abl.*); in (*c. abl.*)
uprightness, prŏbĭtas, ātis, f.
up to, tĕnus (*c. abl.*)

Urbinius, Urbinius, i, m.
urge, urgeo, ursi, 2.
use, ūsus, ūs, m.
use, to, ūtor, usus, 3, dep. (*c. abl.*)
useful, ūtĭlis, e.
useless, ĭnūtĭlis, e.
usual, sŏlītus, a, um.
usually, fĕre.
utter, ēdo, dĭdi, dĭtum, 3.

Vain, vānus, a, um; ĭnānis, e.
vainly, in vain, frustrā; nēquiquam.
Valerius, Vălĕrius, i, m
valley, vallis, is, f.
valour, virtūs, ūtis, f.
value, prĕtium, i, n.
value, to, aestĭmo, 1.
valuable, prĕtiōsus, a, um.
vanish, ēvānesco, ēvānui, 3.
vanity, vānĭtas, ātis, f.
vanquish, vinco, vīci, victum, 3.
variety, vărĭĕtas, ātis, f.
various, varying, vărius, a, um.
Varro, Varro, ōnis, m.
Varus, Vărus, i, m.
vast, ingens, tis.
Veientes, Veientes, um, m.
venture, audeo, ausus, 2, dep.
Venus, Vĕnus, ĕris, f.
very, ipse, a, um.
very small, parvŭlus, a, um.
vessel, nāvis, is, f.; nāvĭgium, i, n.
Vesta, Vesta, ae, f.
veteran, vĕtĕrānus, i, m.
vex, vexo, 1; ango, xi, ctum *and* xum, 3.
vice, vĭtium, i, n.
vicious, prāvus, a, um.
victor, victor, ōris, m.
victorious, victor, ōris, m; victrix, ĭcis, f.
victory, victōria, ae, f.
vigilance, vĭgĭlantia, ae, f.
vigour, vĭgor, ōris, m; vīres, ium, f.
village, vīcus, i, m.
villain, scĕlestus, a, um.
vine, vītis, is, f.
vine leaf, pampĭnus, i, f.
vineyard, vīnea, ae, f.
violate, violo, 1.

English-Latin Vocabulary. 211

violent, vĭŏlentus, a, um.
violence, vis, *acc.* vim, *abl.* vi, f.
virgin, virgo, ĭnis, f.
virtue, virtūs, ūtis, f.
virtuous, prŏbus, a, um.
vision, vīsus, ūs, m; *dream*, somnium, i, n.
visit, vīso, si, sum, 3.
visit (with punishment), afflcio, fēci, fectum, 3.
voice, vox, cis, f.
void, expers, tis.
Volsci, Volsci, ōrum, m.
vow, vōtum, i, n.
vow, to, vŏveo, vōvi, vōtum, 2.
Vulcan, Vulcānus, i, m.
vulture, vultur, ŭris, m.

Wage, gĕro, gessi, gestum, 3.
waggon, plaustrum, i, n.
wailing, plōrātus, ūs, m.
wait, măneo, nsi, nsum, 2.
wait for, expecto, 1.
wake, excĭto, 1 (trans.); *be awake*, vĭgĭlo, 1.
walk, ambŭlo, 1.
walk about, deambŭlo, 1.
wall, mūrus, i, m. ; *town walls*, moenia, ium, n.
wand, virga, ae, f.
wander, erro, 1; văgor, pălor, 1, dep.
wandering, error, ōris, m.
want, ĭnŏpia, ae, f.
want, to. See *to be willing.*
wanting, to be, dēsum, fui, esse.
war, bellum, i, n.
warlike, bellĭcōsus, a, um.
warm, călĭdus, a, um.
warm, to grow, călesco, 3.
warmth, călor, ōris, m.
warn, mŏneo, ui, itum, 2.
warrior, bellātor, ōris, m.
wart, verrūca, ae, f.
wary, cautus, a, um.
wash, lăvo, lāvi, lōtum, 1.
waste, dissĭpo, 1 ; *lay waste*, vnsto, 1.
wastes, dēserta, orum, n.
watch, vĭgĭlia, ae, f.
watch, to, vĭgĭlo, 1.
water, ăqua, ae, f.

watersnake, hydra, ae, f.
wave, fluctus, ūs, m.
wavering, dŭbius, a, um.
way, via, ae, f.; *iter*, itinĕris, n. ; *manner*, mŏdus, i, m.
we, nos, nostri *or* nostrum.
weak, infirmus, a, um.
weaken, mĭnuo, ui, ūtum, 3.
weakness, dēbĭlĭtas, ātis, f.
wealth, ŏpes, um, f. ; dīvĭtiae, arum, f.
wealthy, dīves, ĭtis ; lŏcuples, ētis.
weapon, tēlum, i, n.
wear away, dētĕro, trīvi, trītum, 3.
weary, fessus, a, um.
weave, texo, ui, xtum, 3.
web, tēla, ae, f.
weep, fleo, flēvi, flētum, 2.
weight, pondus, ĕris, n.
weighty, grăvis, e.
well, a, pŭteus, i, m.
well, bĕnĕ.
well, to be, văleo, ui, 2.
well known, it is, constat, 1, impers.
west, occĭdens, tis, m.
wet, mădĭdus, a, um.
wet, to get, mădesco, ui, 3.
whale, bālaena, ae, f.
what (in order of number), quŏtus, a, um ; *what o'clock*, quŏta hora.
when, quum ; ŭbi ; (interrogative), quando; *whenever*, quandocunque.
whence, unde.
where, qua, ŭbi ; (interrogative), ŭbĭ.
wherefore, ĭtăque, ĭgĭtur.
whether, utrum ; num ; sivĕ.
whether of the two, ŭter, tra, trum.
which, qui, quae, quod.
while, dum.
whip, flăgellum, i, n.
white, candĭdus, a, um.
whither, quō.
who, qui, quae, quod ; (interrogative), quis, quid.
whole, totus, a, um.
why, cūr.
wicked, mălus, a, um.
wide, lātus, a, um.
widow, vĭdua, ae, f.
wife, uxor, ōris, f.

English-Latin Vocabulary.

wild, fĕrus, a, um.
wild beast, fĕra, ae, f.
wild boar, ăper, pri, m.
will, vŏluntas, ātis, f.
willing, to be, vŏlo, vŏlui, velle.
willingly, lŭbenter.
window, fĕnestra, ae, f.
win over, concĭlio, 1.
wind, ventus, i, m.
wine, vīnum, i, n.
wing, āla, ae, f.; *of an army*, cornu, ūs, n.
winged, ālĕs, ĭtis ; ālātus, a, um.
winter, hiems, ĕmis, f.
winter quarters, hīberna, ōrum, n.
wisdom, săpientia, ae, f.
wise, săpiens, tis.
wish, vŏluntas, ātis, f.; stŭdium, i, n.
wish, to. See *to be willing*.
wit, ingĕnium, i, n.
with, cum (*c. abl.*)
withdraw, concēdo, cessi, cessum, 3.
wither, marceo, ui, 2.
within, intrā (*c. acc.*); (*adv.*), intus.
without, sĭne (*c. abl.*); (*outside*), extra (*c. acc.*) (*adv.*) extra.
without the knowledge of, clam (*c. abl.*)
withstand, rĕsisto, stĭti, stĭtum, 3 (*c. dat.*)
witness, testis, is, c.
witness, call to, testor, 1 dep.
woe, vae (interjection).
woe. See *grief*.
wolf, lŭpus, i, m.
woman, mŭlier, ĕris, f. ; fēmina, ae, f.
womanly, mŭliebris, e.
wonder, wonder at, mīror, 1 dep.
wonderful, mīrus, a, um.
wonderfully, mīre.
wont, to be, sŏleo, sŏlĭtus, 2.
wood, a, silva, ae, f.
wood, mātĕries, ēi, f.
woodcock, attăgen, ēnis, m.
wooden, ligneus, a, um.
woodman, lignātor, ōris, m.
wool, lāna, ae, f.
word, verbum, i, n.

work, ŏpus, ĕris, n.
work, to, lăbōro, 1.
workman, artĭfex, ĭcis, c.
workshop, offĭcīna, ae, f.
world, mundus, i, m.
worm, vermis, is, m.
worn out, confectus, a, um.
worship, cŏlo, ui, cultum, 3.
worth, to be, văleo, ui, 2.
worthy, dignus, a, um (*c. abl.*)
worthy, to deem, dignor, 1, dep. (*c. abl.*)
would that, ŭtĭnam (*c. subj.*)
wound, vulnus, ĕris, n.
wound, to, vulnĕro, 1.
wrap, involvo, vi, ūtum, 3.
wrath, īra, ae, f.
wreck, naufrăgium, i, n.
wreck, to, frango, frēgi, fractum, 3.
wreath, sertum, i, n.
wretched, mĭser, ĕra, ĕrum.
write, scrībo, scripsi, scriptum, 3.
writer, scriptor, ōris, m.
wrong, a, iniūria, ae, f.

Xanthippus, Xanthippus, i, m.
Xenophon, Xĕnophon, phontis, m.
Xerxes, Xerxes, is, m.

Year, annus, i, m.
yearly, every year, quŏtannis.
yellow, flāvus, a, um.
yesterday, hĕri.
yet, as yet, adhuc; *nevertheless*, tămen.
yield, cēdo, ssi, ssum, 3.
yoke, iŭgum, i, n.
you, vos, vestri or vestrum.
young, iŭvĕnis, e.
young (*ones*), pulli, ōrum, m.
your, vester, tra, trum.
youth, a, iŭvĕnis, is ; adŏlescens, tis, c.
youth, iŭventūs, ūtis, f.
youthful. See *young*.

Zeal, stŭdium, i, n.
Zeno, Zēno, ōnis, m.
Zeuxis, Zeuxis, Zeuxĭdis, m.

www.ingramcontent.com/pod-product-compliance
Lightning Source LLC
Chambersburg PA
CBHW031824230426
43669CB00009B/1217